Perspectives on management and leadership in social work

Perspectives on management and leadership in social work

edited by
Trish Hafford-Letchfield and John Lawler

Whiting & Birch
MMXIII

© Whiting & Birch Ltd 2013
Published by Whiting & Birch Ltd,
Forest Hill, London SE23 3HZ

ISBN 9781861770882

Printed in England and the United States by Lightning Source

For Sylvia Hafford
When I think of a leader, I think of you.
TH-L

For Anne and Adam
The new generation
JL

Contents

The Contributors

Trish Hafford-Letchfield is Reader in Social Work and Teaching Fellow, Department of Mental Health, Social Work, Interprofessional Learning and Chinese Medicine School of Health and Education Middlesex University.

John Lawler trained and practiced as a social worker before moving into academia. He has a particular interest in management and leadership development in public service organisations nationally and internationally and a specific interest in social work management and leadership. He has previously worked in Health and Business Schools at the Universities of Leeds and Bradford.

Garuth Chalfont is a leading practitioner in the art and science of healing gardens, therapeutic spaces and dementia gardens that incorporate the natural world into the healing process. His design philosophy promotes activity with meaning and purpose, for rehabilitation and wellbeing, regardless of disability or impairment. Garuth is the author of several publications in this specialist area.

Lambert Engelbrecht is an Associate Professor in the Department of Social Work at Stellenbosch University, South Africa. His post-graduate studies were all in the field op supervision and management of social workers and students. He has extensive experience of front-line social work, and as manager and supervisor. He published widely on topics related to management and supervision of social workers, and social development. He is rated as an established researcher by the South African National Research Foundation (NRF).

Ivan Gray was formerly Senior lecturer in Leadership and Management at Bournemouth University. He developed and ran the innovative leadership and management programmes for health and social care practitioners at the university, focusing on the development of service improvement oriented research. He is now retired.

Ray Jones is Professor of social work at Kingston University and St George's, University of London. A registered social worker, from 1992 to 2006 he was director of social services in Wiltshire. He was the first chief executive of the Social Care Institute for Excellence, and is a past chair of the British Association of Social Workers. He now oversees child protection improvement in five areas across England.

Sharon Lambley is a lecturer and Director of Continuous Professional Development at the University of Sussex. She is a keen advocate and supporter of good and effective social work management and leadership, and has been teaching and researching in this area of practice since 1991.

John Leinster has been a practicing social worker since 1986. He has worked in a variety of areas including homelessness, criminal justice, mental health, disability and child protection. He had been a social work manager for 15 years and is currently the Principal Social Worker for Child Protection in County Roscommon in Ireland. He is a part-time lecturer in National University of Ireland Galway specializing in Social Work Management and qualified with an M.Litt in 2009.

William McAllan was the learning and development manager for a Scottish local authority social work department. Now retired from this role he retains an interest in all aspects of social work with a particular interest in how social workers engage with research knowledge.

Rhoda MacRae is an independent research consultant. She is a Research Fellow on an ESRC funded Knowledge Exchange project with Social Work colleagues in the School of Social and Political Science, University of Edinburgh. She is also the Lead for the Independent sector in the Reshaping Care for Older People Partnership in North Lanarkshire. Previously she was a Research Fellow at the Social Services Research Centre, University of Stirling and the Institute for Research and Innovation in Social Services (IRISS).

Jonathan Parker is Professor of Social Policy & Social Work and Director of the Centre for Social Work, Sociology and Social Policy at Bournemouth University. He was one of the founders and director of the Family Assessment and Support Unit, a placement agency attached to the University of Hull, and Head of Department of Social Work. Prior to this Jonathan practised in a wide variety of Social Work posts with people with

Learning Disabilities, as a hospital Social Worker, in a generic fieldwork team and with children and families before specialising with people with dementia and as an Approved Social Worker (mental health). He was Chair of the Association of Teachers in Social Work Education until 2005, Vice Chair of the UK higher education representative body, the Joint University Council for Social Work Education from 2005- 2010, and is an Academician with the Academy of Social Sciences.

Stephanie Petrie is a qualified and registered social worker (HCPC SW00246). From 1970 until she became an academic in 1995 she was a social worker and manager of social work and social care services in the statutory and voluntary sectors in North East England and the Midlands. Since becoming an academic she taught on undergraduate and post graduate programmes at five Universities. She also undertook funded research and project evaluations for Government departments, local and health authorities, charities and third sector organisations. Upon retirement in 2011 she was appointed an Honorary Senior Research Fellow in the School of Law and Social Justice at the University of Liverpool and continues to undertake funded research and publish about a wide range of welfare issues.

Lynne Rutter is Lecturer in Postqualifying Social Work, School of Health & Social Care, Bournemouth University. Her research specializes in learning theories and practices, promoting the value of work-based learning.

Mike Webster teaches organisation and management and its practice application in under- and post-graduate social work programmes at the University of Auckland. He was formerly a practitioner and service manager in the Community Probation Service. Mike's doctoral thesis aims to develop a New Zealand model of social work organisational leadership.

Sarah Williams is Senior Lecturer in Postqualifying Social Work, School of Health & Social Care, Bournemouth University. She runs the practice education programmes for qualified health and social care practitioners.

I

Reshaping leadership and management

John Lawler and Trish Hafford-Letchfield

Introduction

Most of us are familiar with the globally iconic tale of the 'Emperor's New Clothes'; a tale of two weavers who promise an emperor a new suit of clothes, said to be invisible to those unfit for their position. The honest response of a child from the crowd however, innocently reveals that the Emperor parading before his subjects in his new 'suit of clothes', is in fact not wearing anything. This tale reminds us of the challenges we have face daily to stay with the courage of our convictions. Sight becomes insight, and in turn prompts action. This folklore tale, we suggest resonates with many contemporary issues within social work management and leadership. Despite many policy initiatives, organisational restructured and so forth, is anything really any different?

Neoliberalism and new public management have continued to have an immense impact on the trajectory of social work as a profession and on the role of leaders and managers in social work (Lawler 2007, Harris, 2003, Dustin 2007). The development of managerialism and the introduction of management techniques are seen to present innovations in social work and social care organisations. However, the extent to which these constitute comprehensive innovations might be debated. Important inter-personal skills which form a key element of professional social work practice might be found in some areas of effective management and leadership. Other initiatives might indeed be seen as innovatory. We need to be able to reflect critically on developments in management and leadership to be able to decide the extent we are witness to 'Emperor's New Clothes' or to genuine change, a distinct and material, so to speak, set of clothes. We need to be able to examine developments in policy and practice in a critical way, not accept a simple binary divide between management and professional practice demands. We need to be able to reflect on the foundations of management and leadership and of professional social work practice and service delivery.

In doing this, we can bring fundamental beliefs and assumptions, and priorities of both management and practice to the fore. The intended result is that we can appreciate better the nuances of the common factors, conflicts, misunderstandings and divergences of managerial and professional perspectives.

The chapters in this book attempt to examine developments by exploring a range of experiences and perspectives – both academic and practice-based, of leadership and management roles and functions in social work. The contexts for these chapters range from the UK to as far afield as New Zealand and South Africa and the contributions call for more liberating and affirming social work services, at variance to some extent, with traditional critiques and rhetoric on its management. Research and debate in the area of social work management and leadership is still in its infancy and our intention in the original journal from which these chapters came and in this book, is to stimulate an increase in confidence both of the leadership and capability of managers in the sector and of the profession's ability to describe and analyse its own experience in these areas. Leaders and managers play a challenging role in developing organisational culture and their voices are crucial to establishing a more critical and realistic dialogue between practitioners and academics. This book is timely as we witness attempts to provide more recognised professional pathways to foster better leadership through workforce development initiatives.

Changing contexts for social work management

The context for the delivery of social work services has changed very considerably over the past two decades and it continues to change. The rise and scope of markets and managerialism have both extended in ways which can barely have been imagined a generation ago. The socio-politico-economic climate has also developed considerably and to some extent the changes in social work organisation, management and delivery reflect those broader changes. Changes have direct consequences and impact. They create pressures for managers and professionals alike, for the design and delivery of services and for service users themselves in terms of the options they might have and the form in which services are used. In general, changes are intended to provide more effective and efficient services. Such changes are also likely to affect the relationships between and among different stakeholder groups.

The current context sees an increase in the marketisation of public services. Since the 1980s, markets have increasingly been seen as the mechanism by which services can be delivered and resources allocated to best effect. After an initial privatisation of many public services, marketisation has continued such that organisations whether in the commercial, public or independent domain are encouraged to compete with other providers (and collaborate at times in developing their own market strengths) so that resources continue to be allocated most efficiently and that services respond to user 'demand' thus in turn continuing an increase in service quality.

Such developments though are not without critics (e.g. Clarke, 2004; Sandel 2012). Some of the criticisms of markets and management might be dismissed as being ideological. However, Sandell (2012) argues that markets themselves are not value-free and that they embody and exemplify particular societal values - we cannot see the development of markets and of managerialism as in themselves neutral. Values in themselves constitute an important part of certain public services and particularly of health and social care services (see e.g. Beckett and Maynard, 2005). Some the values of managerialism and markets might be contradictory at worst or sit uneasily at best, with social work values. The challenge for both managers and social work professionals is to work with the tensions these different sets of values present, if they are not able to reconcile them.

The aim of this chapter is to set out the current context for social work, in particular to consider the role of management and leadership in social work services so that each of the ensuing chapters, which deal more directly with the specific challenges within organisations delivering social work services, can be seen to represent different facets of the same phenomenon. Furthermore, its aim is to provide a framework for how different approaches to management, leadership and practice might be considered, particularly to highlight the fundamental values and assumptions on which activity is based.

Markets and management

Over the past two decades and more, there has been a considerable expansion of neoliberal policies in developed economies (Kennett, 2008). A major component of this is the belief in the market as the most appropriate mechanism to allocate resources in meeting the needs of citizens. The language of the market and of business has become increasingly dominant as markets and quasi-markets in social care have expanded. This has been accompanied by the redefinition of the roles of different players in the public service context and the reconstitution of roles. Those who previously referred to as clients and users are increasingly reconstituted as 'customers'. Whether they see themselves in that role is currently unexplored. Case workers have become case managers, team leaders have become managers (Harris, 2003; Dustin 2008). Customer demands rather than client needs are increasingly the priority. The role of professional workers is also changing. Whereas previously their concern might have been the identification of client need and the delivery of appropriate services, the emphasis is on responding to demands identified and expressed by customers. Services are now becoming individualised and personalised, replacing the previous position of homogeneous services, defined and organised by the providing organisation. There are many positives in such changes, not least the increasing emphasis on an active 'consumer' rather than a passive 'recipient', the attention to individual need and the encouragement to listen to the voice of the user. Markets enable competition and that in turn leads to increasing choice for service consumers as to how their demands might be met. Thus they can choose the service they believe to be most fitting for their own situation (Clarke et al., 2000). So the establishment itself of markets cannot be viewed in isolation from the redefinition of roles of all those involved – funders, providers, purchasers, and consumers - which also signals a change in expectations of those roles.

The growth of markets has been paralleled by the rise of management and managerialism – concepts which would have been quite alien to social work a few decades ago when services were 'administered' rather than managed. Now the language of management is endemic in social work organisation. Social work services though still need to be provided in communities which continue to face many social challenges. At the same time as the influence of management has grown there has been the demand for social work services to become more professional still. Professional staff are under regular scrutiny with the demand that the skills involved in diagnosis, intervention and communication continuously improve.

The combination of managerialism and professionalism presents potential tensions between professional and managerial values and between professional and managerial authority. It might be useful here to refer to a quotation which aptly describes managerialism:

> Managerialism refers to the development of the interest of management in how organizations are managed, stressing the role and accountability of

individual managers and their positions as that – managers – rather than any other role or identity, such as senior professional or administrator. The essence of managerialism is the belief that many organizations have a great deal in common … and, given this people equipped as managers should be able to operate efficiently in any domain – in other words there is a belief in the transferability of these skills to other managerial contexts. (Lawler and Bilson, 2010: 4)

Social workers have always been required to practice in keeping with agency policy and professional guidelines. However with emphasis on management priorities, management efficiency has become a major measure of effectiveness, rather than the attainment of professional objectives. There is thus a danger that professional knowledge and values, and relationship-centred intervention, long the cornerstone of social work practice, are undervalued or disregarded. Managerialism values technical rationality over reflective practice. In other words, the subjective, emotional nature of interpersonal client-worker relationships can increasingly be seen as irrelevant. Ultimately managers have different priorities from social workers (Moore, 2008). Management is concerned with predictability and efficiency and with using management tools to achieve specific ends. Social workers, on the other hand, are likely to favour dialogue over procedure and flexibility and adaptability over predetermined ends.

Managerialism is not value-free being a component, as it is, of a neoliberal agenda which reduces the role of the state through the marketisation of services. Power has arguably shifted from social workers to managers, with the reduction of professional decision-making relating to how resources are allocated. Ultimately, there is the danger that managerial rather than professional action becomes the prime mechanism for developing social policy in this area (Rogowski, 2011).

Analysing management

The differing values of professionalism and managerialism can be explored further by considering important facets of management and professional activity and the assumptions which underpin them. On the one hand, management has a focus on the efficient use of resources and the achievement of organisational (and managerial) goals and outputs; on the other, professionals might be concerned more with the relational process of development in service delivery and with longer term outcomes.

5

In short, it could be argued that management has a concern with tangible and objective outputs whilst professionals might value more subjective assessments of efficacy. We can explore such different focuses of interest and their underlying influences, through considering different perspectives from which management can be examined.

Burrell and Morgan (1979) co-authored an important book which sought to consider the different approaches of a variety of sociological and organisational theories. Their analysis highlighted different ontological and epistemological bases on which different approaches were founded and thus the assumptions each of them made. They summarised these approaches using a matrix, sociology of regulation versus radical change as one dimension, against a continuum of subjective-objective perspectives as the other. Others have adopted and adapted this approach in different contexts including that of social work (Whittington and Holland, 1985; Howe, 1987; Payne, 2005; Poulter, 2005). The dimensions used might have altered slightly but the overall approach of Burrell and Morgan still resonates. More recently this approach has informed other work such as that of Lawler and Bilson (2010) who present a conceptual framework to help understand and organise different approaches to management and leadership in social work. The framework helps to distinguish the different foundations and concerns of each theoretical approach. The framework is presented in Fig. 1 overleaf.

The vertical axis represents a range of approaches from Reflective-pluralist at one end, to Rational-objectivist at the other. Rational-objectivist perspectives take a realist position of assuming an objective, stable and knowable reality. Such perspectives have a concern with planning, predictability, regulation and control. On the other hand, Reflective-pluralist approaches assume a more interpretative 'reality' or range of socially constructed and individually perceived realities and take account of emergence and complexity. The horizontal axis represents the focus being on the individual and individual interactions at one end, and the organisation as a whole at the other.

To illustrate this, an approach such as trait theory of leadership, would be an example belonging in Quadrant A (focusing on objective criteria at the individual level); classical bureaucracy would exemplify Quadrant B (a universal, prescribed approach focusing on the organisation); Symbolic interactionism and dialogical approaches to communication would characterise Quadrant C; and soft systems approaches to organisation would belong in Quadrant D.

Managerialist practices, in general, illustrate a focus on rational and

Figure 1 *Matrix for categorisation of management and leadership theories*

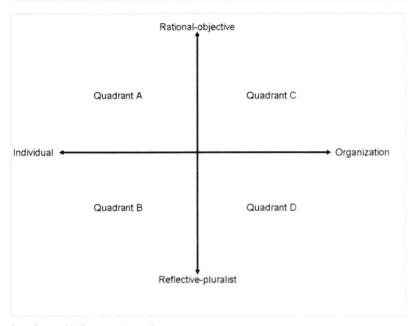

(Lawler and Bilson, 2010 p16)

objective planning and control and regulation. This can be counter to emancipatory theories applied to social work practice which present specific challenges to regulation and control. There is a need to consider both rational-objectivist approaches and reflective approaches if we are to understand social work management more fully and if we are to promote the development of more effective management practice in that context.

Aronson and Smith, (2011) argue that managerialism presents management as predominantly promoting stereotypically masculine values. Thus it can be characterised as being logical, unemotional, with a focus on using objective data to inform decision-making. Furthermore, a prime driver in traditional management studies has been the pursuit of generalizable models or practices which apply regardless of context – a 'best way' of managing. In this approach emotionality and intuition are discounted or discouraged - the 'positivist, value-free model of scientific knowledge (is) enthroned, marginalizing other approaches' (Adler et al., 2007, p. 180). Reflective-pluralist approaches do not promote a 'blue-print' or single 'best way' for organisation or management but accept different influences and interactions. They also accept that organisations might pursue a wider range of goals or outcomes than solely ensuring that the most efficient systems are in operation.

Relational issues are more highly valued in the reflective-pluralist approach which accepts more subjective assessments of activity and performance and more emergent properties in organisations which can be directed as they develop, towards desired outcomes, in an organic manner, rather than being prescribed through comprehensive planning. Management, from this perspective relies on the establishment of an effective working relationship between manager and professional, as in the social worker and service user relationship (Ruch, 2011). Rather than relying on planning and monitoring as the means to do this as an objectivist would, this is done through a dialogical process.

There is a particular point in highlighting the different approaches to management and leadership and noting the different foundations and priorities of practice. As noted above, the influence of managerialism can be profound and can also be accepted unquestioningly. As Aronson and Smith note, the discourse of managerialism is unsurprisingly adopted quickly by social work managers with a consequent influence on the perceived identities of the managers themselves. The point of considering the foundations of different approaches is to some extent to problematise the concepts we are using – that is to examine the concepts and the foundations on which they are based and to highlight different interpretations of them and different consequences of their application, rather than accept them without question. In this way we may develop clearer and more detailed understandings both of the concepts and the consequences of translating them into operational contexts.

Critical management

This approach can be seen in the development of Critical Management Studies (CMS) over recent decades. CMS provides different perspectives from which to analyse the concept of management and its component theories. It represents an eclectic range of approaches from the more structural, objectivist approaches, drawing on, for example, Marxist analyses (Adler, 2007) to more subjectivist approaches drawing, for example, on the work of Lacan (see, e.g., Arnand & Vanheulen, 2007). Given its eclectic foundations, an authoritative definition is difficult but Grey (2005) presents the following overview:

CMS represents the possibility of drawing together those elements within business schools (and cognate areas) who share some oppositional tendencies. That is: oppositional to established power and ideology: to managerial privilege; to hierarchy and its abuse: to put it at its most generic, not only the established order but the proposition that the established order is immutable (p. 187).

There are parallels here in that CMS challenges orthodox thinking and practice in a similar way to the manner in which the radical social work movement provided a challenge to orthodox thinking and practice in social work from the mid 1970s (Bailey & Brake, 1975). The parallel is that both present challenges to power - explicit and implicit –both question established practice.

Fleming and Mandarini (2009,) argue that a prime role of CMS is to problematise management both in theory and in practice. In particular they argue much management theory and practice is de-politised, that is that the power dynamics in particular concepts are underplayed or ignored but are of fundamental importance if we are to understand the situation fully. They argue that managerialism represents and privileges a set of particular values, such as the legitimacy or primacy of 'business methods', efficiency, and economy, which are being internalised in public service. This, in turn, is likely to affect social work attitudes and practice directly and intentionally and, as importantly, indirectly. For example, Adler et al. (2007) illustrate how managerialism can affects teams resulting in 'the oppressive internalization of business values and goals by team members, who then begin exploiting themselves and disciplining team players in the name of business performance' (p. 179). A critical approach to management has the intention of highlighting such dynamics not necessarily in a subversive way but so that innovations, for example to practice, can be made with a fuller understanding of the potential benefits and drawbacks to all concerned and thus in a spirit of emancipation rather than exploitation.

CMS has continued the themes highlighted in the 20th century, for example in relation to labour process theory (Braverman, 1974) where workers were seen as alienated actors in the production process. In this scenario workers came under the direct control and surveillance of their employers and supervisors and their activities were strictly prescribed and regulated. In the context of post-industrial social work - a welfare service with significant aspects of co-production, professional autonomy and intangible outputs - one might expect less direct supervision of work and less surveillance and control. However, as writers such as Adler et al. (2007) and Fleming and Madarini (2009) point out, within a managerial world, professional and service work is likely to be as scutinsed as ever, as might be evidenced by a focus on the achievement of work targets, adherence to protocol etc. There is some evidence, for example, in the work of Aronson and Smith (2011) of social work managers developing 'manager identities', which are not exclusively managerial. They seek to achieve required managerial/organisational goals but their 'manager identities' maintain their own values and form some protection against the pressure from more powerful managerial values for social workers to continue their professional activities and maintain professional values. Individual social workers' subjective values and feelings of esteem are protected while working towards the objective goals and performance of management.

A consideration of CMS brings us back to the framework illustrate in Figure 1. As professionals, managers and academics we need to recognise the assumptions which inform our actions and what we regard as relevant experience and evidence which supports those assumptions. What constitutes evidence to an objectivist is likely to be very different from how evidence is viewed from a subjective perspective. The informed manager will recognise the legitimacy of each approach dependent on the particular context and will manage accordingly, with exclusive reliance on neither objectivist nor subjective perspective. There are times when objective views are most useful, e.g. in measuring the usage of physical resources, financial data etc. and times when subjective impressions are more useful e.g. the inspiration of staff.

One can see a difference of approach to managerialism when taking a critical management perspective. The literature on management and leadership in social work, as we have already noted, is still developing, that using critical management as its main perspective is at an earlier stage of development. Each of these different perspectives offers important new insights into how management and leadership are developing in social work and also insights into how they might develop in more creative, less restrictive ways than those prescribed by strictly managerial approaches. Some of these creative and imaginative approaches are evidenced in this book. The following chapters illustrate creativity and imagination both in how social work management can and might operate and in terms of how it might be theorised. The original versions of these chapters formed two Special Editions of *Social Work and Social Sciences Review* (2010) Vol. 14, 1 & 2. These chapters have been revised for this edited book. In some cases an updated introduction has been used to highlight changes since the original publication, in other cases the chapter itself has been revised.

References

Adler, P.S., Forbes, L.C., & Willmott, H. (2007). Critical management studies. *Academy of Management Annals*, 1(1), 119-179.

Aronson, J., & Smith, K. (2011). Identity work and critical social service management: Balancing on a tightrope? *British Journal of Social Work*, 41(3), 1-17.

Arnaud, G., & Vanheule, S. (2007). he division of the subject and the organization: A Lacanian approach to subjectivity at work. *Journal of Organizational Change Management*, 20(3), 359-369.

Bailey, R., & Brake, M. (1975). *Radical social work*. London: Edward Arnold.

Beckett, C. And Maynard, A. (2995) *Values and Ethics in Social Work: An Introduction*. London: Sage

Braverman, H. (1974) *Labor and monopoly capital : the degradation of work in the twentieth century*. New York, London. Monthly Review Press.

Burrell, G. and Morgan, G. (1979) *Sociological Paradigms and organisational Analysis: elements of the sociology of corporate life*, London: Heinemann.

Clarke, J. (2004) 'Dissolving the Public Realm? The Logics and Limits of Neo-liberalism.' *Journal of Social Policy* 33: pp 27-48

Dustin. D. (2008) *The McDonaldization of Social Work*. Aldershot: Ashgate

Fleming, P., & Mandarini, M. (2009). New perspectives on work and emancipation. In Alvesson, M., Bridgman, T., & Willmott, H. (Eds). *The Oxford Handbook of Critical Management Studies*. Oxford: Oxford University Press. 328-344.

Grey, C. (2005). Critical management studies: Towards a more mature politics. In D. Howcroft & Trauth, E.M. (Eds). *Handbook of critical information systems research: Theory and application*. Aldershot: Edward Elgar. 174-194.

Kennett, P. (Ed.) (2008). *Governance, Globalization and Public Policy Cheltenham*: Edward Elgar Publishing.

Harris, J. (2003). *The social work business*. London: Routledge.

Howe, D (1987) *Introduction to Social Work Theory: Making Sense in Practice*. Aldershot: Wildwood House.

Lawler, J. (2007) 'Leadership in Social Work: A Case of Caveat Emptor?' *British Journal of Social Work* 37, (1), 123-141

Lawler, J. and Bilson, A. (2010) *Social Work Management and Leadership: Managing Complexity with Creativity*. Abingdon, Routledge

Moore, G. (2008). Re-imagining the morality of management: A modern virtue ethics approach. *Business Ethics Quarterly*, 18(4), 483-511.

Payne, M. (2005) *Modern Social Work Theory*, Basingstoke: Macmillan Palgrave.

Poulter, J. (2005) 'Integrating theory and practice: A new heuristic paradigm for social work practice', *Australian Social Work*. 58(2): 199-211.

Rogowski, S. (2011). Managers, managerialism and social work with children and families: The deformation of a profession? *Practice*, 23(3), 157-167.

Ruch, G. (2011). Where have all the feelings gone? Developing reflective and relationship-based management in child-care social work. *British Journal of Social Work*. First published online October 5, 2011. doi:10.1093/bjsw/bcr134.

Sandel, M (2012) *What Money Can't Buy: The Moral Limits of Markets*. Allen Lane.

Whittington, C. and Holland, R. (1985) 'A Framework for Theory in Social Work', *Issues in Social Work Education*, 6(1): 41-46.

2

The 'commodification' of 'children in need' in welfare markets:
Implications for managers

Stephanie Petrie

The situation in 2013

The stimulus for the following chapter was primarily my experience as a social worker through the gradual move from the Welfare State to welfare 'markets' in the UK. Subsequent research as an academic persuaded me that the nature of the relationship between the professional adult and children receiving 'welfare' services of all kinds had been fundamentally altered with the imposition of the 'market' paradigm. In other words children and young people had simply become commodities with an exchange value subject to contracts between assessors of need and providers of services. There was evidence to suggest this had a deleterious effect on children and young people in the UK compared to similar countries.

Since publication, however, the UK landscape for social work and indeed welfare as a whole has been affected by a seismic shift in political configuration and economic policies that are affecting children and their families especially harshly. Furthermore these changes are not limited to the UK as the entirety of the European Union (EU) is facing political and economic turmoil affecting its' very future as the impact of 'austerity' policies bear down on the majority of country populations (Petrie, 2013). The chapter that follows was concerned with the implementation gap between policies and legislation and allied professional practices constrained by the welfare 'market' however the current situation for children and young people is now catastrophic because of the wider impact of neo-liberal 'market' forces.

Neo-liberal economic policies have been adopted by most complex affluent societies in the West during the last 30 years and substantial studies (Stukler, et al., 2009; Wilkinson and Pickett, 2010; Dorling, 2011) have now shown decisively that the primary achievement of 'free markets' has been to widen the gap between the rich and the poor. Evidence shows this trend has been to everyone's detriment in relation to population health and social stability (ibid). Not only is there a failure of the 'market' paradigm as a satisfactory mechanism for the distribution of health and welfare services the 'market' as an economic regulator is in meltdown in country after country. As the global economic crisis that began in 2008 has deepened it is clear that neo-liberal economics and an unregulated global financial sector have delivered economic chaos and as ever children are the first to suffer at times of social upheaval. There is a domino effect from developed to developing countries impacting adversely on children and their families already living on the margins of survival (Green, et al., 2010) but it is also clear that the lives of the poorest children in the UK have worsened too and that many more will become poor over the next few years. The impact of 'austerity' policies in the UK can be seen if we consider two of the services for 'children-in-need'; child protection and childcare.

'Markets' and services for children in the UK

The 'New' Labour governments (1997-2010) continued the 'marketisation' policies introduced by the Thatcher/ Major governments from 1979 onwards and widened their applicability to public sector health and welfare services. Management by government-set performance indicators was also a feature of this approach and ultimately generated professional unease especially in relation to services for 'children-in-need'. The general election of 2010 saw the defeat of 'New' Labour whilst the opposition Conservatives had an insufficient majority to form a government. Consequently a Coalition government was formed between the Conservatives and Liberal Democrats. Despite enormous variations in their manifestos they share a commitment to 'austerity' policies. In effect, although the indebtedness of countries such as the UK has been due to the large-scale mismanagement of the banking and financial industries, major cuts in public sector services are seen to be inevitable.

Child Protection

A major review of child protection systems, policies and procedures in the UK led by Professor Eileen Monro was commissioned in 2010 by the outgoing 'New' Labour government. The findings confirmed that there had been a diminution of professional decision-making and an over-reliance on centralised bureaucratic and prescriptive policies and procedures during the previous decade. These findings and the proposals of the Monro Review (DoE, 2011a) were endorsed by the Coalition government:

> The Government commends Professor Munro's thorough analysis of the issues and accepts her fundamental argument ... We believe we need to move towards a child protection system with less central prescription and interference, where we place greater trust and responsibility in skilled professionals at the front line (DoE, 2011b, p.1).

Ironically if the political landscape had remained unchanged the proposals of the Monro Review would no doubt have contributed to strengthening the professional 'helping' relationship discussed in detail in the chapter that follows. This is because State investment into a range of community-based services, such as Surestart, would have continued offering the professional 'helper' a range of options in their work with children and their families. It now seems likely that the Review will be used to justify 'austerity' policies that have substantially diminished State investment in children, in effect throwing the baby out with the bath water. Professional fears have been expressed that the Review will be used to savagely reduce child protection guidance in a way that will undermine cross-agency collaboration (Community Care 2012a) whilst public sector cuts have reduced frontline services and increased workloads (2012b). Furthermore the link between poverty and child-maltreatment is well-known (NSPCC, 2008; Leventhal, et al, 2012) and it is equally clear that 'austerity' policies will increase child poverty in many European countries including the UK (unicef, 2012).

Childcare

The assumption that the best way out of poverty for children is parental employment led to the Welfare Reform policy direction initiated by 'New' Labour and embraced by the current Coalition government. Policies and legislation resting on this assumption turn a correlation (that fewer children live in poverty if their parents are employed), into a causality that does not take account of the differing needs of individual children during their childhoods. Welfare Reform legislation links eligibility for financial assistance to parental work availability rather than children's 'needs' with strong elements of both compulsion and penalty that can include a reduction in benefit payable. Being a lone parent of young children is no longer an exemption from job seeking. From when the youngest child is five-years-old (and legislation is already in place to reduce this further) a lone parent has to be in paid work or actively demonstrate they are seeking employment. Changes in housing benefit, child benefit and disability benefits have also reduced the income of working parents. The cost, availability and quality of childcare for children and after school care for older children whilst parents work however acts as a barrier to employment. A recent report for the Department for Education (Brind, et al., 2012) shows that the sector, composed mainly of women working in private day nurseries and as child-minders, is poorly-funded, poorly-paid and overworked. Nevertheless UK parents pay substantially more than their EU counterparts with yearly fees for 25 hours childcare of between £5103 and £15,000 (Daycare Trust 2011). There are indications that the costs of childcare are forcing parents out of the labour market (Daycare Trust 2012; Ahmad, et al., 2010; Petrie, Campbell, 2009) even when jobs are available (unemployment at time of writing stands at nearly 3 million (ONS, May 2012)). Policy solutions suggested remain focussed on making the 'market' more effective and show little concern or even interest in the development needs of children. It has been proposed that one way to make the sector more profitable and thus financially viable is by reducing regulation and restrictions on staff/child ratios (Truss, 2012) and another is through long-term government loans (between 11 and 20 years) to parents - another debt burden (Shorthouse, et al., 2012). The current system of 15 hours of free early education in place shows how the 'market' continues to disadvantage poor children as the subsidy can be used to offset fees for the first year of private primary education for children with an early birthday whilst parents of children who attend state school receive nothing. There is snowballing evidence of the damage caused to the most vulnerable in European societies, especially children, by slavish adherence to neo-liberal 'market' economics yet 'austerity' policies are set to continue.

Concluding comments

Whatever services for children are considered the pattern is the same; availability and quality are reducing dramatically. The impact of 'austerity' policies and savage cuts in public sector services and State funding in EU countries such as Greece, Spain, France and Portugal as well as the UK are disastrous leading to widespread citizen unrest. The latest report from the UN Children's Fund (UNICEF) states:

> Because children have only one opportunity to develop normally in mind and body, the commitment to protection from poverty must be upheld in good times and in bad. A society that fails to maintain that commitment, even in difficult economic times, is a society that is failing its most vulnerable citizens and storing up intractable social and economic problems for the years immediately ahead (UNICEF, 2012, p.1).

At this moment it seems that our children are no longer even 'commodities' – they have become collateral damage in the 'austerity' war. The question now is not merely whether or not the 'helping' relationship has been adversely affected by the 'market' but whether or not the 'market' mechanism prevents children and young people 'in-need' having access to a 'helping' relationship at all.

References

Ahmad, S., Graham, C., Lance Jones, B., Petrie, S., Reith, L., (2010), *Lone Parent Advancement – A Report of Local Action Research: Are We Nearly There Yet? Managing Children and Work*, Liverpool: University of Liverpool

Brind, R., Norden, O., Oseman, D., (2012), Childcare Finances Provider Survey, London: Department for Education

Community Care, (2012a), 'Fears over plans to 'slaughter' child protection guidance'. http://www.communitycare.co.uk/Articles/28/03/2012/118112/fear-over-plans-to-slaughter-child-protection-guidance.htm. Accessed 4.6.2012

Community Care, (2012b), 'What difference has Monro made to frontline services?' http://www.communitycare.co.uk/Articles/28/05/2012/118250/What-difference-has-Munro-made-to-frontline-social-work.htm. Accessed 4.6.2012

Daycare Trust (2012), *Childcare costs survey 2012*. http://www.daycaretrust.org.uk/pages/childcare-costs-survey-2012.html. Accessed 4.6.2012

Daycare Trust (2011), 'New Research from Daycare Trust and Save the Children' http://www.daycaretrust.org.uk/news.php?id=54. Accessed 4.6.2012

Department of Education, (2011a), *The Monro Review of Child Protection: Final*

Report. A child-centred system. Cmnd., 8062, May 2011. http://www.education. gov.uk/munroreview/downloads/8875_DfE_Munro_Report_TAGGED. pdf. Accessed 7.09.2011

Department of Education, (2011b), *A child-centred system. The Government's Response to the Monro Review.* *http://www.education.gov.uk/munroreview/ downloads/GovernmentResponsetoMunro.pdf.* Accessed 7.09.2011

Dorling, D., (2011), *Injustice: why social inequality persists*, Bristol: The Policy Press

Green, D., King, R., Miller-Dawkins, M., (2010),*The Global Economic Crisis and Developing Countries*, Oxfam International Research Report, May 28th. http:// www.oxfam.org/sites/www.oxfam.org/files/global-economic-crisis-and-developing-countries-2010.pdf. Accessed 4.6.2012

Leventhal, J.M., Martin, K.D., Gaither, J.R., (2012), 'Using US Data to Estimate the Incidence of Serious Physical Abuse in Children', *Pediatrics*, 129, 3, 458-464

National Society for the Prevention of Cruelty to Children (NSPCC) (2008), *Poverty and Child Maltreatment: child protection research briefing*, London: NSPCC. Office of National Statistics (ONS), 'Labour 'market' Statistics May 2012'. http://www.ons.gov.uk/ons/rel/lms/labour-'market'-statistics/ may-2012/index.html. Accessed 4.6.2012

Petrie, S.,(ed.) (2013), *Critical Policy Research: Praxis, Analysis and Politics*, Houndmills, Basingstoke: Palgrave Macmillan

Petrie, S., Campbell, P., (2009), *Lone Parent Advancement – A Greater Merseyside Profile: a contextual report supporting further local action research*, Liverpool: University of Liverpool

Shorthouse, R., Masters, J., Mulheirn, I., (2012), *A Better Beginning; Easing the cost of childcare*, London: Social 'market' Foundation

Stuckler, D., Basu, S., Suhrcke, M., Coutts, A., McKee, M., (2009), 'The public health effect of economic crises and alternative policy responses in Europe: an empirical analysis, *The Lancet*, 374 (9886), pp. 315-23

Truss, E., (2012), *Affordable Quality: new approaches to childcare*, London: centreforum

Unicef (2012) *Innocenti Report Card 10: Measuring Child Poverty*, Florence, Italy: unicef innocent research centre

Wilkinson, R., Pickett, K., (2010), *The Spirit Level: why Equality is Better for Everyone*, London: Penguin

The 'commodification' of 'children in need' in welfare markets: Implications for managers

The true measure of a nation's standing is how well it attends to its children – their health and safety, their material security, their education and socialization, and their sense of being loved, valued and included in the families and societies into which they are born (UNICEF) 2007, pp.1).

Introduction

The impact of the market paradigm and performance indicator management in welfare[1] has commodified 'children in need', undermined the 'helping relationship'[2] and is a significant factor in the well-documented poor outcomes for children and young people in the UK that will be discussed later. This paper has been informed by my professional experience as a social worker, manager and policy officer, and subsequent research as an academic during the changing landscape of welfare in the UK since the 1970s.

Although there are now four administrations in the United Kingdom since devolution in 1999 the UK will be used throughout as the over-arching term when discussing issues prior to devolution or where policies and practices are similar. Notwithstanding the different combinations of laws and policies. England, Northern Ireland, Scotland and Wales share comparable approaches to 'children-in-need (sec.17, Children Act (CA) 1989). For example apart from some country-specific amendments the CA 1989 remains the overarching legal framework for 'children in need' and applies to all administrations. By statute each country now has a commissioner for children and a four administration collaborative approach was adopted to review of the implementation of the United Nations Convention on the Rights of the Child (UNCRC) (1989) to which all countries are signatories (DCSF,WAG, TSG, NIE, 2009).

Major policies are also congruent in many respects. For example in England the five objectives of *Every Child Matters* (DfES, 2005a) are for children and young people to be healthy; stay safe; enjoy and achieve; make a positive contribution and achieve economic well-being. Similar aims are evident in Northern Ireland, *Our Children and Young People: Our pledge*

(OFMDFM, 2005); in Scotland, *Getting it Right for Every Child* (TSG, 2008) and in Wales *Children and Young People: Rights to action* (WAG, 2004).

As a foundation for arguments later in the paper the main changes for welfare management, organisational structures and culture brought about by the gradual move from the Welfare State to welfare markets that have influenced all four countries will be reviewed. This is followed by an analysis of the impact of markets on children and young people. Current challenges and possible future strategies for managers of services for 'children in need' will conclude the paper highlighting at this point the diverging approaches to welfare provision for 'children in need' emerging in the four administrations.

From the Welfare State to welfare markets

My interest in the consequences for children and young people of the introduction of the market paradigm into children's services has been stimulated by two aspects of my professional career.

First was my experience of working within different approaches to welfare. I began working as a child care officer when the Welfare State was the primary mechanism for delivering welfare and continued working throughout the shift towards what Le Grand calls 'quasi-markets'(Le Grand, 1990, 1993). At that time I became aware that the organisational structures and management processes being developed by local authorities in response to the Children Act (CA) 1989 were mirroring those required for adult services by the National Health Service and Community Care Act (NHS & CC) 1990, although there was no statutory duty to do so (Petrie and Wilson, 1999). The key market characteristics that impacted on children's welfare services in all administrations were:

- an increase in the mixed economy in welfare;
- internal and external markets between assessors of 'need' and providers of services and
- the introduction of cost considerations at individual level when professional assessments of need were made.

Secondly the changing nature of the 'helping relationship' in human services in the UK, particularly in social work, was immediate and significant. Not only did the organisation of children's services change but this triggered a shift in professional language and interactions suggesting a fundamental alteration in the nature of the 'helping relationship'. 'Clients' became 'service-users' and 'partnership' the primary service model (Petrie, 2007). A contract rather than grant-aid became the vehicle through which the relationship between third sector providers and the State was managed changing their role and leading to short-term services (Gutch, 1992). Terms such as 'partnership', were not evident in statute and had not been clearly defined in policies and as a result attempts to operationalise these imperatives were difficult as neither agencies nor service-users shared the same understanding of what was meant in practice (Novak, *et al.*, 1997). Care management emerged and post-holders held budgets that were used to purchase services on behalf of service-users; a new and highly significant change in direction for welfare professionals. As the regulatory duties of local authorities increased the surveillance aspects of welfare were codified and, more rigidly than ever before, separated from other educative, supportive and advocacy functions (Petrie, 1995). There was increasing evidence that the main preoccupation of welfare managers was the meeting of performance indicators or contractual targets set by national or local government (Townley, 2001; Laming, 2003).

As an academic in England I have three main areas of study: children's day care; child protection services; and services in the community for 'children in need'. All of these areas overlap, for example children's day care is a service often used as part of a child protection plan or to enable parents to enter the labour market. Children and young people, including young parents, encountered during these studies indicated they often met professional adults who did not respond to their unique circumstances and with whom they were unable to establish a consistent, respectful and helpful relationship (Bell, *et al.*, 2004; Fiorelli & O'Donnell, 2004; Petrie, *et al.*, 2006). This was unexpected as the 'partnership' focus of 1990s welfare 'best practice' had been superseded by an emphasis on 'participation' (DfES, 2005b).

By the beginning of the new millennium there had been many developments in ways of involving children and young people in policies and services in the UK. Consultation with young service-users had become a contractual requirement for most service providers and was mandated by statute in some circumstances (Franklin, 2002). These legislative and strategic imperatives generated a proliferation of initiatives designed to empower children and young people and bring their voices into policy and service planning processes. Despite a presumption about what participation means and involves (DfES, 2005b) there are still contested issues evident in welfare provision (Evans & Spicer, 2008).

Some children and young people experience participation as tokenistic – in place to meet contractual or legislative requirements but giving them no real say in the decision-making that affects their lives (Hill, 2006; Woolfson, *et al*, 2009). This may be because legislation and policies are not formed or implemented in a social and cultural vacuum. Welfare practices are affected by how children and young people are constructed and understood by the powerful adults around them. It has been argued that children and young people are a marginal group with little power whose realities have been unrecognised and whose competencies are discouraged (Qvortrup, 2004). Those who are 'different' because of ethnic origin, migrant status, physical or learning impairments are even more marginal (Kohli 2006, Clarke 2006). Children and young people in contemporary UK society are confronted by many, and often conflicting, demands and requirements imposed by adults. Although the debate on the meaning and nature of citizenship has begun to consider children and young people (Lawy & Biesta, 2006) they are still regarded as non-adults. These contradictions are apparent when services for 'children in need' are considered.

The lives children and young people in the UK

The concept of a 'child in need', which includes young people in early adulthood in specified circumstances, was brought into UK law by section 17 of the CA 1989 as a legal passport to state provided or paid for services in the community. A 'child in need' includes all disabled children (sec. 17 (10) (c)) and children at risk of significant harm (sec. 47) but must also include all 'children in need' in the community. A range of services have to be provided by statutory, third sector and 'for-profit' organisations although the local authority retains responsibility. The over-arching principle of the CA 1989 is that a child's welfare shall be paramount (Part 1, section 1) and this is reflected in the policies for children and young people in all four administrations. This principle is supported by resource allocation as investment in children in the UK is higher than the OECD average standing at £90,000 per child from birth to 18 years compared to £80,000 (OECD, 2009).

Nevertheless the well-being of children and young people in the UK, compared to their European peers, is deficient in several key areas according to three recent international comparative studies of more than 20 affluent countries, the findings of all three being based on comparable national statistics. They reveal higher rates: of teenage pregnancy, underage drinking, and young people not in education, employment or training (OECD, 2009); infant mortality and low birth weight (CPAG, 2009); and child poverty (UNICEF, 2007) than most countries sampled other than the USA. 'Well-being' is a socially constructed term but is defined as 'the many different factors which affect children's lives: including material conditions; housing and neighbourhoods; how children feel and do at school; their health; exposure to dangerous risks; and the quality of family and classmate relationships children develop (CPAG, 2009a, pp.2)'. Child abuse scandals have also drawn attention to systemic failings in services for 'children in need'. Public inquiries and government inspections have leveled criticism at all agencies involved, including health, education, probation and non-statutory organisations as well as children's services (Laming, 2003; The Lord Laming, 2009, Ofsted, 2008). Poor management; shortages of staff, both in terms of numbers and skills; poor communication within and between agencies and so on are common themes. The lack of consistency in the professional relationship with 'children in need', that has been revealed in many inquiries and inspections, is particularly concerning. Continuity of knowledge about a child as a necessary condition for decisions supporting optimal childhood development has been well understood for many decades.

Conditions necessary for the optimal development and well-being of children and young people

Professionals and managers responsible for services for 'children in need' can draw on many decades of research evidence as to what is required for optimal childhood development. There is greater consensus about what is needed by children in order to achieve their potential than in almost any other area of research into human well-being. These needs are common to all children whatever their society, ethnic origin, culture, affluence level, physical or learning capacities. Key theorists and researchers have demonstrated that as well as basic needs for food, shelter and so on, children also need a consistent and positive emotional relationship with one or a small number of adults especially during their early years (Bowlby, 1965; Erikson, 1965; Piaget, 1970; Ainsworth, *et al.*, 1978; Oaklander, 1978; Robertson & Robertson, 1989; Kellmer-Pringle, 1992; Fahlberg, 1994, Crittenden, 2008). Although all children are similar each child is unique and their development patterns vary as do the demands they place on those who care for them. Individual characteristics such as ethnicity, culture, gender, affluence, and physical or learning impairments also affect a child's developmental needs and pathways and the potential harms they face, as do the societies in which they live.

Professionals and their managers are charged with making decisions that safeguard 'children in need' and promote their well-being. This can best be achieved through decision-making that rests on a consistent 'helping relationship', as many decades of research into the effectiveness of human services has shown (Petrie, 2007). This requires continuity over time even when the identified problems appear to have been resolved. Organisational and management effectiveness is judged, however, by a complex array of performance indicators and inspections focused on outputs that can be measured quantitatively. Managers are additionally pressurised by other forces as the control and punishment of the young and professionals judged as inadequate are often the primary objectives of public and political opinion. The market polarises responses to the most difficult situations because 'children in need' have to fit adult constructions – are they 'at-risk' or 'in need?' victims or criminals? socially achieving or socially excluded? Outcomes have to be subject to quantitative measurement and so the operation of the market requires 'children in need' to be categorised and prioritised before they can receive a service.

The problems of managing services for 'children in need', it seems, have deeper roots than resource shortages or organisational configuration. These problems lie in the way in which the market paradigm in welfare has not only altered the way in which services are configured and distributed but altered the fundamental relationship between professional adults and 'children in need'. The discourse of consumption and the market paradigm, within which policies are formulated and services managed, pervades all aspects of our social life and, according to some commentators has had a profoundly negative effect on UK society (Bauman, 1995; Leonard, 1997; Bauman, 1998; JRF, 2008).

Children, young people, consumption and the market paradigm

The impact of the market paradigm on children and young people has barely been explored and inquiry has tended to focus on commercial goods and services. Martens *et al.*, (2004) argue there are a number of methodological and theoretical limitations in research examining the impact of consumption and markets on children and young people as they have received little theoretical attention within the sociology of consumption and the sociology of childhood has concentrated primarily on the production of consumption:

> [M]uch work on children's consumption shares an apparently uniform point of departure in that it focuses on the relationship between the market and children to the neglect of other pertinent social relationships (Martens et al., 2004, pp.158).

Academic interest has focused mainly on the type of commodities consumed such as toys, clothes, computer games and so on and the activity of children and young people as consumers (Gunter & Furnham, 1998). The effects of consumption, such as whether violent computer games stimulate violent behaviour, have also been studied (Anderson & Bushman 2001; Mitchell & Ziegler, 2007). Scant attention, however, has been paid to the symbolic meanings given by children and young people to the goods and services they consume although the 'commodification' of childhood (Langer, 2002; Cook, 2004) has been explored. It has been argued that the consuming experience has 'a *psycho-social* impact (Miles, 1998, pp.5)' and is a bridge between the individual and society. Psychological and social identities are simultaneously constrained and enabled through the consuming experience.

According to some commentators (Cook 2004; Crewe & Collins; 2006, Boden, 2006), children's identity and status are becoming inseparable from branding and investment. Some such as Seabrook (1985) perceive the impact on children of markets and consumerism as entirely negative. He argues that, as in the nineteenth century, children are still working for capital but as consumers not labourers and furthermore that poor children are not expected to desire the same goods and services as their more affluent peers. Langer (2002), however, argues that children can use consumer culture as a social resource 'a way of moving from "I" to "We" (2002, pp.71)'. It has also been suggested that

> children's consumption is the means ... [whereby] parents and children gain a sense of acceptance and belonging within their desired social group (Martens, et al., 2004, pp.169)

and perhaps strengthen their mutual bond. Martens, *et al.*, (2004) refer to Bourdieu's concept of '*habitus*' to illustrate how children learn competence in consumption not only through their families but also through social networks and institutions. The nature of the consuming experience in complex affluent societies is mediated by such factors as economic and social status, gender, ethnicity, physical or learning impairments and other signifiers of difference.

The variations experienced by some children as they move towards adulthood, therefore, may have negative consequences for them. Indeed the 'psycho-social' impact of the consuming experience is often negative for 'children in need' who are unable to act as consumers in ways that are considered appropriate or desirable within their social location. For example clothing is an important contributor towards identity construction:

> In late modernity, the visual styles adopted by young people through the consumption of clothing are regarded as having become increasingly central to the establishment of identity and to peer relations (Furlong & Cartmel, 2007, pp.83).

Young women described this to me most powerfully in relation to poverty, fashion and bullying in school (Petrie, *et al.*, 2006). But children have other roles in markets too as there is evidence to suggest that in some transactions they have become mere commodities with an exchange value.

The 'commodification' of children in markets

Legal and medical ethics theorists and business analysts (Yngvesson, 2002; Dorow, 2006; Baird, 1996; Shuster, 2003; Spar, 2006) have shown that children have been 'commodified' in relation to the trans-national trade in adoptable children, surrogacy and cloning. It is easy to see in relation to these market transactions (David and Kirkhope, 2005) how children have a use-value and are subject to commercial exchange. In other markets, such as the sex and leisure industries, young people, especially young women, have become 'commodities' also in order to meet adult needs with extreme and harmful consequences for some. During one study with which I was involved (Bell, *et al.*, 2004) a disclosure by a young woman was linked to the disappearance of the teenager Charlene Downes. This investigation led to the establishment of a multi-agency project aimed at preventing the child sex industry in the town (*Blackpool Gazette*, 2004a, 2004b). It was commonly stated by young people that under-age young women are encouraged as customers by nightclubs and pubs, in seaside and rural localities,

> 'If you're a girl and smile at the bouncers you get in unless you look like 10
> ... Easy. The thing is if you're attractive then you're in (Year 10, Young Men,
> Bell, *et al.*, 2004, pp.26)'.

Young people were acutely aware of their 'market value' in these circumstances.

In many transactions in markets, therefore, children and young people have become mere commodities with an exchange value. This process can be conceptualised in a similar way to the 'commodification' of body parts – a prominent theme in contemporary debates about the body:

> [A] process of objectification or reification is required, in which case it is first
> necessary mentally or physically to separate the materials from the body so
> that they may become objects. Once objectified ... a body part may have a
> social life as a thing and, ultimately, as a commodity ... There is in this process
> a potential violation to personal identity ... this is quite apart from any
> scientific or economic exploitation that may occur (Seale, et al., 2006, pp.26).

It is clear, therefore, that children's locus within markets of all kinds is evident and multi-faceted. They are consumers, perhaps powerful and discerning or exploited and manipulated or are objectified and constructed as commodities with an exchange value.

The 'commodification' of children in welfare markets

In welfare markets 'children in need' have no purchasing power and little or no choice about the kind or length of services they receive and so cannot act as consumers. Furthermore a deficit construction of children is embedded in the welfare market paradigm. Although the legal definition of a 'child in need' has remained the same since the CA 1989 it is the powerful discourse of adults that constructs the child inhering in policies, legislation and practices. The 'child in need' has been constructed as a social problem with costs attached; for control, treatment or protection. Public interest and welfare policies target issues such as teenage pregnancy, HIV/AIDS, sexual behaviour and exploitation, drug and alcohol consumption, obesity, anorexia/ bulimia, behaviour in school and educational under-achievement, anti-social behaviour and so on. Emphasis is placed on the cost-burden to society of what children do or do not do and how to change their behaviour. The current discourse constructs children as 'bad', 'mad' or 'sad'. Children as individuals or in groups are dangerous, frightening or victims. Attention and resources are given to ways in which children can be controlled, because of 'criminal' behaviour, treated because of 'psychiatric disorder' or saved from child abuse. Although the focus of this paper is on welfare services for 'children in need' in the community it is interesting to note the approach in the major policy for children in care in England *Care Matters: Time for Change* (DfES, 2007). The policy rests on a deficit model of children since low levels of educational achievement and high rates of those not in employment or training, and high rates of criminal activity are of primary concern. Proposals for action focus mainly on administrative and structural change including an 'Annual Stocktake' of the outcomes for children in care. The first of these has taken place (DCSF, 2009) and two of the four key messages are concerned with strengthening inspections and regulations. Will further regulation and attention paid to structure and process fundamentally improve outcomes for 'children in need?'

'Children in need' have become objects of market interactions in transactions between welfare purchasers and providers albeit for services which are meant to safeguard and promote their well-being. The operation of welfare markets however contributes to the process of objectification by codifying and quantifying 'needs' against which children are ranked and prioritised (Burden, *et al.*, 2000; Lyon, *et al.*,2003; Johnson & Petrie, 2004). In order to operate within market mechanisms services are predicated on commonalities and distributed according to adult needs although children's optimal development and well-being requires an individualised response to their individual needs. To fit within welfare assessment templates in statute and policies the 'child in need' has been objectified, standardised, costed and subject to quality control mechanisms. The Laming Inquiry identified this approach to assessment as highly unsatisfactory and a contributory factor in the appalling suffering and death of Victoria Climbié. 'The use of eligibility criteria to restrict access to services is not found in either legislation or in guidance and its ill-founded application is not something I support (Laming, 2003, pp.13)'. Short-term and fragmented services for 'children in need' framed around crude definitions of problematics and developed to suit the needs of adults cannot provide the well-researched conditions needed for optimal development. Performance indicators, imposed on local authorities and derived from macro patterns of 'need' such as indicators of deprivation distort responses by individual workers to individual children and their families. The emphasis, despite child-centred rhetoric, is on achieving the targets set by governments which has created 'short-termism' in services for children. The Association of Directors of Social Work in Scotland in a submission to TSG argue for:

> A move from 'short termism' to 'long termism': Children grow up over a period of 20 years or more. A series of short term initiatives aimed at having specific targeted outcomes don't allow for the building of strong community foundations to deliver long term support and development to children and their families [necessary] to see improved outcomes over time (Main:2006, pp.2)

Short-termism undermines the possibility of effective 'helping relationships' between professional adults and 'children in need.'

The demise of the 'helping relationship'

Concern has been raised from different quarters and disciplines about the changing construction of the welfare professional and their relationship with the recipients of welfare. It has been argued (Leonard, 1997; Walklate, 1999; Orme, 2001; Watson, 2002; Orme, 2002; Powell & Gilbert; 2006) that the centrality of the 'helping relationship' in welfare has been adversely affected by the market paradigm. This shift has occurred because the focus of policies, inspections and guidance has been on multi-agency work within a market paradigm:

> ...[These] are mostly structural changes attempting, probably with great difficulty, to alter the way in which adult professionals relate to each other. They will not necessarily alter the way in which they relate to children (Petrie & Owen, 2005, pp.132).

In all studies with which I have been involved children and young people, including young parents, gave great importance to the quality of the 'helping relationship' which they shared with welfare professionals. No single agency or professional predominated when positive or poor services were described. If respect was not present in their relationships with professional adults, however, services did not engage them:

But some teachers insult you and then the people who've been insult [sic], they don't like the lessons and they skive off it. (School F, Year 9, Petrie, et al., 2006, pp.33).

Midwives and health professionals, I found them degrading actually, putting us down because of our age – their comments and looks and attitudes towards us (Young Father, Bell, et al., 2004:38).

Managers' attention has been directed to improving communication between professionals as a primary objective. The welfare market processes focus on relationships between assessors and providers formalised in contracts concerned with costs and timescales. These adult concerns have not improved the ability of organisations to provide 'children in need' with a consistent long-term relationship with a skilled and competent professional.

The mixed economy in welfare has led not only to a proliferation of providers but also to a fragmentation of professional roles and functions. Although the neo-liberal government headed by Margaret Thatcher first introduced the market paradigm into public sector services the New Labour government elected in 1997 embraced this approach arguably creating additional difficulties for welfare professionals:

A continuing commitment by New Labour to the mixed economy of welfare introduced with the community care reforms of the Conservative administration led to a plethora of providers or 'stakeholders'. These bodies and individuals on the one hand had to be regulated, and on the other were to be involved in the evolving arrangements to achieve the necessary standards (Orme, 2001:613).

Multi-agency work is supposed to bring together a range of skills and breadth of knowledge whilst simultaneously unifying different professional cultures and values yet, as outlined earlier, evidence of poor outcomes for 'children in need' continue to emerge. The operational effectiveness of welfare markets for all services have been critiqued comprehensively almost since their emergence in the early 1990s (Clarke & Newman, 1993a, 1993b; Flynn & Hurley, 1993; Young and Wistow, 1996; Boyne, *et al.*, 2003; Micheli, *et al.*, 2007), but particular damaging consequences for children are embedded in the methods of costing services and distributing resources (Wilson & Petrie, 1998; Statham, *et al.*, 2001; Platt, 2001; Skinner, 2003; Margo, *et al.*, 2006). Performance indicator management, the deficit model of children inhering in welfare markets, and the 'commodification' of 'children in need' in market interactions have all combined to undermine the professional 'helping relationship' – the essential element in effective services for children and young people.

Implications for managers

Welfare in the UK has undergone a fundamental reconstruction in its relationship to the state and to welfare recipients because social and political attitudes towards welfare provision have changed since the late 1970s (Bauman, 1998). I have argued in this paper that 'children in need' are now commodities to be exchanged for payment between needs assessors and welfare providers mediated by short-term contracts. Furthermore the market paradigm operates on a construction of the 'child in need' as a costly social burden rather than a potential social asset. Different professions involved with 'children in need' are in danger of losing their distinctive skills and knowledge and although regulation of welfare has increased professionalism has diminished.

Despite their laudable aims the current policy programmes for children and young people in all four countries in the UK , have failed to prevent the deepening divide between children, young people and professional adults; the widening gap between professional knowledge and operational demands or redirect the attention of managers away from the demands of politicians towards 'children-in-need.' Yet there are indications that some administrations in the UK are seeking to move away from the market paradigm in welfare. For example in a review of social work by the Scottish Executive, Roe (2006) highlights research findings revealing the importance of the quality of the 'helping relationship' in successful outcomes in human services, evident in research into the helping professions for the last 40 years (Petrie, 2007). One reason why social workers leave the profession, it was suggested in the review, is that they can no longer work in this way:

> The inability to operate according to core principles may also in part account for the fact that many social workers leave the profession ... the situation in which they practice does not allow them to fulfil their commitment to key principles (Asquith, et al., 2005, 4.7).

Wales has made a clear commitment to move away from the market paradigm in public services (Gibbons, 2007), based on the Beecham Report two years earlier:

> In England, the Government is seeking to respond to the new public service challenges through a customer model which emphasises choice as the means to meet consumer expectations with competition, contestability and elements of market testing as the way to achieve efficiency ... this has not found favour in Wales, on grounds of both principle and practicality (Beecham Report 2006:5)

And England, at least as far as domiciliary social care for adults is concerned, is now modifying the market (BBC, 2nd Feb 2010).

The market paradigm in welfare has been driven by ideology not evidence and there is no statutory requirement to separate the management of assessment from the management of commissioning or provision in children's services. Fragmenting decisions about children's lives in this way runs contrary to all that is known about how children develop and relate to those around them. Managers must prioritise safeguarding 'children in need' by safeguarding the consistent, long-term 'helping relationship' between professionals and young service-users. Without a major effort to detach welfare from party political agendas and recover distinct and necessary professional identities in ways similar to our European neighbours, outcomes for children and young people in the UK will continue to be poor.

Notes

1   Within this article 'welfare' refers to aspects of social work/ social care, health and education services for 'children in need' and their families in the community.
2   I define a 'helping relationship' as an interpersonal, accountable relationship between a welfare professional and a 'child in need' that improves the child's well-being whilst 'managing expectations and reducing complexity' (Luhmann (1979) cited in Powell & Owen, 2006, pp.113)

References

Ainsworth, M., Blehar, M., Waters, E., and Wall, S. (1978) *Patterns of Attachment*. Hillsdale, NJ: Erlbaum

Anderson, C. and Bushman, B. (2001) Effects of violent video games on aggressive behaviour, aggressive cognition, aggressive affect, physiological arousal and prosocial behaviour: A meta-analytic review of the scientific literature,. *Psychological Science*, 12, 5, 353-359

Asquith, S., Clark, C., and Waterhouse, L. (2005) *The Role of the Social Worker in the 21st Century: a Literature review*. Edinburgh: University of Edinburgh

Baird, P.A. (1996) Ethical Issues of Fertility and Reproduction. *Annual Review of Medicine*, 47, 107-116

Bauman, Z. (1995) *Life in Fragments: Essays in Postmodern Morality*. Oxford:Blackwell

Bauman, Z. (1998) *Work, consumerism and the new poor*. Buckingham: Open University Press

BBC News (2010) Free social care delay outvoted. http://news.bbc.co.uk/1/hi/health/8492473.stm [Published, 2.2.2010, accessed, 4.2.1010]

Beecham Report (2006) *Beyond Boundaries. Citizen-centred local services for Wales*. Cardiff: Beecham Review Secretariat

Bell, J., Clisby, S., Craig, G., Measor, L., Petrie, S., and Stanley, N. (2004) *Living on the Edge: Sexual behaviour and young parenthood in seaside and rural areas*. University of Hull Working Papers in Social Sciences and Policy. Hull: University of Hull

Blackpool Gazette (2004a) A murky world of child prostitution. http://www.blackpoolgazette.co.uk/viewarticle.aspx?sectionid=62&articleid=879860 [Published 29.10.04, accessed 29.10.09]

Blackpool Gazette (2004b) Evil trade. http://www.blackpoolgazette.co.uk/viewarticle.aspx?sectionid=62&articleid=879872 [Published 29.10.04, accessed 29.10.09]

Boden, S. (2006) Dedicated followers of fashion? The influence of popular culture on children's social identities. *Media, Culture & Society*, 28, No.2, 289-298

Bowlby, J. and Fry, M. (1965) *Child Care and the Growth of Love*,. (2nd ed) Harmondsworth: Penguin

Boyne, G., Farrell, C., Law, J., Powell, M., and Walker, R. (2003) *Evaluating Public Management Reforms: Principles and practice* . Buckingham: Open University Press

Burden, T., Cooper, C., and Petrie, S. (2000) *Modernising. Social Policy: Unravelling New Labour's Welfare Reforms*. Aldershot: Ashgate

Child Poverty Action Poverty Group (CPAG) (2009a) *Child Wellbeing and Child Poverty: Where the UK stands in the European table.* London: CPAG

Clarke, H. (2006) *Preventing Social Exclusion of Disabled children and Their Families. Literature review paper produced for the National Evaluation of the Children's Fund.* Birmingham: University of Birmingham

Clarke, J., and Newman, J. (1993a) The right to manage: A second managerial revolution? *Cultural Studies,* 7, 3, Oct., 42-44

Clarke, J., and Newman, J. (1993b) Managing to survive: Dilemmas of changing organisational forms in the public sector. in R. Page, N. Deakin (eds.) (1993) *The Costs of Welfare* .Aldershot: Avebury (pp. 6-63)

Cook, D.T. (2004) *The Commodification. of Childhood: The children's clothing industry and the rise of the child consumer.* Durham, NC: Duke University Press

Crewe, L. and Collins, P. (2006) Commodifying children:Fashion, space, and the production of the profitable child. *Environment and Planning,* 38, 7-24

Crittenden, P.M. (2008) *Raising Parents. Attachment: Parenting and child safety.* Cullompton, Devon: Willan Publishing

David, M., and Kirkhope, J. (2005) Cloning/ stem cells and the meaning of life. *Current Sociology,* 53, 2, Monograph 1, 368-381

Department for Children, Schools and Families (DCSF) (2009) *Care Matters: Ministerial Stocktake Report 2009.* Nottingham: DCSF

Department for Children, Schools and Families, Welsh Assembly Government (WAG) The Scottish Government (TSG) Northern Ireland Executive (NIE) (2009) *Working Together, Achieving More,* DCSF: Nottingham

Department for Education and Skills (DfES),(2007) *Care Matters: Time for Change.* Norwich: TSO

Department for Education and Skills (2005a) *Every Child Matters: Aims and outcomes.* http://www.everychildmatters.gov.uk/aims/ [Accessed 27.1.2010]

Department for Education and Skills (2005b) *Every Child Matters: Participation of children and young people.* http://www.everychildmatters.gov.uk/ participation/ [Accessed 27.1.2010]

Department of Health (1991) *Child Abuse. A study of inquiry reports 1980-1989.* London: HMSO

Dorow, S.K. (2006) *Transnational Adoption: A cultural economy of race, gender, and kinship.* New York: New York University Press

Erikson, E. (1965) *Childhood and Society.* Harmondsworth: , Penguin

Evans, R. and Spicer, N. (2008) Is Participation Prevention? *Childhood,* 15, 1, 50-73

Fahlberg, V. (1994) (UK ed.) *A Child's Journey through Placement,* BAAF: London

Fiorelli, L. and O'Donnell, K. (2004) Trials of being a teenage mother. *Blackpool*

Gazette 27th October, pp.10-11

Flynn, N. and Hurley, D. (1993) *The Market for Care: Public sector management.* London: LSE

Franklin, B. (Ed.)(2002) *The New Handbook of Children's Rights*, London: Routledge

Furlong, A. and Cartmel, F. (2007) *Young People and Social Change: new perspectives.* (2nd ed.) Maidenhead: Open University Press

Gibbons, B. (2007) *A Strategy For Social Services in Wales over the Next Decade; Fulfilled lives, supportive communities.* Cardiff: Welsh Assembly Government

Gunter, B. and Furnham, A. (1998) *Children as Consumers. A psychological analysis of the young people's market.* London: Routledge

Gutch, R. (1992) *Contracting Lessons for the US.* London: NCVO

Hill, M. (2006) Children's voices on ways of having a voice: Children's and young people's perspectives on methods used in research and consultation. *Childhood*, 13, No.1, 69-89

Johnson, S. and Petrie, S. (2004) Child protection and risk-management: The death of Victoria Climbié', *Journal of Social Policy*, 33, 2, 179-202

Joseph Rowntree Foundation, What are today's social evils? http://www.socialevils.org.uk/# [Accessed 29.10.09]

Kellmer-Pringle, M. L. (1992) *The Needs of Children.* (3rd ed.) London: Routledge

Kohli, R.K.S. (2006) The sound of silence: Listening to what unaccompanied asylum-seeking children say and do not say. *British Journal of Social Work*, 36, 5, 707-721

Laming Report (2003) *The Victoria Climbié Inquiry: report of an inquiry by Lord Laming*, Cmnd. 5730. London: HMSO

Langer, B. (2002) Commodified enchantment: children and consumer capitalism. *Thesis Eleven*, 69, May, 67-81

Lawy, R and Biesta, G. (2006) Citizenship-as-practice: The educational implications of an inclusive and relational understanding of citizenship. *British Journal of Educational Studies*, 54, 1, 34-50

Le Grand, J. (1990) *Quasi-Markets and Social Policy.* Studies in Decentralization and Quasi-Markets, 1. Bristol: SAUS

Le Grand, J. (1993) Paying for or providing welfare. in R. Page and N. Deakin (Eds.) *The Costs of Welfare.* Aldershot: Avebury (pp. 87-106)

Leonard, P. (1997) *Postmodern Welfare: Reconstructing an emancipatory project.* London: Sage

Lyon, C., Cobley, C., Petrie, S., and Reid, C. (2003) *Child Abuse*, (3rd ed.) Bristol: Family Law/ Jordans

Main, S. (2006) *Education Committee: Inquiry into early years education and childcare.* Written submission from the Association of Directors of Social

Work. Edinburgh: ADSW

Margo, J., and Dixon, M., with Pearce, N. and Reed, H. (2006) *Freedom's Orphans: Raising youth in a changing world*. Newcastle-upon-Tyne: ippr, north

Martens, L., Southern, D., and Scott, S. (2004) Bringing children (and Parents) into the sociology of consumption. *Journal of Consumer Culture*, 4, 2, 155-182

Micheli, P., Neely, A., Kennerley, M. (2007) Have performance measurement systems helped or hindered public services? *CIMA Insight*, April. http://www.cimaglobal.com/cps/rde/xchg/SID-0AAAC564-496C4CFC/live/root.xsl/Insight052807_2898.htm [Accessed 29.10.09]

Miles, S. (1998) *Consumerism as a Way of Life*. London: Sage

Mitchell, P., Ziegler, F. (2007) *Fundamentals of Development: the psychology of childhood*. Hove: Psychology Press

Novak, T., Owen, S., Petrie, S., and Sennett, S. (1997) *Children's Day-care and Welfare Markets: Research study funded by NHS Executive (Northern and Yorkshire)*. Hull: University of Lincolnshire and Humberside

Oaklander, V. (1978) *Windows to our Children: Gestalt therapy approach to children and adolescents*. Highland, NY: Gestalt Journal Press

Office of the First Minister and Deputy First Minister (OFMDFM) (2005) *Our Children and Young People – Our Pledge*. Belfast: Children and Young People's Unit

Ofsted (2008) *Learning lessons, taking action: Ofsted's evaluations of serious case reviews 1 April 2007 to 31 March 2008*. London: Ofsted

Organisation for Economic Co-operation and Development (OECD) (2009) *Doing Better for Children*. Paris: OECD

Orme, J. (2001) Regulation or fragmentation? Directions for social work under New Labour. *British Journal of Social Work*, 31, 611-624

Orme, J. (2002) Social work: Gender, care and justice. *British Journal of Social Work*, 32, 799-814

Petrie, S. (1995) *Day-care Regulation and Support. Local authorities and day-care under the Children Act 1989*. London: Save the Children

Petrie, S. (2007) Partnership with parents. in A. James and K.Wilson (Eds.) *The Child Protection Handbook*. (3rd ed.) Elsevier: Edinburgh, (pp.377-379)

Petrie, S., Hughes, G., and Bennett, K.M. (2006) *Report for Blackpool Council on the Educational Achievement of Young Women at Key Stage 4*. Liverpool: University of Liverpool

Petrie, S. and Owen, S. (Eds.) (2005) *Authentic Relationships in Group Care for Infants and Toddlers: Resources for Infant Educarers (RIE). Principles into practices*. London: Jessica Kingsley

Petrie, S. and Wilson, K. (1999) Towards the disintegration of child welfare services. *Social Policy and Administration*, 33, 2, 181-196

Piaget, J. (1970) (trans. M. Cook) *The Origins of Intelligence in Children.* New York: International Universities Press

Platt, D. (2001) Refocusing children's services: evaluation of an initial assessment process. *Child and Family Social Work*, 6, 2, 139-148

Powell, J. and Gilbert, T. (2006) Performativity and helping professions: Social theory, power and practice. *International Journal of Social Welfare*, 15, 1-9

Powell, J. and Owen, T. (2006) Trust', professional power and social theory lessons from a post-Foucauldian framework. *International Journal of Sociology and Social Policy*, 26, 3/4, 110-120

Qvortrup, J. (2004) Editorial: The waiting child. *Childhood*, 11, 3, 267-273

Robertson, J. and Robertson, J. (1989) *Separation and the Very Young.* London: Free Association Books

Roe, W. (2006) *Report of the 21st Century Social Work Review.* Edinburgh: Scottish Executive

Seabrook, J. (1985) *Landscapes of Poverty.* Oxford: Blackwell

Seale, C., Cavers, D., and Dixon-Woods, M. (2006) Commodification. of body parts: By medicine or by media,. *Body and Society*, 12, 1, 25-42

Shuster, E. (2003) Human cloning: Category, Dignity, and the role of bioethics. *Bioethics*, 17, 5-6, 517-525

Skinner, C. (2003) New Labour and family policy. in M. Bell and K. Wilson *The Practitioner's Guide to Working with Families.* Basingstoke: Palgrave Macmillan (pp. 19-38)

Spar, D.L. (2006) *The Baby Business: How money, science and politics drive the commerce of conception.* Boston: MA: Harvard Business School Publishing

Statham, J., Dillon, J., and Moss, P. (2001) *Placed and Paid For: Supporting families through sponsored day care,* London: HMSO

The Lord Laming (2009) *The Protection of children in England: A Progress Report,* London: TSO

The Scottish Government (2008) *Getting it Right for Every Child.* Edinburgh: TSG

Townley, B. (2001) The Cult of modernity. *Financial Accountability and Management*, 17, 4, 303-310

United Nation Children's Fund (UNICEF) (2007) *Child Poverty in Perspective: An overview of child well-being in rich countries.* Florence: Innocenti Research Centre

Walklate, S. (1999) Is It Possible To Assess Risk?. in *Risk Management: An International Journal*, 1, 4, 45-53

Watson, D. (2002) A Critical perspective on quality within the personal social services: Prospects and concerns,. *British Journal of Social Work*, 32, 877-891

Welsh Assembly Government (2004) *Children and Young People: Rights to Action*. Cardiff: WAG

Wilson, K. and Petrie, S. (1998) No place like home: Lessons learned and lessons forgotten – the Children Act 1948. *Child & Family Social Work*, 3, 3, 183-188

Woolfson, R.C., Heffernan, E., Paul, M., and Brown, M. (2009) Young people's views of the child protection systems in Scotland', *British Journal of Social Work Advance Access*, published Oct 2009, 1-17

Yngvesson, B. (2002) Placing the gift child. in transnational adoption. *Law & Society Review*, 36, 2, 227-256

Young, R., and Wistow, G. (1996) Growth and stability for independent sector providers? *The Mixed Economy of Care Bulletin*, 5, 18-20

The body of this chapter was first published in 2010 in *Social Work & Social Sciences Review* vol. 14(1) pp.9-26. Stephanie Petrie was then a Senior Lecturer in the School of Law and Social Justice, University of Liverpool.

3

Complexity approach to frontline social work management:
Constructing an emergent team leadership design for a managerialist world

Michael Webster

The situation in 2013

The 2010 article which follows provoked the development of a conceptual framework for social work leadership. The 'complex argument' (Hafford-Letchfield & Lawler, 2010, p.7) advanced in the original article is intended to become more accessible by articulating this framework, and briefly unpacking its key elements. For this purpose, figure 1 provides a schematic representation of the framework.

The constituent elements in figure 1 underpin the development of a social work leadership model. I suggest that five strands in the literature present a distinctive configuration—a platform—from which conceptualisation of social work leadership may be derived. The article essentially canvassed aspects of this configuration; a more coherent design will hopefully be evident in this development.

Strand one:
Are leadership and management interchangeable terms?

This perennial debate has resulted in a range of opinion at divergent points on a continuum. Thus, e.g., Coulshed, Mullender, Jones and Thompson (2006) assert that the terms are practically synonymous; at the other end of the continuum, Zaleznik (2010) perceives them as radically different. Adopting a mid-point perspective, Jackson and Parry (2011, p.19) suggest that to separate leaders and managers is to 'ghettoize' them, proposing

Figure 1. Conceptualising social work leadership

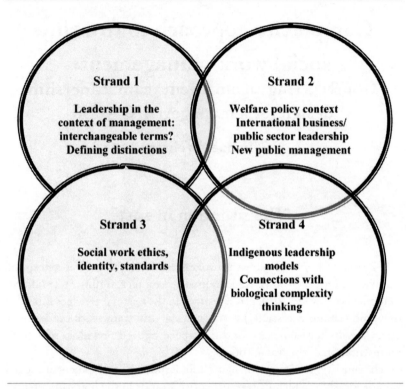

Strand 1

Leadership in the
context of management:
interchangeable terms?
Defining distinctions

Strand 2

Welfare policy context
International business/
public sector leadership
New public management

Strand 3

Social work ethics,
identity, standards

Strand 4

Indigenous leadership
models
Connections with
biological complexity
thinking

that managers exercise organic (i.e. informal) as well as positional (i.e. formal) leadership actions. This approach may be seen through a social constructivist lens, recognisable to social workers as an ecological framework (Bronfenbrenner, 2005). Grint (2005, p.1473) argues that leadership actions are socially constructed by the problems faced by organisations; that decision-making in ambiguous circumstances is the order of the day and is to be seen, he suggests, as emanating from leadership asking the right questions rather than determining the right answers.

This mid-point perspective informs the developing framework proposed in this introduction. A 'leader-management' approach (Bass & Bass, 2008, p.655) argues that management activities—the classic functions of planning, organising, leading and controlling—focus on 'things' such as designing job descriptions and organisational structures; leadership interacts with people. Motivating people and resolving conflict, for example, require communication skills to achieve desired agency objectives. These are leadership actions. That said, managerial restructuring of organisations may in fact produce greater transformation than person-to-person or person-to-persons leadership interactions. Leadership exercises influence and power in the organisational culture domain where uncertainty is seen (Grint, 2005; Uhl-Bien, Marion, & McKelvey, 2007). Organisational culture is created by people, not 'things;' leadership actions fit naturally into that domain.

Strand two:
Western leadership literature

Western leadership models have exercised enormous influence on the social work profession. Leadership thinking has shifted from early twentieth century 'trait' ideas analysing attributes of leaders, to focus on leader-follower relationships: an organic, complexity mode which proposes that leadership actions may emerge from workers at diverse levels in the organisation, described as complex adaptive systems thinking (e.g., McMillan, 2008; Plowman et al., 2007). Complexity thinking coincided with the emergence of transformational and transactional perspectives. Transformational leadership actions build or change organisation culture; transactional actions operate within existing norms (Bass & Avolio, 1993). The connections between leadership actions, organisational culture and a systems approach noted in the original article have also emerged in social work literature (e.g., Jaskyte & Dressler, 2005). Social workers think systemically from the 'person-in-social-context' perspective (Jarvis, 1995, p.79) thus finding congruence with systems thinking.

In contrast, public sector literature proposes that leadership occurs within the context of management, linking it with Fayol's (1967) conceptualisation of leading as one of the four classic management functions. The 'new public management' (NPM) (Hood, 1991) revolution of the last three decades falls within this category. In its broadest terms, NPM proposes that private sector management should be applied to the public sector by a focus on results rather than process. The British academic Pollitt (1990) characterises NPM as Taylorist 'scientific management' of a century ago; in the New Zealand context, Boston, Martin, Pallot and Walsh (1996) see NPM as instrumental in transforming public sector policies, practice and culture including many social work agencies located in the public sector. Public sector—NGO contracts extended this transformation to the not-for-profit arena. Leadership actions and conceptualisations of leadership by social workers need to be seen through the lens of these seminal organisational changes.

Strand three:
Welfare policy context: Historical and current influences on social work leadership

Tennant's (2007) analysis of New Zealand welfare policy, drawing on the British context, takes into account legislative and organisational changes, informed by three policy levels: welfare regimes, including state—NGO interactions; ideological and political conflicts; and welfare implementation. She notes that in a 'maturing welfare state,' diverse needs were acknowledged and specialised services emerged. This expansion occasioned 'an expanding welfare bureaucracy' characterised as 'systematized efficiency' (Tennant, 2007, pp. 119, 120). Tennant also observes that management was noted to be capable of inflexibility in state sector and NGOs alike, suggesting a transactional leadership style. It is in this welfare policy context that social work leadership occurs.

The effects of the 1980s NPM transformation rippled through social work agencies. Welfare policy, organisational culture change, leadership actions, tensions between the social work profession and NPM effectively coalesced to create social work agencies which in organisational design and accountability terms would have been unrecognisable to a previous generation of practitioners. Tennant draws attention to public funding of social work services by NGOs as 'the contract crunch' (2007, p.193), and succinctly expresses the prevailing NPM ideology—with a marginal leavening of social work understandings of 'empowerment' and 'bicultural journeys'—in her description of

> Consultants and change managers, mission statements, brand identities and
> empowerment models, bicultural journeys, quality assurance and assertions
> of excellence: the mantras of the late 1980s and 1990s [as] striking to anyone
> studying the records and annual reports of voluntary organisations.

Strand four:
social work ethics, identity, standards and management relating to leadership thinking

The International Federation of Social Workers (IFSW) (2012) code of ethics expects that organisational leadership activities will be integrated with professional practice ideals. Social work ethics enshrine notions of integrity; the British Association of Social Workers (2012) for example, identify qualities of integrity as 'honesty' and 'reliability'. In an unpublished social work master's thesis, Appleton (2010, p.105) articulates the 'multiple contexts influenced by our personal integrity, our professional integrity and the integrity of the helping professions,' and includes management practice in these 'multiple contexts.' The literature suggests that ethical considerations are inseparable from leadership and that qualities such as authenticity, spirituality and servant leadership express ethical leadership (Freeman, 2011; Luthans & Avolio, 2003).

Social work ethical codes mandate recognition of indigenous populations as marginalised groups (Briskman, 2007), connecting with the fifth literature strand. As a 'core purpose' of the profession, managerial leadership may be perceived as the executive agent in implementing such core purposes as 'engaging in social and political action ... to effect change by eliminating inequalities' (Sewpaul & Jones, 2005, p.219). Ethical social work leadership appropriately addresses indigenous inequalities. A holistic model emerges in which social work ethics, identity and standards are integrated with organisational leadership and indigenous perspectives.

Strand five:
Indigenous leadership models: connections with biological complexity thinking

By virtue of their organic nature, indigenous leadership models carry affinity with social work ecological thinking (Bronfenbrenner, 2005). Western leadership and management thinking has also embraced indigenous perspectives by suggesting, for example, that organisations may be seen as 'living' organisms (De Geus, 1999). Complexity-based whole systems development as 'biological' processes sees them as developmental: outcomes cannot be predicted (Olson & Eoyang, 2001). Such leadership styles are transformational (Burns, 1978) in that they change cultures. These observations demonstrate the emerging conceptual connections between Western complexity leadership thinking and indigenous 'living' images of organisational leadership.

These connections are illustrated, in the New Zealand context for example, by the Māori leadership perspective offered by Tipu Ake (Te Whaiti Nui-a-Toi, 2001). Leadership in Tipu Ake (Figure 2) is seen as collective, operating as an agent filtering fresh ideas into the organisation, or organism. In the Australian aboriginal context, Ivory (2008) notes that leadership derives from organic 'webs of nodal networks' (2008, pp.253-4). Similarly, North American indigenous leadership identifies values of spirituality and holistic worldview as underpinning leadership validity (Calliou, 2005, p.58). A generic understanding of indigenous perspectives therefore proposes that leadership is collective; it is organic; and it privileges holistic, spiritual thinking.

Figure 2. Tipu Ake

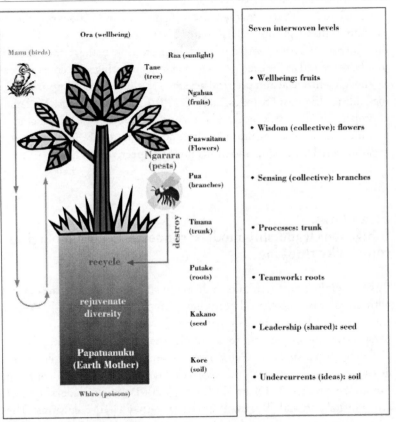

Source: Te Whaiti-Nui-A-Toi, 2001.

Conclusion:
A distinctive configuration for social work leadership

The framework proposed is intended as a contribution towards developing a social work conceptualisation of leadership. The configuration is located in organisational leadership theory, the broad social service and health policy context, social work ethics and identity, and indigenous models of leadership. Qualities associated with authenticity, ethics, indigenous, shared and exemplary leadership are increasingly appearing in the literature (Van Dierendonck, 2011). It is in that direction that future social work leadership may develop.

References

Appleton, C. (2010). *Integrity matters: An inquiry into social workers' understandings.* Massey, Palmerston North.

Bass, B. M., & Avolio, B. (1993). Transformational leadership and organizational culture. *Public Administration Quarterly, 17(1),* 112-121.

Bass, B. M., & Bass, R. (2008). *The Bass handbook of leadership: theory, research, and managerial applications* (4th ed.). New York Free Press.

Boston, J., Martin, J., Pallot, J., & Walsh, P. (1996). *Public management: The New Zealand model.* Auckland: Oxford University Press.

Briskman, L. (2007). *Social work with indigenous communities.* Sydney: Federation Press.

British Association of Social Workers. (2012). *Code of ethics: Key principles.* Birmingham: British Association of Social Workers.

Bronfenbrenner, U. (Ed.). (2005). *Making human beings human: Bioecological perspectives on human development.* Thousand Oaks: Sage.

Burns, J. M. (1978). *Leadership.* New York: Harper and Row.

Calliou, B. (2005). The culture of leadership: North American indigenous leadership in a changing economy. In D. Champagne, K. Torjesen & S. Steiner (Eds.), *Indigenous peoples and the modern state* (pp. 47-68). Walnut Creek, CA: Altamira Press.

Coulshed, V., Mullender, A., Jones, D. N., & Thompson, N. (2006). *Management in social work* (3rd ed.). Basingstoke; New York: Palgrave Macmillan.

De Geus, A. (1999). *The living company : Growth, learning and longevity in business.* London: Nicholas Brealey.

Fayol, H. (1967). *General and industrial management* (C. Storrs, Trans.). London: Pitman.

Freeman, G. (2011). Spirituality and servant leadership: A conceptual model and research proposal. *Emerging Leadership Journeys, 4(1),* 120-140.

Grint, K. (2005). Problems, problems, problems: The social construction of 'leadership'. *Human*

Relations, 58(11), 1467-1494.

Hafford-Letchfield, T., & Lawler, J. (2010). Reshaping leadership and management: The emperor's new clothes? *Social Work & Social Sciences Review, 14*(1), 5-8.

Hood, C. (1991). A public management for all seasons? . *Public Administration, 69*(1), 3-19.

International Federation of Social Workers. (2012). *Code of ethics.* Berne, Switzerland: International Federation of Social Workers.

Ivory, B. (2008). Indigenous leaders and leadership: Agents of networked governance. In J. Hunt, D. Smith, S. Garling & W. Sanders (Eds.), *Contested governance: Culture, power and institutions in indigenous Australia* (pp. 233-264). Canberra, Australia: Australian National University.

Jackson, B., & Parry, K. (2011). *A very short, fairly interesting and reasonably cheap book about studying leadership.* London, England: Sage.

Jarvis, P. (1995). *Adult and continuing education : theory and practice* (2nd ed.). London ; New York: Routledge.

Jaskyte, K., & Dressler, W. (2005). Organizational culture and innovation in nonprofit human service organizations. *Administration in Social Work, 29*(2), 23 - 41.

Luthans, F., & Avolio, B. (2003). Authentic leadership development. In K. S. Cameron, J. E. Dutton & R. E. Quinn (Eds.), *Positive organizational scholarship: Foundations of a new discipline* (pp. 241-258). San Francisco: Berrett-Koehler.

McMillan, E. M. (2008). *Complexity, management and the dynamics of change: Challenges for practice.* Abingdon: Routledge.

Olson, E. E., & Eoyang, G. H. (2001). *Facilitating organization change [electronic resource] : lessons from complexity science.* San Francisco: Jossey-Bass/Pfeiffer.

Plowman, D. A., Solansky, S., Beck, T. E., Baker, L., Kulkarni, M., & Travis, D. V. (2007). The role of leadership in emergent, self-organization. *Leadership Quarterly, 18*(4), 341-356.

Pollitt, C. (1990). *Managerialism and the public services: The Anglo-American experience.* Oxford: Basil Blackwell.

Sewpaul, V., & Jones, D. (2005). Global standards for the education and training of the social work profession. *International Journal of Social Welfare, 14*(3), 218-230.

Te Whaiti Nui-a-Toi (2001). Tipu Ake ki te Ora: Growing the future - An organic leadership model for innovative organisations and communities. In P. Goldsbury (Eds.), Available from http://www.tipuake.org.nz/tipu_life_cycle.htm

Tennant, M. (2007). *The fabric of welfare: Voluntary organisations, government and welfare in New Zealand, 1840-2005.* Wellington: Bridget Williams Books.

Uhl-Bien, M., Marion, R., & McKelvey, B. (2007). Complexity leadership theory: Shifting leadership from the industrial age to the knowledge era. *Leadership Quarterly, 18*(4), 298-318.

Van Dierendonck, D. (2011). Servant Leadership: A Review and Synthesis. *Journal of Management, 37*(4), 1228-1261.

Zaleznik, A. (2010). Managers and leaders: Are they different? In J. McMahon (Ed.), *Leadership classics* (pp. 86-98). Long Grove, IL: Waveland Press.

Complexity approach to frontline social work management:
Constructing an emergent team leadership design for a managerialist world

Introduction

Recognition of management as a 'core purpose' of social work in 2004 by the International Federation of Social Workers (IFSW) and International Association of Schools of Social Work (IASSW) (Sewpaul & Jones, 2005, p.219) legitimates exploration of the values, place and function of social care leadership and management. Such exploration recognises that in day-to-day practice, organisational imperatives emanating from an agency's requisite outputs and key performance indicators frequently exercise disproportionately high influence on service quality to consumers. The voice of the profession is commonly a poor relation to senior management expectations which exert significant pressure on frontline managers and practitioners. In this context, the mediating function of middle and frontline managers assumes pivotal significance in translating those expectations into workable approaches designed to meet consumer needs while balancing the profession's ethic of empowering service delivery against new public management's demand for 'efficiency, economy and effectiveness' (Boston, Martin, Pallot, & Walsh, 1996; Coffey, Dugdill, & Tattersall, 2009). Middleman and Rhodes (1980, p.52) capture this tension in their insightful statement that

> the supervisor-worker relationship is the key encounter where the influence of organisational authority and professional identity collide, collude or connect.

This paper analyses professional and organisational influences converging at that 'key encounter.' The author proposes that management premised on social work values at that critical interaction between supervisor and frontline worker requires a paradigm shift whereby social work managerial *philosophy* determines organisational *design* and thus practice. Social work academic thinking assumes that management as a business school discipline governs managerial theory and practice in social care organisations (Tsui

& Cheung, 2009); the respected British social work management academic text Coulshed, Mullender, Jones, and Thompson (2007, p.171), for example, contextualizes performance management in social work agencies by using Drucker's (1954) 'management by objectives' ('MBO').

However, critical reflections in social work literature are emerging on such approaches as Taylor's (1967) early 20th century 'scientific management,' resurrected since the 1970s as 'new public management' (NPM). Fiona Gardner's (2006) innovative treatment of 'creating connections for practice' offers analysis and vision for human service management by applying practice values and perspectives to the management task. This paper suggests that contributions such as Gardner's represent an incipient paradigm shift in moving scholarly and practitioner discourse away from fitting social care management thinking into historic managerial theory. Instead, conversations reflecting management 'as a conceptual field of practice *within* the principles and practices of social work' (Webster & Tofi, 2007, p.49, italics added) are needed. Although not a social work educator, Weymes (2001, p.320) articulates a purposeful working definition of organisational leadership that social workers would endorse:

> Today, the literature is … implying a move from 'leaders and followers' to leaders as *inspirational players* … the success of an organisation is vested in the formation of *sustainable relationships*, with the primary purpose of leadership being to influence the *feelings and emotions* of those associated with the organisation; to *create the emotional heart* of the organisation and thus to determine the tenor of the relationships between the people inside and outside the organisation (italics added).

The organic qualities identified express a transformational social work vision of leadership and management, illustrating Bass and Avolio's (1993, p.112) transformational qualities of 'idealized influence, inspirational motivation, intellectual stimulation, and individualized consideration.'

Constructing a management model unique to social work calls for explicit adoption of the profession's underpinning values to influence management behaviours. From a New Zealand perspective, this paper proposes that constituents of this construction are drawn from the professional body's bicultural social work code of ethics (Aotearoa New Zealand Association of Social Workers [ANZASW], 2008); indigenous approaches to organisation and management (Te Whaiti Nui-a-Toi, 2001); and management as a distinct discipline integrated with overarching 'whole systems' change management approaches (Attwood, Pedler, Pritchard, & Wilkinson

2003). These elements provide a framework in which management as a field of practice is located. Indigenous Maori living organisation images synergise with emergent complexity (Olsen & Eoyang, 2001; Lewin & Regine, 2001; Uhl-Bien, Marion, & McKelvey, 2007), servant leadership (Liden, Wayne, Zhao, & Henderson 2008), spirituality (Fawcett, S., Brau, Rhoads, Whitlark, & Fawcett, A., 2008) creating a management tapestry. Transcultural storytelling as powerfully contributing to cultural transformation is advocated. Gardner (2006) argues that telling stories develops clarity and makes sense of the narrative, acknowledging that stories *are* complex, messy, and continuing rather than well ordered and coherent. This paper argues that a narrative tapestry provides a potent balance to the re-emergence of a Taylorist scientific model which has contributed to deskilling social work practice under the guise of new managerial effectiveness, efficiency and economy.

Construction of this paper

The author proposes that three components define the professional, organisational and political cultures in which frontline social work managers function. The first is the managerialist environment in which social work agencies typically operate – alternatively termed 'new public management' (NPM). The second is found in the tensions which arise from the interaction between social work ethical values and NPM (Stewart & Webster). The third integrates a 'current realities' conceptual diagnosis emanating from the first two and constructs an emergent social work model of management. This paper suggests that cultural diagnosis – behaviours, values, beliefs and assumptions (Schein, 2004) – must precede application of philosophy, a process paralleling Senge's (1990) argument that 'learning disabilities' require treatment if learning systems tools are to be effective.

Figure 3 below illustrates the tensions arising from these components requiring synthesis for a frontline social work model of management.

Figure 3. Synthesising tensions for a frontline social work model of management

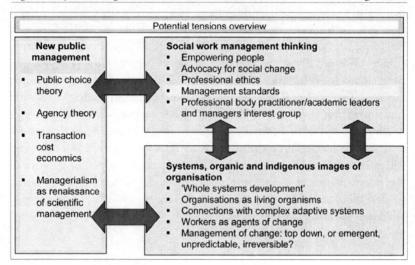

The pervasive reality of NPM:
Implications for coalface service delivery

NPM influence on statutory social work agencies – and via principal-agent relationships to non governmental organisations – has been extensively examined by social work academics. Even in the last two years, published papers have inter alia addressed 'Taylorist managerial control' (Carey, 2009) and 'Taylorised' ie 'deskilled' practitioners (Fitzgibbon 2008); 'staffing crisis' in UK social services caused by a drive for greater efficiencies, effectiveness and economies (Coffey, et al., 2009); and professional-bureaucratic tensions arising from information communication technology [ICT] (Burton & Van den Broek, 2009). Taylorist managerial discourse illustrates the NPM 'analytically driven movement of unusual coherence' noted by Hood's (1991) examination of the New Zealand model.

This paper focuses on frontline manager-practitioner interactions, analysing managerialist policy and practice influencing coalface service delivery to enable organisational diagnosis and redesign. The objective for this exercise is to apply social work values to 'moments of truth:' worker-consumer interactions epitomising the culture of the organisation (Grönroos, 1990, as cited in Moullin 2002, p.25). Interactions at odds with social work ethics may suggest organisational dysfunctionality at the worker-consumer 'moment of truth.'

This paper applies Boston et al's (1996) analysis of an overarching NPM descriptor relevant to frontline practice – the argument for transferable management between public and private sectors. It is not an exhaustive treatment.

Interoperability of public and private management?

The notion of interoperability of public and private management and a shift in emphasis from process accountability to accountability for results (Boston et al., 1996, p.26) represents a *non sequitur* for social care leadership and management. This rubric effectively reduces the frontline management task to one of accountability for measuring outputs and performance targets, replacing accountability for social work processes via professional supervision (O'Donoghue, Baskerville, & Trlin, 1999, pp.8-9). Arguably, frontline managers may become fixated checking data on computer monitors at the cost of maintaining social capital with practitioners, neglecting 'leadership behaviors that foster participatory management' (Elpers & Westhuis, 2008, p.40).

'Participatory management' resonates with Follett's notion of 'power with' as distinct from 'power over' (Graham, 1995) leadership value in social care organisations. These concepts are illustrated by Erez, Lepine, and Elms' (2002) investigation into team performance and membership satisfaction, suggesting that leadership behaviours are mediated through team design. Erez and his colleagues (2002, p.942) unexpectedly found that

> peer ratings for evaluation and reward ... promoted workload sharing, voice, and cooperation, and ... translated into higher levels of performance and member satisfaction.

Limitations associated with the study included 'fairly homogeneous ethnic background' of the teams unlikely be replicated in the workplace, and a 'quasi-experiment' with tertiary students 'did not consider a team structure where the leader was also responsible for providing specific evaluations of his or her subordinates' (Erez et al., 2002, pp.944-945).

Notwithstanding these limitations, potential benefits accruing from applying peer ratings and rotated leadership in a workplace social work team warrant critical evaluation. While clearly predicated on a high level of trust, this approach is philosophically congruent with the profession's empowerment ethos expressed in Follett's management model.

Implementation would require genuine power sharing and strengthened negotiating skills. Team members' ownership of responsibility would enhance qualities of team cohesion, add to group capacity for leadership skill development and integrate professional and organisational fields of practice through appreciative inquiry (Cooperrider, Whitney, & Stavros, 2008) – management's variant of strengths based practice.

An unintended serendipity of peer rating and rotated leadership also emerges. Erez et al (2002, p.942) note 'higher levels of team performance' as the approach is implemented. Skilful facilitation processes strengthen a professional ethic and also engender NPM efficiencies and effectiveness. Complexity perspectives of change emerge, demonstrating that even in a new managerialist world a living, organic approach to achieving requisite outputs is possible. This paper suggests however that the model proposed is likely to encounter inertia at best – and hostility at worst – if implemented among social workers with a cynical perspective of management initiatives. A pilot project with practitioners who combine a professional ethic for empowering individuals and challenging unjust structures (ANZASW, 2008), with innovation or pacesetting may be appropriate. Wood and Alterio (1995, 2.12.2) describe 'innovators' as professionals who 'push frontiers, creating and testing ... new knowledge and ideas'; pacesetters 'welcome ... new ... ideas but wait until they have been well tested by innovators before adopting them' (Wood & Alterio 1995, 2.12.3). Strategies needed to implement Wood and Alterio's 'Z-Zoner' model are canvassed later in this paper.

Morgeson, DeRue, and Karam (2010, pp.7-9) address team dynamics by examining leadership actions enabling a team to meet its 'critical needs' (eg 'psychological safety'), thereby 'fostering team effectiveness.' These authors suggest that 'in any given team there are multiple sources of leadership.' These sources enable expression of worker 'voice' articulated by Erez et al. (2002) in earlier discussion – that is, emergent leadership qualities articulating social work practice values. Citing Attwood et al. (2003, pp.58-74), McNabb and Webster (2010, p.44) identify these qualities and values as

'Humanising servant leadership;' 'holding frameworks' for shared ... 'mission' by 'appropriate dialogue'; 'diversity' as a source of 'innovation and learning'; holding the dynamic tensions between 'autonomy and direction' ... communication modes; 'building a learning community' informed by 'living' organisational images.

Ethics, the organisation and the individual: Tensions in workplace settings

This paper's second component comes out of almost a century of ethics by professional social work (Reamer, 1998). The place of ethics in developing 'effective practice' and 'improving organisational culture' at the frontline manager-practitioner level is predicated on Banks' (2008, p.1238) definition of 'social work ethics' as

> a specialist area of professional ethics comprising the study of the norms of right action, good qualities of character and values relating to the nature of the good life that are aspired to, espoused and enacted by social workers in the context of their work.

This definition usefully integrates ethical values of social work conduct and personal character attributes of the social worker applied to the organisation which legitimates practice. The use of self has long been seen as tacitly informing professional practice (Davies, 1994; Reupert, 2007). In this paper, it is used to define the 'moment of truth' between practitioner and consumer expressing organisational culture demonstrated in the quality of that interaction. Arnd-Caddigan and Pozzuto (2008, p.235) capture that emergent interaction by defining self as 'a function of relationships with others in which the self is continually created, maintained and re-created.' The author suggests that tacit skills reflecting professional ethics will be unconsciously integrated into a worker-consumer encounter as a behavioural expression of the assumptions, values and beliefs (Schein, 2004) which make up the culture of the employing organisation. Efficacious management is a prime contributor to that culture as the 'container' in which complex adaptive systems operate (Lewin & Regine, 2001). The question is: Are emergent processes in bicultural practice envisioned in the ANZASW (2008) Code of Ethics capable of thriving in an NPM context?

Ethics in a managerialist environment

Social work practice by members of the ANZASW is governed by the Association's Code of Ethics (ANZASW, 2008). Although the purpose of an ethical code is to engender trust in professionals by society and service consumers, managerialist prescriptive codes may diminish trust (Banks, 2004). The issue of trust in ethical decision making by social workers has also been raised as a concern in the New Zealand context of social work registration in 2003 which has arguably reduced the focus on social justice, where ethical issues abound (O'Brien, 2005; Orme & Rennie, 2004; Pitt, 2005).

Issues of trust in decisions by social workers in the context of these disparate ethical and organisational forces are analysed in this section of the paper which examines

+ the purpose of codes of ethics generally and the Bicultural Code adopted by the Aotearoa New Zealand Association of Social Workers in particular
+ tensions of deprofessionalisation and practice (Banks, 2004)
+ ethics and ethical dilemmas in day-to-day practice

Purpose of codes of ethics

The ANZASW Code's purposes include:

+ Benchmarks for client protection against unethical behaviours
+ Inspire professional behaviour reflecting core values and integrity of practice
+ Promote a standard of professional behaviour amongst members
+ Underpin everyday practice (ANZASW 2008, 6)

These purposes filter through the Code's recognition of the 'unique constitutional foundation of ... Te Tiriti o Waitangi' [The Treaty of Waitangi]' calling *inter alia* for application of indigenous Maori 'social work models of practice' (ANZASW, 2008, p.6). Social work's commitment to indigenous practice perspectives almost inevitably produces conflict with a 'discourse of modernisation' (Banks, 2004, p.41). 'Pressure points' of efficiency, performance and practice model standardisation (Banks, 2004, p.42) may be represented by competency-based training driven by employers, rather than professional standards inclusive of Treaty-based practice.

This paper suggests that the managerial agenda meets professional ethics at this practice interface; that the NPM agenda is not only exercised through exception reporting and imposed top down processes ('pressure points') but more potently through a sense of powerlessness by social workers leading to a culture of alienation. Staff turnover, resulting in the loss of institutional and practice wisdom, is tangible evidence of such alienation. The author recalls fifty percent turnover over three years in his statutory agency's local area from 1998 on as NPM became the dominating culture. A memorable statement revealing this agenda was, perhaps unwittingly, articulated by the general manager of the agency that she was 'driven by numbers.'

Burton and Van den Broek (2009, p.1326) illustrate Banks' (2004) observations around 'efficiency, audit and managerial control' by describing how reliance on information communication technology (ICT) for quality assurance and accountability purposes has shifted 'professional values ... to organisational and bureaucratic accountabilities.' They note 'substantial changes in work practices, processes and relationships for social workers ... tensions between professional and bureaucratic accountabilities have intensified.' These changes, not merely ideological, influence day-to-day practice: for example, ICT ability to measure outputs may reduce attention to 'user outcomes' (Burton & Van den Broek, 2009, p.1328).

Ethics in day-to-day practice

Computer-driven demands for data, for example, may undercut ethics' intentions to 'underpin everyday practice' (ANZASW, 2008, p.6). Frontline practitioners may perceive senior management information demands as exerting such pressure (Banks, 2004) that direct client contact becomes ethically uninformed. Banks (2008, p.1241) cites a Canadian study (Rossiter et al., 2000) reporting that 'codes are not used in practice and practitioners are often only dimly aware of their existence.'

This paper suggests that the plethora of reporting requirements by managerial demands for quantitative data has significantly affected social work's dual ethical focus on consumer empowerment and challenging unjust structures (ANZASW, 2008). Newly recruited workers may perceive ethics as a debating point rather than as an integrative force for practice – arguably representing an institutionalised cultural shift in which the education, experience, and personalities of social work recruits is located – the worker's 'capacity'. Banks (2009, p.9-10) articulates an emergent notion of capacity as 'moral competence' whereby a 'process of continuous reflexive sense-making ... may even involve re-evaluating and giving up previously held ideals and principles.' It is precisely this potential susceptibility to prevailing NPM organisational cultural suasion that may displace a new recruit's commitment to the social work ethic in favour of quantitative reporting as evidence of good practice.

Gray captures this susceptibility in her graphic depiction of current social work practice struggling to constructively integrate professional ethical values in the context of powerful organisational 'prescriptive' imperatives (Gray, 2009, p.3). Gray argues (p.13) that applying a care ethic to social work practice in 'risk-aversive, managerial social service environments' cannot be implemented, but pathways to 'compassion, consideration and care of others' by practitioners can be facilitated through 'values education' (virtues ethicists) or in 'caring relationships' (care ethicists).

Integrating a virtue or care ethic into social work practice implies that the moral and ethical legitimacy of the profession is at stake if that ethic is marginalised (Bisman, 2004). Values, argues Bisman (p.120), must drive the quest for the knowledge base of social work; and social work leadership is responsible for society's response to 'human well-being.' This paper applies Bisman's advocacy for societally-directed values leadership by the profession to the organisational sphere – that the ethical values intrinsic to worker-client interactions are evaluated in the light of 'the requirements of occupational roles' (Clark, 2006, p.80). In short, the ethical values-based coalface delivery of services to consumers must be congruent with organisational structures, policies and the quality of manager-worker relations.

The insights afforded by Gray, Bisman and Clark connect with Banks' emergent approach to ethical competence capacity building in the professional organisation. An emergent vision of ethics and organisation is also implicit through Hugman's (2003, p.8) postmodern interpretive discourse in which he notes that ethics are 'non-rational', that 'an exhaustive set of 'laws' cannot be applied and that 'contradictions are irresolvable' How might these perceptions be applied in the frontline perspective?

Such 'irresolvable' issues are polarities to be managed, distinguishable from problems capable of solution (Johnson, 1992). Polarities cannot be neatly analysed with diagnostic tools such as strengths/weaknesses/ opportunities/threats frameworks and do not readily allow clear, feasible options for action. Johnson argues that collaborative management 'relying on mutual assistance, support, cooperation, or interaction among constituent members' (Encarta Dictionary) is required to address polarities – for example, ongoing tensions between strengths perspectives (Saleebey, 2006) and risk assessment (Webb, 2006). Witkin's (2000) expressive phrase 'ethics-r-us' calls for 'ethics talks,' an implicit argument for a polarity discourse between practitioners, supervisors, senior managers and board governance scaffolding discussion to an emergent social work model of management.

Framework for an emergent social work model of management

In his cultural diagnostic tool, Schein (2004, p.17) draws from social anthropology in defining organisational culture as

> A pattern of shared basic assumptions that the group learned as it solved its problems of external adaptation and internal integration that has worked well enough to be considered valid and therefore to be taught to new members as the correct way to perceive, think and feel in relation to those problems.

Schein (2004, p.26) identifies three 'levels of culture.' (1) Assumptions – the 'unconscious, taken-for-granted ultimate source of values and actions' – are expressed in (2) values and beliefs which in turn result in (3) artefacts i.e. observable behaviour and physical objects. Although Schein implies that behaviour influences values which in turn influence assumptions, he nonetheless argues that leaders must be able to understand those assumptions if they are to be challenged and changed (pp.36-37). In contrast, Attwood and her colleagues (2003, p.138) suggest that in earnest discussions about changing the culture ... so often nothing really feels the change, especially the culture.' These authors propose that cultures will change as people in organisations tackle 'significant concrete tasks' (pp138-139). The author suggests that to actualise social work's commitment to change – including social workers' function as change agents within their own agencies – both Schein and Attwood et al. carry validity. Discourses of the profession's philosophical underpinnings are integral to intellectual debates practitioners need; but equally, 'the journey of a thousand miles starts with a single [physical] step.' Action steps authenticate practice integrity, obligating critical evaluation of organisational values against those of the profession.

With Schein, Attwood et al. in mind, this paper asks: How might the constituencies discussed in this paper be crafted into a workable model for coalface service delivery? Revisiting figure 3, these constituencies are:

+ Tensions contributing to frontline practice stressors caused by conflict between professional social work ethical codes and 'scientific' Taylorist managerialism (Banks, 2004; Bisman, 2004; Boston et al., 1996; Clark, 2006; Gray ,2009; Hood, 1991; Hugman, 2003)
+ An emergent, organic perception of agencies as organisations, integrating 'whole systems' thinking and complex adaptive approaches (Attwood et al,. 2003; Lewin & Regine ,2001; Morgan 1 997; Olson & Eoyang, 2001; Uhl-Bien et al,. 2007) with indigenous 'living' lenses through which organisation is viewed (Te Whaiti-Nui-a-Toi, 2001).
+ Constructing a diversity-based social work management model via practitioner-academic collaboration in the context of the ANZASW Leaders and Managers Interest group (ANZASW, 2008; McNabb & Webster, 2010; Sewpaul & Jones, 2005): workers as agents for 'second order' culture change (Van de Ven & Poole, 2009) using complexity thinking

The author proposes Attwood et al's (2003) 'whole systems development' as an enabling framework to apply these constituencies by generating 'containers' (Olson and Eoyang, 2001) in which worker creativity can flourish. By thus recognising diversity thinking, this emergent approach facilitates culture change embodying the social work vision for leadership expressed by Weymes (2001) and McNabb and Webster (2010). The author also suggests that this pathway synergises with servant leadership, workplace spirituality, and storytelling.

A way forward: Applying a 'whole systems development' framework

The 'five keys of whole systems development' identified by Attwood et al. (2003, p.xv) (figure 4 below) emanate from emergent notions of organisation described as 'complex adaptive systems' ('CAS') (Attwood et al. 2003, p.23) which apply a biological rather than a 'mechanistic process' (Lewin & Regine, 2001, p.24). Complexity theory explores leadership actions and workforce diversity by focusing on interactions between individual 'agents' in a CAS (Lewin & Regine, 2001, p.27). In describing complex systems, Morgan (1997, p.34) evokes biological images of 'relations among *molecules, cells, complex organisms, species,* and *ecology* [as paralleling] *individuals, groups, organisations, populations (species) of organisations,* and their *social ecology.*'

Figure 4
The five keys of whole systems development

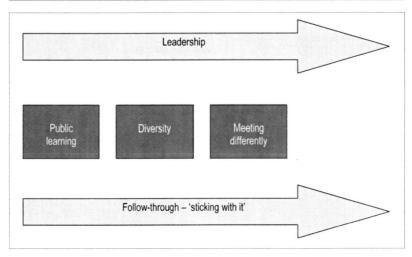

Source: Attwood, M., Pedler, M., Pritchard, S., & Wilkinson, D. (2003). *Leading Change: A guide to whole systems working.* (p.xv). Bristol: Policy Press. Reproduced by permission

This paper suggests that whole systems development offers an integrated framework to create a 'container' (Olson & Eoyang, 2001) for change whereby change agents can facilitate an emergent frontline team leadership model. Olson and Eoyang (2001, pp.11-12) propose that self-organising patterns are shaped by these 'containers' which set boundaries and may be geographic, eg department or team; behaviourally-based, eg professional identification; or conceptual, eg identity, purpose, procedures or budgets. Pathways for change – enabled by mutual group trust – avoid prescription in favour of an emergent approach employing the referent power given to those we admire or respect rather than coercive, expert, legitimate or reward power (French and Raven, 1959).

The whole systems framework provides human service change agents with the elements for creating an emergent team leadership model through an environmental scan: the 'balcony view' (Heifetz & Laurie, 1997 as cited in Attwood et al., 2003, p.61). Although there are five 'keys', the focus in this paper on 'leadership design' and journal space limitations concentrates attention on the leadership key.

Figure 5

Framework for creating Z-Zoners

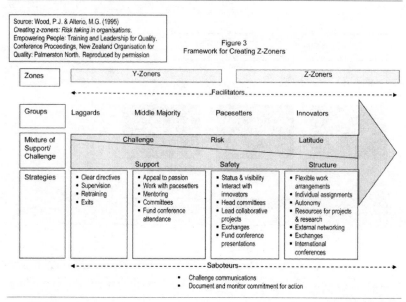

Source: Wood, P.J. & Alterio, M.G. (1995)
Creating z-zoners: Risk taking in organisations.
Empowering People: Training and Leadership for Quality.
Conference Proceedings, New Zealand Organisation for
Quality: Palmerston North. Reproduced by permission

Figure 3
Framework for Creating Z-Zoners

Zones	Y-Zoners		Z-Zoners

← — — — — — — — — — — — — — Facilitators — — — — — — — — — — — — — →

Groups	Laggards	Middle Majority	Pacesetters	Innovators
Mixture of Support/ Challenge	Challenge	Risk	Latitude	
	Support	Safety	Structure	
Strategies	• Clear directives • Supervision • Retraining • Exits	• Appeal to passion • Work with pacesetters • Mentoring • Committees • Fund conference attendance	• Status & visibility • Interact with innovators • Head committees • Lead collaborative projects • Exchanges • Fund conference presentations	• Flexible work arrangements • Individual assignments • Autonomy • Resources for projects & research • External networking • Exchanges • International conferences

← — — — — — — — — — — — — — Saboteurs — — — — — — — — — — — — — →

* Challenge communications
* Document and monitor commitment for action

Leadership

Attwood and her colleagues (2003, p.30) implicitly suggest that providing solutions for managing organisational change carry high failure rates. Kotter (1995) admits that most change programmes fail. What is needed, say Attwood et al. (2003, pp.31, 32), is that the leader asks the right systemic questions:

1. How can I best use my position ... to assist us all to make sense of what is going on, so that together we can contribute to sustainable change?
2. How do I lead this organisation so that we can make the best possible contribution to the improvement and wellbeing of those we serve?
3. How can I share my ideas and emerging goals in ways that do not stultify debate but assist learning about the 'bigger picture'?
4. How do I ensure that we implement plans that we have agreed with partners?

This paper proposes four pathways for change leaders to actualise responses to these questions: Servant leadership (Greenleaf, 1977; Liden et al., 2008); the Z-Zoner model (Wood & Alterio, 1995); workplace spirituality (Fawcett et al., 2008); and storytelling (Gardner, 2006). Because affinities exist between servant leadership and workplace spirituality they will be considered together.

The last section of this paper is not prescriptive, suggesting instead that practitioners acting as change agents might find that values and behaviours outlined provoke thinking and potential application.

Servant leadership and workplace spirituality

Research carried out by Liden and his colleagues (2008, p.162) suggests that servant leadership 'focuses on developing employees to their fullest potential in … task effectiveness, community stewardship, self-motivation, and future leadership capabilities.' This is no easy option. Together with notions of 'value creation' and 'emotional healing,' servant leadership articulates conceptual skills to push practitioners out of their comfort zones. Expectations of personal and career growth, of problem-solving and task completion are equally important, for example, as 'putting subordinates first' (Liden et al. 2008, 166).

Servant leadership synergises with qualities of workplace spirituality, which carries capacity for organisational 'creativity and innovative solutions' (Fawcett et al. 2008, 420), Fawcett and his colleagues equate workplace spirituality with a 'values-based organisation' (2008, 425), identifying fifteen workplace attributes which also connect with Wood and Alterio's (1995) Z-Zoner approach. Summarised, these attributes are valued work which extends worker capacity and recognise efforts made; depth of collegial interactions; managers who empower, guide and as leaders provide 'clear and consistent' behaviours; fostering collaboration, respect, commitment to a mission surpassing monetary reward; consumer orientation; learning from mistakes; self-management. Applying leadership wisdom which come out of these attributes creates perceptions of 'affirmation, belonging and competence' ((Fawcett et al., 2008, p.425, p.428), illustrating relationship/ task dimensions in Blake and Mouton's (1985) 'managerial grid'.

Z-Zoner model

Wood and Alterio's (1995) Z-Zoner framework (Figure 3) offers potential strategies for actions arising from servant leadership and workplace spirituality. This paper suggests that the framework applies to rotated

Assumptions

In 'normal' times – if there is such a thing – as well as in times of change, subordinates cannot understand a chief executive's isolation. I've given everything to this organisation – hard work, intellectual grunt, and playing the political game. It's a competitive and hierarchical world. I have to rely on my own judgment in making decisions because no one else has the complete picture. I'm paid to think. What I need from my staff is a return on the investment we've made in them – training, salary, subsidised university courses. It's a fair contract. No subordinate can understand the pressures of my position. Only fellow chief executives appreciate the stresses that come with the territory. Whatever management's perceptions, those of us delivering frontline services to consumers know that without our work there would be no organisation to manage. The success of the enterprise depends on our knowledge, skill base and commitment to the task at hand. Unpredictable behaviour by our consumers requires continual upskilling and ability to respond to surprises. We work best in interdependent teams which value collaboration, transparency and trust. Operational 'how to' manuals cannot cover every eventuality.

Designing processes which implement scientific, technological solutions for operations are models of precision and simplicity guaranteed to deliver to customers. We think of ourselves as engineers, providing best design solutions to master environmental challenges. Problem-solving is enjoyable and should exclude worker input – people are the problem because they make mistakes. Harmony in designed processes is the ideal model to produce outcomes which improve on existing services.

leadership (Erez et al., 2002), emergent leadership (Uhl-Bien et al., 2007) as well as conventional line management structures. Indeed, the author argues that the Z-Zoner approach facilitates emergent collaborative decision-making and in a social work agency environment acts as additional leverage for implementing Follett's power sharing approach (Graham, 1995). Rotated leadership advocated by Erez et al. (2002) implicitly requires team 'buy-in' for implementation. Combination with a peer reward system plainly reinforces equity outcomes. Conventional line manager decisions are arguably more susceptible to dissatisfaction: rotated leadership projects the message that all team members will eventually be stretched by decision-making leadership responsibility. Strategies suggested for 'laggards' and 'saboteurs' by Wood and Alterio may in fact carry added weight if exercised by collegial leadership, as 'blame' messages directed towards the hierarchy are effectively targeting colleagues.

This paper suggests that a collegial power-sharing culture contributes to the creation of 'containers' – noted previously – in which workers can be professionally stretched in 'safe' spheres of action (Olson and Eoyang, 2001). A feedback loop to Attwood et al's call for workers to tackle 'significant concrete tasks' (2003, p.138, p.139) is also discernible as an agent for culture change: tangible actions are arguably as, or more, powerful than another talkfest about agency climate.

Storytelling

Storytelling is emerging in organisation literature as a sense making phenomenon in which events and changes are interpreted by individuals at different hierarchical levels (Gardner, 2006). Beech, MacPhail, and Coupland (2009, p.337) identify 'dialogical stories' enabling alternatives to the dominant discourse – a practical route to Gardner's (2006) call to develop clarity and make sense of the narrative. Perceptions of the 'self' by others are constituted in stories of organisational change and reactions of players to each other (Beech et al. 2009, p.338). An example, translated from the organisational literature, follows overleaf.

'Assumptions' retells in narrative form Edgar Schein's 'executive, operator and engineer subcultures' (Schein 2004, pp.198-199). It illustrates the powerful images created by the 'silo' effect and lack of mutual understanding between interdependent groups in the organisation – human and social services no less than profit-making corporations. Narratives can be fixed-point observations – what Beech et al. (2008, p.337) describe as 'monological ... stories ... told from one perspective ... not amenable to questioning or criticism.' 'The ant' (http://www.scribd.com/The-Ant/d/12991307) is an amusing example; but the fixed-point message is unmistakable.

Beech et al. adopt emergent thinking in their discourse, observing that narrators in 'self-sealed stories' did not engage, precluding 'dialogue' (2009, p.349). Drawing on Shotter (2006), they contrast 'aboutness monological thinking' which fails to relate to others as 'living objects' with 'withness dialogical thinking' which engenders 'touch, contact' and leads to a genuine response between the parties. This paper proposes that the change agent in human services – manager, supervisor or frontline practitioner alike – can create a dialogue of engagement as an emergent 'container' to build a team leadership design.

Conclusion

The author suggests that most social work practitioners and managers are committed to integrate the historic ethos of the profession into organisational reality. However, the sheer demands of day-to-day practice with consumers, staff or other stakeholders, part-time academic study or participating in yet another project team, may preclude initiating cultural change. An emergent complexity approach to frontline management thinking simultaneously carries both significant risk of failure and potential for creative culture change by those most directly responsible for coalface service delivery: the practitioners and their immediate team leaders. The author proposes that the ideas expressed in this paper integrate recognition of the realities of NPM – so focused on outputs, measurements and key performance indicators – with opportunity for an emergent creativity in the construction of a social work vision for frontline management and service delivery. That construction provides an alternative to the route so many of us have taken exemplified by George Orwell's (1946) 'Boxer' in *Animal Farm*: 'I will work harder.' Using a commonplace expression, this is a 'win-win' outcome for all parties.

References

Aotearoa New Zealand Association of Social Workers. (2008) *Code of Ethics* (revised ed.). Christchurch: ANZASW

Arnd-Caddigan, M., and Pozzuto, R. (2008) Use of self in relational clinical social work. *Clinical Social Work Journal*, 36, 3, 235-243

Attwood, M., M. Pedler, M. Pritchard, S., and Wilkinson, D. (2003) *Leading Change: A guide to whole systems working*. Bristol, UK: Policy Press

Banks, S. (2009) Integrity in professional life: Issues of conduct, commitment and capacity. *British Journal of Social Work*, bcp152

Banks, S. (2008) Critical commentary: Social work ethics. *British Journal of Social Work*, 38, 6, 1238-1249

Banks, S., and Williams, R. (2005) Accounting for ethical difficulties in social welfare work: Issues, problems and dilemmas. *British Journal of Social Work*, 35, 7, 1005-1022

Banks, S. (2004) *Ethics, Accountability and The Social Professions*. Basingstoke: Palgrave Macmillan

Bass, B.M., and Avolio, B.J. (1993(Transformational leadership and organisational culture. *Public Administration Quarterly*, 17, 1, 112-121

Beech, N., MacPhail, S.A., and Coupland, C. (2009) Anti-dialogic positioning in change stories: Bank robbers, saviours and peons. *Organisation*, 16, 3, 335-352

Bisman, C. (2004) Social work values: The moral core of the profession. *British Journal of Social Work*, 34, 1, 109-123

Blake, R. and Mouton, J. (1985) *The Managerial Grid III: The key to leadership excellence*. Houston: Gulf Publishing

Boston, J., Martin, J., Pallot, J., and Walsh, P. (1996) The ideas and theories underpinning the New Zealand model. in J. Boston, J. Martin, J. Pallot, and P. Walsh (Eds.) *Public Management: The New Zealand model*. Auckland: Oxford University Press (pp. 16-40)

Burton, J., and Van den Broek, D. (2009) Accountable and countable: Information management systems and the bureaucratization of social work. *British Journal of Social Work*, 39, 7, 1326-1342

Carey, M. (2009) The order of chaos: Exploring agency care managers' construction of social order within fragmented worlds of state social work. *British Journal of Social Work*, 39, 3, 556-573

Clark, C. (2006) Moral character in social work. *British Journal of Social Work*, 36, 1, 75-89

Coffey, M., Dugdill, L.. and Tattersall, A. (2009) Working in the public sector: A case study of social services. *Journal of Social Work*, 9, 4, 420-442

Cooperrider, D.L., Whitney, and J.M. Stavros, J.M. (2008) *Appreciative Inquiry Handbook: For leaders of change*. (2nd ed.) Brunswick, OH; San Francisco: Crown Custom Publishing; Berrett-Koehler

Coulshed, V. and Mullender, A., with Jones, D.N. and Thompson, N. (2006) *Management in Social Work*. (3rd ed.) Basingstoke: Palgrave Macmillan

Davies, M. 1994. *The Essential Social Worker*. (3rd ed.) Aldershot: Arena

Denhardt, R.B., Denhardt, J.V., and Aristigueta, M.P. (2009) *Managing Human Behavior in Public and Nonprofit Organisations*. (2nd ed.) Thousand Oaks, CA: Sage

Drucker, P. (1954) *The practice of management*. New York: Harper & Row

Elpers, K., and Westhuis, D.J. (2008) Organisational leadership and its impact on social workers' job satisfaction: A national study. *Administration in Social Work*, 32, 3, 26-43

Erez, A., Lepine, J.A., and Elms, H. (2002) Effects of rotated leadership and peer evaluation of the functioning and effectiveness of self managed teams: A quasi experiment. *Personnel Psychology*, 55, 4, 929-948

Fawcett, S., Brau, ,J., Rhoads, G., Whitlark, D. and Fawcett, A. (2008) Spirituality and organisational culture: Cultivating the ABCs of an inspiring workplace. *International Journal of Public Administration*, 31, 4, 420–438

Fitzgibbon, D.W. (2008) Deconstructing probation: Risk and developments in practice. *Journal of Social Work Practice*, 22, 1, 85-101

French, J.R.P. and Raven, B.H. (1959) The bases of social power. In *Studies in social power*, ed. D. Cartwright. Ann Arbor, MI: University of Michigan, Institute of Social Science Research

Gardner, F. (2006) *Working with Human Service Organisations: Creating connections for practice.* South Melbourne: Oxford

Graham, P. (Ed.) (1995) *Mary Parker Follett – Prophet of Management: A celebration of writings from the 1920s.* Boston: Harvard Business School Press

Gray, M. (2009) Moral sources and emergent ethical theories in social work. *British Journal of Social Work*, bcp104

Greenleaf, R.K. (1977) *Servant Leadership: A journey into the nature of legitimate power and greatness.* New York: Paulist Press

Hood, C. (1991) A public management for all seasons? *Public Administration*, 69, 1, 3-19

Hugman, R. (2003) Professional ethics and social work, Living with the legacy. *Australian Social Work*, 56, 1, 5-15

Johnson, B. (1992) *Polarity Management: Identifying and managing unsolvable problems.* Amherst, MA: HRD Press

Kean, J. (2007) Professional ethics versus institutional expectations. *Social Work Review*, 19, 2, 37-41

Lewin, R.A., and Regine, B. (2001) *Weaving Complexity and Business: Engaging the soul at work.* New York: Texere

Liden, R.C., Wayne, S.J., Zhao, H., and Henderson, H. (2008) Servant leadership: Development of a multidimensional measure and multi-level assessment. *The Leadership Quarterly*, 19, 2, 161-177

McNabb, D. and Webster, M. (2010) Qualities and practices of professional social work leadership in an interdisciplinary mental health service: An action learning approach. *Action Learning: Research and Practice*, 7, 1, 41-57

Middleman, R. and Rhodes, G. (1980) Teaching the practice of supervision. *Journal of Education for Social Work*, 16, 51-59

Morgan, G. (1997) *Images of Organisation.* (2nd ed) Thousand Oaks, CA: Sage

Morgeson, F. P., DeRue, D.S., and Karam, E.P. (2010) Leadership in teams: A functional approach to understanding leadership structures and processes. *Journal of Management*, 36, 1, 5-39

Moullin, M. (2002) What is quality in health and social care? in *Delivering Excellence in Health and Social Care: Quality, excellence, and performance measurement* Maidenhead, New York: Open University Press; McGraw-Hill Education (pp.5-35)

O'Brien, M. (2005) A just profession or just a profession? Social work and social justice. *Social Work Review.* 17, 1, 3-22

O'Donoghue, K., Baskerville, A.D., and Trlin, M. (1999) Professional supervision in the new managerial climate of the Department of Corrections. *Social Work Review*, 11, 1, 8-15

Olson, E. and Eoyang, G. (2001) *Facilitating organisation change: Lessons from complexity science.* San Francisco: Jossey-Bass/Pfeiffer

Orme, J., and Rennie, G. (2004) *The Role of Registration in Assuring Ethical Practice.* Presented to the Global Social Work Congress, ' Reclaiming Civil Society', 2-5 October, Adelaide, Australia

Orwell, G. (1946) *Animal farm.* New York: Harcourt, Brace

Pitt, L. (2005) Social work registration: Knowledge and power. *Social Work Review.* 17, 3, 41-42

Pollitt, C., and Bouckaert, G.(2004) *Public Management Reform: A comparative analysis.* (2nd ed.) Oxford: Oxford University Press

Reamer, F.G. (1998) The evolution of social work ethics. *Social Work,* 43, 6, 488-500

Reupert, A. (2007) Social worker's use of self. *Clinical Social Work Journal,* 35, 2, 107-116

Saleebey, D. (Ed.) (2006) *The Strengths Perspective in Social Work Practice.* (4th ed.) **Boston: Pearson/Allyn & Bacon**

Schein, E.H. (2004) *Organisational Culture and Leadership.* (3rd ed.) San Francisco: Jossey-Bass

Senge, P. 1990. *The Fifth Discipline: The art and practice of the learning organisation.* New York: Doubleday/Currency

Sewpaul, V., and Jones, D. (2005) Global standards for the education and training of the social work profession. *International Journal of Social Welfare,* 14, 3, 218-230

Stewart, J., and M. Webster. (2009) *Where the rubber meets the road: Professional ethics, the organisation and the individual.* Presented to the 20th Asia Pacific Social Work Conference, Auckland, 11-13 November, 2009

Taylor, F.W. (1967) *The Principles of Scientific Management.* New York: Norton

Te Whaiti Nui-a-Toi (2001) *Tipu Ake ki te Ora.* (Retrieved March 26, 2007 from http://www.tipuake.org.nz/tipu_life_cycle.htm

Tsui, M.-S., and Cheung,F .C.H. (2009) Social work administration revisited: A re-examination of concepts, context and content. *Journal of Social Work,* 9, 2, 148-157

Van de Ven, A.H. and Poole, M.S. (2009) Explaining development and change in organisations. In *Organisation change: A comprehensive reader*, ed. W. W. Burke, D. G. Lake & J. W. Paine, 859-892. San Francisco: Jossey-Bass

Webb, S.A. (2006) *Social Work in a Risk Society: Social and political perspectives.* Basingstoke; New York: Palgrave Macmillan

Webster, M., and Tofi, H.J. (2007) Postgraduate social work management education in Aotearoa New Zealand: A unique framework for the study of management. *Social Work Review,* 19, 3, 48-57

Weymes, E. (2001) Relationships not leadership sustain successful organisations. *Journal of Change Management,* 3, 4, 319-331

Witkin, S. L. (2000. Ethics-R-Us. *Social Work,* 45, 3, 197-200

Wood, P., and Alterio, M. (1995) Creating z-zoners: Risk taking in organisations. In *Empowering People: Training and Leadership for Quality. Conference Proceedings,* New Zealand Organisation for Quality: Palmerston North

Uhl-Bien, M., Marion, R., and McKelvey, B. (2007) Complexity leadership theory: Shifting leadership from the industrial age to the knowledge era. *Leadership Quarterly,* 18, 4, 298-318

The body of this chapter was first published in 2010 in *Social Work & Social Sciences Review* vol. 14(1) pp.27-46. Michael Webster was then a Lecturer, School of Counselling, Human Services and Social Work, Faculty of Education, University of Auckland, New Zealand.

4

A strengths perspective on supervision of social workers within a social development context:
A best practice vignette

Lambert Engelbrecht

Introduction

The emergence of new public management measures as an operationalisation of neoliberal ideas is evident in various social work contexts all over the world. Consequential changes in conditions of service delivery, control and accountability create an infusion of supervision mechanisms for bureaucratic standardisation in social service delivery; and have the potential to exchange the traditional client-practitioner relationship for marketisation, resulting in a buyer-seller relationship (Bradley et al, 2010; Hughes and Wearing, 2007). Indeed, this growing global discourse has an immense impact on management and leadership practices in social work as welfare organisations and social workers are subjected to ever increasing performance pressures, exacerbated by a dominant deficit-based work orientation (Engelbrecht, 2010). These stressors, coupled in many instances with a traditional Western paternalistic and imperialist male worldview of social work supervision (O'Donoghue, 2002) as imbedded in the management and leadership models employed at social welfare organisations, need to be addressed by a critical theory beyond a deficits approach as an interpretative framework.

A strengths perspective, defined as a theory of social work practice by authors such as Healy (2005), with a focus on strengths, competencies, capacities, capabilities and resilience instead of on problems and pathology is a challenge posed to social service providers (Cohen, 1999). In response to this challenge, this chapter attempts in a vein similar to Ferguson's Critical Best Practice (CBP) approach (Ferguson, 2003) to present an example of a best practice in an inductive mode. This is done by integrating the supervision of social workers and strengths-based social work practices to offer an alternative management paradigm. The South African welfare context, as a showcase for a paradigm shift of welfare service delivery from a social treatment model to a developmental service delivery model (Patel, 2005), serves in this chapter as an example of a best practice vignette of a strengths perspective on supervision employed at a welfare organisation.

The chapter begins with an overview of a strengths perspective: in social work practice; as an alternative management paradigm; and on supervision of social workers. Subsequently, these aspects are elucidated by means of the best practice vignette. It is concluded that a strengths perspective has transformational potential; and as a proactive response to neoliberal global and local market demands, compels managers to employ strengths-based interpretative frameworks for assessments and personal development plans of supervisees in order to develop a facilitative alternative management paradigm. More specifically, the focus on current situations and the creation of a vision and challenges for future work endeavours is imperative, as well as addressing the question on who is taking ownership of the supervision process. It is emphasised that a focus on social workers' strengths does not mean an abdication of their responsibility for the development of own competencies.

A strengths perspective in social work practice

The roots of the strengths perspective reach deep into the history of social work, as represented by social work pioneers such as Hollis (1966) and Perlman (1957) who urged social workers more than four decades ago to focus on clients' strengths. A revival of the strengths perspective was initiated largely by scholars of the University of Kansas. Weick et al (1989) first offered an exposition of the perspective, followed by texts on the assumptions and principles of strengths-based practices with at-risk populations, by scholars such as Saleebey (1992, 1996, 1999, 2002, 2008) and Chapin (1995). Social workers throughout the world re-examined the strengths-based ideas and found them to be compatible with their own beliefs (Cohen, 1999). This evolving perspective provided practitioners with an alternative to the prevailing deficit-based practice models practiced in many countries in the world. Cohen (1999) even construed the strengths perspective as a rebellion against the dominant medico-scientific paradigms, which reduces people's symptomatology to problems.

A synthesis of conceptualisations on the strengths perspective adheres to a multifaceted philosophy which moves away from pathology and deficits towards practices which focus on the strengths, assets, capacities, abilities, resilience and resources of people; and is eminently based on key concepts such as empowerment, capacity, ownership, partnership, facilitation and participation; it concerns itself with a language of progressive change; it is compatible with social work's commitment to the person-in-environment; and it can be applied in a number of contexts and situations (Gray and Collet van Rooyen, 2002; Oko, 2000; Rapp, 1998; Saleebey, 2008). However, a core implication of the perspective is that '…it is impossible to make a one-to-one comparison with the medical model or to talk about which works better' (Saleebey 2002: 30). A strengths perspective is thus rather a critical, radical approach. Consequently it not only challenges medico-scientific or psychosociological approaches, but also anti-oppressive practice models that regard service users as oppressed and engender notions of powerlessness, positivism, ardent feminism and structuralism which might conceivably influence social workers (Gray and Collet van Rooyen, 2002).

Be that as it may, Rapp (1998) postulates that the strengths perspective is not a theory: it is merely a practice perspective in social work and does not consist of a definite process of facilitation (Weick and Saleebey, 1998). Therefore the strengths perspective is simply '…a way of thinking about what you do and with whom you do it. It provides a distinctive lens for examining the world of practice' (Saleebey, 2002:20). However, concerns about the perspective may be rooted in both the overall assumptions and its implementation in various contexts. Saleebey (2002) points out for example that the perspective has been accused of being merely a mantra to encourage positive thinking and a disguised attempt to reframe misery. In turn, scholars such as Gray and Collet van Rooyen (2002) produced specific examples from practice to show that the strengths perspective is more than mere positive thinking. Furthermore, since the products of strengths-based practices are defined within diverse contexts (Oko, 2000), the application of the perspective reaches beyond a welfare service delivery model which is based only on a social treatment approach, and which is informed by a medical model with its emphasis on remedial treatment, social pathology and individual clinical practice. The strengths perspective thus plausibly informs a developmental approach to social welfare as instituted in South Africa (RSA, 2006).

A strengths perspective within a social development context

South Africa adopted a social development approach to social welfare after the country's democratisation in 1994. This approach embraced a people-centred approach to social and economic development with the aim to redress the past imbalances in the country. As an approach to social service delivery, social development transcends the residual approach that has dominated social welfare discourses of the past, and instead proposes a welfare system that facilitates the development of human capacity (RSA, 1997). This context implies that developmental social work per se promotes social and economic inclusion through enhanced personal functioning, strengthening of human capital, well-being and the livelihood capabilities of individuals, groups and communities that contribute to social justice and human development (Patel, 2005). Notably, the Integrated Service Delivery Model towards improved social services (RSA, 2006) of the South African National Department of Social Development, which has the role and responsibility to inter alia provide strategic direction for social service delivery, recognises the need for integrated strengths-based approaches to service delivery. It is against this background that Engelbrecht (2010) concludes that a strengths perspective and related concepts are peculiar to a social development approach to social welfare and should therefore be essential in constructing an appropriate theoretical conceptual framework as an alternative management paradigm for social work service delivery.

A strengths perspective as an alternative social work management paradigm

Traditionally social work organisations operate in rigid bureaucratic contexts characterised by social control functions in which an ideology of pathology and managed cared predominates (Gray and Collet van Rooyen, 2002). This tradition is critiqued by authors such as O'Donoghue (2002) as a paternalistic and imperialist male worldview, echoing the values and attitudes which Patel (2005) regarded as an inheritance from a social treatment model and which requires a shift in paradigm. A shift in management paradigm presupposes flexibility and adaptability by a learning organisation and is offered as a solution to how organisations can increase their chances for survival and strengthen their market position (Hafford-Letchfield et al, 2008). An alternative social work management paradigm within a social development context thus necessitates strengths-based learning organisations which systematically identify and supply leverage to both organisational strengths and individual strengths of staff in the pursuit of their mission and vision. The management paradigm of the organisation should furthermore consciously be designed with a focus on strengths that are evident both in what the organisations do (social service delivery) as well as how they lead and how they manage. Contrary to classical theories in human service organisations, a strengths-based management paradigm evidently falls within a human resources model of organisational management, as Lewis et al (2007) state that 'the purpose of the human resources approach is to develop organisational forms that build on the worker's strength and motivation'. A human resources model of organisational management moreover provides the theoretical foundation for Engelbrecht's (2010) contextualisation of social work supervision as an integrated part of the middle managers' human resources function. This argument echoes the claim by Hafford-Letchfield et al (2008) that supervision provides an alternative mechanism capable of fostering the ideal of a learning organisation.

A strengths perspective on supervision of social workers

Cohen (1999) regards a strengths perspective on supervision of social workers as particularly relevant as strengths-based supervision similar to strengths-based practices is consistent with the mission of social work (Hare, 2004). Since the principles of strengths-based practices are also consistent with a social development approach, which is anchored firmly in South Africa's Integrated Service Delivery Model (2006), generalist social workers in the country are enjoined to employ strengths-based practices in their interventions. These social workers are subject to supervision as amended by a Social Service Professions Act (RSA, 1978).

Supervision in South Africa is generally defined by a normative or administrative function, a formative or educational function and a restorative or supportive function. However, recent research by Engelbrecht (2010) reveals that the way in which these supervision functions are depicted, tends to consider supervisees to be in deficit despite organisations' social development approach, which may be regarded as contradicting clinical intervention and correlating supervision practices. This arises from the fact that the functions of supervision as expounded by Kadushin (1976) are intrinsically based on a traditional problem-oriented paradigm (Perlman, 1957) of social work practice. In this connection, Cohen (1999) advised that problem-solving supervision may undermine strengths-based practices considering the parallels that exist between the process of supervision and the process of practice. He specifically postulates that '...problem-centred supervision would render strengths-based practice very difficult indeed and could result in the strengths-oriented supervisee developing either a powerful resistance to the supervision or a grand confusion in his or her work with clients' (Cohen, 1999: 462). Indeed, this problem-centred framework is '...a kind of cultural discourse' (Saleebey, 2002: 273) and needs to be redefined with fundamental principles constituting a strengths perspective on social work supervision.

The following synthesis of fundamental principles regarding the scope of supervision, role of the supervisor and theoretical undergirding of supervision may contribute to building a strengths perspective on social work supervision: the scope of supervision should not be crisis-driven as this would suggest a problem orientation; the supervisor needs to assume a facilitation role by adopting a strengths vocabulary; and the theoretical undergirding of supervision should be based on competencies and outcomes (Engelbrecht, 2004). These fundamental principles ought not to be regarded as a denial of the supervisee's learning needs, but should rather be regarded as a conscious choice and effort to focus on talents, skills and competencies as opposed to spending supervision time and energy on deficits. The following best practice vignette is an illustration of one organisation's efforts to instil a strengths perspective on the management of their supervision practices.

Best practice vignette

Social work as a profession in South Africa was born out of disquiet about poverty by Afrikaner women's welfare organisations after the end of the Anglo-Boer war in 1902. This culminated in the foundation of the NGO represented in this vignette. Supervision of social workers in the organisation emerged prominently as a form of in-service training in the early 1960s and has since then been regarded as a middle management activity internal to the organisation (Engelbrecht, 2010). All front-line social service professionals employed by the organisation receive supervision from middle managers in accordance with organisation policies. The professional organisational structure of the organisation comprises a director, three senior managers, 20 supervisors who function as middle managers and 115 front-line social workers, 28 auxiliary social workers and 25 community development workers. The social workers render generalist and integrated social work services to more than 407 200 service users through case work, group work and community work methodologies, across four provinces in South Africa.

The country's embrace of a social development approach to social welfare after the end of the Apartheid political system in 1994 informed strengths-based social work practices in the organisation concerned, as a result of state subsidy implications and by means of a range of government enforceable policies. All social workers employed by the organisation receive in-house training in strengths-based social work practices and are expected to reflect this perspective in their interventions as indicated in organisational manuals and documents.

Despite the structured introduction of strengths-based social work practices in the organisation, Engelbrecht's (2010) research on the interplay between the historical development, current practices and future challenges of social work supervision reveals a discrepancy between the strengths-based practices of front-line social workers and the deficit, paternalistic management orientation of the supervision they receive, resulting in a growing uneasiness amongst workers (compare Cohen, 1999 and O'Donoghue, 2002).

The organisation furthermore draws mainly on the seminal work of Botha (2002), a local pioneer in social work supervision, whose composition of the supervision process is based on Perlman's (1957) problem solving process and Kadushin and Harkness' (2002) exposition thereof. This education model, as construed by Botha (2002: 104) '...comprises details related to the welfare organisation (place), the individuals, families, groups, communities (client system), the needs or problems of the client system (problems), the social work process (process), and the social worker (personnel)'. Although this education model provides a definite, comprehensive, unique framework for holistic supervision practice, the philosophical underpinning of this frame of reference by a strengths perspective on supervision (Cohen, 1999), competence supervision model and outcomes based orientation (Engelbrecht, 2004) is ambiguous and needs to be transformed to be compatible with a strengths perspective.

The preceding context prompted the organisation concerned to redefine itself as a strengths-based learning organisation, and to initiate processes to transform its problem and deficit oriented management and supervision practices to be congruent with the ideal of strengths-based social work intervention practices. This revaluation initiated the construction of interpretative frameworks using an inductive methodology by means of workshops with the supervisors in order to facilitate an alternative management and supervision paradigm. Since no concrete examples of interpretative frameworks for a strengths perspective on supervision could be found, the workshop participants decided to delineate the organisation's management of supervision to a two-step process and associated product, namely a strengths-based assessment of social workers and a strengths-based personal development plan (PDP). The rationale for this action was that an initial strengths assessment of each social worker may inform that worker's PDP, which subsequently may augment the content of each supervision session with a social worker, ultimately resulting in evidence-based material for performance appraisals. The interpretative frameworks of the strengths-based assessment of social workers and PDP will be illustrated in the following exposition.

Botha's (2002) education model was transformed into an interpretative framework for the strengths-based assessment of social workers, due to the holistic nature of the model, and the supervisors' familiarity with the model. The strengths-based assessment of social workers serves mainly as a process of information gathering to compile a strengths register of assets, talents, competencies and capabilities, which may be recognised and actively engaged in the PDP and subsequent supervision sessions of the social worker. Essential to every component of the strengths assessment is that associated knowledge, skills and values be established which should be situation-specific, according to the social worker's work context. Therefore, only explanatory examples will be presented.

The first component of the strengths assessment is defined as the strengths in the social worker's knowledge, skills and values regarding his/her characteristics in terms of aspects such as self-knowledge, leadership qualities, communication, loyalty and so on. The second component deals with the worker's strengths with reference to his/her practices within the specific organisation. These strengths may allude to the worker's understanding and execution of policies, legislation and statutory processes, budgets, administrative procedures etc. The third component entails the worker's strengths in knowledge, skills and values with regards to the dynamics of service users, which may include their culture, developmental phases, socio-economic status and of course also their specific capabilities. The fourth component pertains to the strengths in knowledge, skills and values of the worker regarding the range of challenges faced by service users, such as poverty, homelessness, abuse and the like. The last component deals with the worker's strengths regarding the actual intervention with the service user, the scope of which stretches from the utilisation of methodologies and securing resources to the integration of theory and practice. The preceding components are however intertwined and should be assessed as a coherent meaningful whole, but retaining specific content. The knowledge, skills and values regarding the different components may also overlap most of the time and be diffused, and should rather be perceived as provoking pointers for interpretation of the components. The matrix below portrays the interpretative framework of a strengths-based assessment of a social worker:

Strengths-based assessment	Social worker characteristics	Organisation	Service users	Challenges of service users	Intervention with service users
Knowledge -------- Skills -------- Values	e.g.: - self-knowledge - leadership - communication - loyalty - creativity - adaptability	e.g.: - policies - legislation - statutory processes - budgets - administration	e.g.: - culture - developmental phases - socio-economic status -capabilities	e.g.: - poverty - homelessness - abuse - troubled relationships - family violence	e.g.: - methodologies - models, theories and perspectives - integration of theory and practice

An interpretative framework of a strengths-based assessment of a social worker

Flowing from the strengths-based assessment's interpretative framework, the supervisors of the organisation concerned identified ten competencies as the basis for each social worker's PDP, which is peculiar to the organisation's domain within the social development approach. Echoing a conceptualisation of competencies articulated by Hafford-Letchfield et al (2008), the managers define competencies within the organisation as what the worker knows and can do and how he/she values it; and how these are demonstrated at the end of a period of supervision. The competencies are thus focussed on work-based evidence and provide an independent set of criteria against which performance is measured and recorded. In short: the competencies are not a job description, but are seen as providing a common language for the organisation to define organisation-specific practices as determined by the organisation's vision, mission and service plan. The competencies identified by the managers focus in essence on the social worker's implementation of policies and legislation; methodologies; assessments; contracting with service users; engagement with service users; integration of theories, perspectives and models; utilisation of organisation-specific intervention programmes; the social worker's documentation; management of service delivery programmes and evaluation and monitoring of service delivery programmes.

Each competency informs specific outcomes, which are, in turn, based on the social worker's strengths-based assessment and situational work context. The participating managers interpret an outcome as a demonstration of achievements culminating in a reliable, valid, authentic, current and sufficient context, stemming from a particular competency (compare

Letchfield et al, 2008). The outcomes ought to contain a verb to denote action, an object or noun and as far as possible a word or parameter with which to qualify it (Engelbrecht, 2004).

Supervision activities, based on each outcome, to be conducted during supervision sessions are furthermore facilitated as part of the supervision contract between the supervisor and the worker according to a mutually agreed assessment method, which ultimately underpins the performance appraisal of the particular social worker. Supervision activities may consist of various strategies and techniques such as role plays, reviews of documents and oral presentations, and assessment methods may comprise checklists, direct observations, portfolios and so on. The compilation of portfolios is favoured as basis for a performance appraisal as it might serve as a showcase for social workers to demonstrate their strengths and associated competencies in practice. The following diagram graphically illustrates the interpretative framework of a strengths-based personal development plan (PDP):

Competencies	Specific outcomes	Supervision activities	Assessment method
1. Policies and legislation	e.g.: 1.1. Practice reflects ability to work in accordance with statutory requirements	1.1 Self-study of applicable statutory documents such as:.................	1.1 Present court reports of ..... (service user) and identify ......(social worker's) ability (strengths and challenges) to work in accordance with statutory requirements
2. Methodologies			
3. Assessments			
4. Contracting with service users			
5. Engagement with service users			
6. Integration of theories, perspectives and models			
7. Utilisation of specific intervention programmes			
8. Documentation			
9. Management			
10 Monitoring and evaluation			

An interpretative framework of a strengths-based personal development plan

It is imperative to reiterate that the organisation's two-step process and product, encompassing the strengths-based assessment of a social worker and the strengths-based personal development plan were founded on fundamental strengths-based principles regarding the scope of supervision, the role of the supervisor and the theoretical undergirding of supervision.

These strengths-based principles are aimed at creating supervisees' independence, and optimising participation in the supervision process, while at the same time also respecting their self-determination. The purpose is to lead to capacity building of supervisees, so as to develop their self-control regarding their reactions and decisions. It is believed that this aim can only be achieved if the supervisor lets go of the power associated with the title of "supervisor". The supervisor must therefore assume a facilitation role, and nurture a partnership relationship with the supervisee. This relationship is also aimed at facilitating supervisees' responsibility for self-development, which implies that they accept co-responsibility for their own development and supervision; that the traditional vertical supervisee-supervisor interaction must change into a horizontal dialogue; that supervisees must be cognitively and affectively empowered and motivated to accept challenges with confidence; and that the supervisee's work environment must be mobilised as a resource for support. These principles, originally constructed to empower social workers (Engelbrecht, 2004), also imply that within a paradigm of developing and activating the possibilities, capabilities and potential of supervisees, the primary focus of supervision must be on the current situation and the creation of a vision and challenges for future work endeavours.

With the above-mentioned principles as backdrop, a comparison between the differences in operationalising traditional supervision and strengths-based supervision is evident in order to elucidate the transformation from problem-centred to strengths-based supervision. Some differences are illustrated below as example and are framed particularly to address practical issues raised by both supervisees and supervisors in the organisation when employing strengths-based supervision (Engelbrecht, 2009). These issues translated to questions such as: who takes responsibility for the education in supervision? Is the supervisor the only all-knowing expert in the supervisor-worker-relationship? Who takes responsibility for critical reflections on interventions? Who is talking the most and who is listening? Who is making the decisions? Who is controlling the supervision process?

TRADITIONAL SUPERVISION	STRENGTHS-BASED SUPERVISION
The supervisor educates and the supervisee is being taught.	Both the supervisor and the supervisee are involved in the education and they learn from each other.
The supervisor is the all-knowing expert and the supervisee is the layperson.	The supervisor admits that he/she is not the all-knowing expert and appreciates and utilises the supervisee's knowledge and experience.
The supervisor takes full responsibility for the critical reflection on interventions.	The supervisor and the supervisee are jointly involved in critical, reflective and imaginative thinking.
The supervisor mostly talks and the supervisee listens.	Both the supervisor and the supervisee talk and listen.
The supervisor makes the decisions and the supervisee implements them.	The supervisor and the supervisee make joint decisions, based on what is meaningful to both.
The supervisor controls the supervision process and the supervisee is being controlled.	The supervisor and the supervisee strive to meet each other's needs instead of administering the control of the process.

Comparison between the differences in operationalising traditional supervision and strengths-based supervision

The illustration above reveals that in the employment of strengths-based supervision numerous issues may be identified, but the ultimate core question is: Who is taking ownership of the supervision process? The answer to this question as proffered with acclamation by the supervisors of the organisation, is unequivocally that a strengths perspectives on supervision of social workers holds that ownership of the supervision process implies a shared agenda between the supervisee and the supervisor and that the focus on workers' strengths does not mean an abdication of responsibilities for the development of own competencies.

In addition it should be noted, that when operationalising a strengths perspective on supervision, the goal, processes, functions and related strategies of management and supervision of social workers remain. Be that as it may, this best practice vignette shows that it also remains a constant challenge for leadership, management and supervision in social service delivery to transform an organisation's vision and mission towards a strengths perspective as an alternative management paradigm.

Conclusion

This chapter presents a strengths perspective on supervision within an interpretative framework, which is a key element in a social development approach to social work practice in South Africa, and which also finds resonance with supervision in other contexts. Without a strengths perspective, managers, supervisors and social workers are left with theories that emphasise deficits in social work management and service delivery. The arguments in this chapter show that the strengths perspective, in Saleebey's (2002: xiv) words '...has been quietly fostering a small revolution in which the hegemony of deficit explanations is beginning to weaken, belief in resilience is rebounding and collaborative practice is growing'. Moreover, the said author suggests that one should not be fooled by the seeming simplicity of the strengths perspective.

The best practice vignette presented here, confirms that the strengths perspective has transformational potential if the focus is on current situations and the creation of a future vision and challenges for supervisees. Additional prerequisites are that the supervisee should take ownership of the employment of the supervision process – and most importantly – should take responsibility for the development of own competencies.

Hence, as a proactive response to neoliberal global and local market demands, a strengths perspective compels managers to employ strengths-based interpretative frameworks for assessments and personal development plans of supervisees in order to develop a facilitative alternative management paradigm. This reveals true transformational leadership.

References

Botha, N.J. (2002) *Supervision and consultation in social work.* Bloemfontein: Drufoma

Bradley, G., Engelbrecht, L.K. and Höjer, S. 2010. Supervision: a force for change? Three stories told. *International Social Work,* 53,6, 773-790

Chapin, R.K. (1995) Social policy development: The strengths perspective. *Social Work,* 40, 4, 506-514

Cohen B-Z. (1999) Intervention and supervision in strengths-based social work practice. *Families in Society,* 80, 5, 460-466

Engelbrecht, L.K. (2004) Operationalising a competence model of supervision to empower social workers and students in South Africa. *Social Work/ Maatskaplike Werk,* 40,2, 206-216

Engelbrecht, L.K. (2009) *The status of supervision in the ACVV.* Cape Town: ACVV Head Office

Engelbrecht, L.K. (2010) Yesterday, today, and tomorrow: Is social work supervision in South Africa keeping up? *Social Work/Maatskaplike Werk,* 46, 3, 224-242

Ferguson, H. (2003) Outline of a critical best practice perspective on social work and social care. *British Journal of Social Work,* 33,1005-1024

Gray, M. and Collet van Rooyen, C. (2002) The strengths perspective in social work: Lessons from practice. *Social Work/Maatskaplike Werk,* 38,3, 193-201

Hafford-Letchfield, T., Leonard, K., Begum, N. and Chick, N.F. (2008) *Leadership and management in social care.* London: Sage publications

Hare, I. (2004) Defining social work for the 21st century. The International Federation of Social Workers' revised definition of social work. *International Social Work,* 3,47,406-424

Healy, K. (2005) *Social work theories in context. Creating frameworks for practice.* Houndmills: Pagrave-Macmillan

Hollis, F. (1966) *Casework: A psychosocial therapy.* New York: Random House

Hughes, M. and Wearing, M. (2007) *Organisations and management in social work.* London: SAGE Publications

Kadushin, A. (1976) *Supervision in Social Work.* New York: Columbia University Press.

Kadushin, A. and Harkness, D. (2002) *Supervision in social work.* (4th ed.) New York: Columbia University Press

Lewis, J.A., Packard, T. and Lewis, M.D. (2007) *Management of human service programs.* (4th ed.) Belmont: Thomson Brooks/Cole

Oko, J. (2000) Towards a new model of practice. In P. Cox, S. Kershall and J. Trotter *Child sexual assault: Feminist perspectives.* London: Palgrave

O'Donoghue, K. (2002) *Global-vision, local-vision, personal-vision and social work supervision.* Paper presented to Aotearoa New Zealand Association of Social Workers Conference, Christchurch, 31October- 2 November

Patel, L. (2005) *Social Welfare and Social Development.* Cape Town: Oxford University Press

Perlman, H.H. (1957) *Social casework: A problem-solving process.* Chicago: The University of Chicago Press

Rapp, C.A. (1998) *The strengths model: Case management with people suffering from severe and persistent mental illness.* New York Oxford University Press

RSA (Republic of South Africa) (1978). Ministry for Social Development. South African Council for Social Service Professions. *Social Service Professions Act* (100 of 1978). [Amended National Welfare Act (Act 100 of 1978).] Pretoria: Government Printers

RSA (Republic of South Africa) (1997). Ministry of Welfare and Population Development. *White Paper for Social Welfare.* Notice 1108 of 1997, Government Gazette, Vol. 386, No. 18166 (August 1997). Pretoria: Government Printers

RSA (Republic of South Africa) (2006). Department of Social Development. *Integrated Service Delivery Model.* Pretoria: Government Printers

Saleebey, D. (1992) *The strengths perspective in social work practice.* New York: Longman

Saleebey, D. (1996) The strengths perspective in social work practice: Extensions and cautions. *Social Work,* 41,3, 296-305

Saleebey, D. (1999) The strengths perspective: Principles and practices. In B.R. Compton and B. Galaway. *Social work processes.* Pacific Grove: Brooks Cole

Saleebey, D. (2002) *The strengths perspective in social work practice.* (3rd ed.) Boston: Allyn & Bacon

Saleebey, D (2008) *The strengths perspective in social work practice.* (5rd ed.) Boston: Allyn & Bacon

Weick, A., Rapp, C, Sullivan, W.P. and Kisthardt, W. (1989) A strengths perspective for social work practice. *Social Work,* 34, 6, 350-354

Weick, A. and Saleebey, D. (1998) Postmodern perspectives for social work. In R.G. Meinert, J.T. Pardeck and J.W. *Murphy Postmodernism, religion and the future of social work.* New York: Haworth Pastoral Press

This chapter is based on an article first published in 2010 in *Social Work & Social Sciences Review* vol. 14(1) pp.47-58. Lambert Engelbrecht was then a Senior Lecturer in the Dept of Social Work, Stellenbosch University, Republic of South Africa.

5
Managing at a distance in social work and social care

Ray Jones

The situation in 2013

This paper on 'Managing at a Distance' was prepared just before the new Conservative Cameron Coalition government came into power in the United Kingdom. It has led to some change in the landscape for social work and social care which has modified the context for managers and leaders.

Firstly, the Coalition government inherited an international financial crisis which had been created by big banking corporations which spanned national boundaries and which had become reckless. As the complex vehicles the banks had created to move and make money started to collapse the whole edifice of international and national finance started to crumble. There were options in how this might be addressed. One possibility would have to been to constrain the accumulation of wealth by those who were already very rich and to look for some modest redistribution to inject spending power into depressed economies. A second option would have been to follow the Keynsians and to inject energy into flagging economies through expenditure on public works and infrastructure. A third possibility was to batten down the hatches, to very dramatically and quickly reduce public borrowing and expenditure, with the consequence that economic policies disadvantaged the poorest who were the heaviest users of public services and leave the rich untouched (and with even less direct tax to pay). This latter option was chosen by the Conservative and Liberal coalition government. The consequence for the managers of public services was less money resulting in inevitable service cuts. For managers of social work and social care services in particular it meant less money for services at a time of escalating demand as increasing poverty of children, families, disabled and older people all created more need and more referrals for assistance.

The management task, therefore, has become focussed on managing greater demand with less money. It has become even more important in this context that managers stay close to their front-line colleagues, are explicit and public about the realities of what can be achieved, and avoid piling the pressure and blame on front-line teams and services. 'Managing at a distance' in this context requires closing the distance so that front-line workers and managers do not feel stranded with the impossibilities and pain created by national government decisions and policies.

Secondly, the Coalition government has, not always explicitly, sought to break up the coherence of the welfare state. There is increasing complexity with academies and free schools being financially rewarded for moving outside the community of schools previously brought together by local councils. There is the chaos of disjointed and damaging reform of the National Health Service. What drives government policy is a belief that competition and fragmentation will drive the three 'Es' of economy, efficiency and effectiveness. This is unproven and uncertain. The track record of the privatised and separated gas, electricity and water public utilities and of rail services is hardly reassuring or inspiring in terms of current cost or quality. One 'E' which is proven, however, is the loss of 'Equity' as those who can afford to pay more (e.g. in private education or private health care) secure their own services and other publicly-funded services deteriorate and are more heavily rationed.

Again, the consequence of the complexity, confusion and chaos being created is experienced by public sector managers. For managers in social work and social care services for children it means schools focussing overwhelmingly on nationally bench-marked and reported academic attainment rather than being local partners and a community resource for children, and now looking primarily after their own rankings and ratings. In services for adults it means health and housing partners competing with each other in an economic market place and with greater gain to be had by focussing on the more financially lucrative options which includes increasing services for those who can pay and will pay more.

It is front-line workers across agencies who see their working relationships being fragmented and who have to learn the new routes to capture the commitment and attention of partners. Managers need to stay close to their front-line services to help keep them linked within the rapidly changing territories of inter-agency working. Managers need themselves to work across these reshaping agency boundaries to make as much sense as possible of what may be becoming increasingly incoherent.

Thirdly, the Coalition government has clearly indicated its intention to reduce what might be seen as bureaucratisation and proceduralisation. This ranges from looking to reduce nationally-determined regulation within the economy, relaxing planning controls and restricting the role and remit of national inspectorates. From health and safety, to where houses are built, to what employers can do to employees, to what financial services can do, rolling back the role of government and its regulations and inspectorates is seen to free up opportunity and to reduce red tape.

It is also seen to create more opportunities within social work and social care for professional rather than procedural practice. The Munro review of child protection, and the Coalition government's response including dramatically reducing the 'Working Together' child protection statutory guidance, is evidence of this government commitment.

But lighter touch regulation and inspection, and less prescribed practice, places an even greater onus and responsibility on managers to ensure performance and quality at the front-line. But less reporting to inspectors and fewer data returns to government should create more space, and a greater awareness and opportunity, for managers to manage rather than report. Again, staying close to the front-line while also giving front-line managers and teams the space to shape and to use professional competencies should be a part of the new script.

So the Coalition government is creating a social work and social care glass which is partly full and partly empty. It may be rather less than half-full but the responsibilities and opportunities for managers now may be even greater than before.

Managing at a distance
in social work and social care

Management may be thought about as the manager overseeing and directing others who are in a subordinate relationship. The picture might be of the manager or supervisor on the shop floor or alongside the production line in direct contact with other workers, giving instructions and observing their actions. Leadership might conjure up the picture of the battlefield with orders being given by the commander requiring an immediate acceptance and response at a time of crisis.

But rarely, if ever, is it like this. Even within routinised industrial work workers create their own meaning, and determine their own actions and strategies, sometimes in opposition to the intentions of managers (see, for example, the early seminal studies by Burns & Stalker, 1961; Goldthorpe & Lockwood, 1968). On the battlefield everyone has to use their initiative as an immediate response to what is happening (Montgomery, 1961).

And within social work and social care even when the manager is on site, based within the service centre such as a residential care home for which they have a responsibility, they will not be observing all that is happening. It is their subordinate colleagues providing the care for residents who determine the immediate quality of care and the experience of the residents. The shift and rota system within care homes also means that, at most, the manager will be at work for only about a third of the time the service is in operation.

For fieldwork services the team manager will have even less direct knowledge of the practice of members of their team, who will be unseen in much of their contact with service users which takes place away from the office or in discrete office interviews.

It is, however, the first line managers in social work and social care services who still have most direct contact with the practitioners who are undertaking direct work with, or providing the hands on care for, service users, and who are also most likely to have at least some contact themselves alongside other workers with service users. The role of front-line service managers is crucial in determining service quality and performance and also the experience of service users and of those workers who provide the service (see Reynolds et al, 2003; Kearney, 2004; Coulshed et al, 2006; Social Work Task Force, 2009).

For more senior managers their management and leadership will be at even more of a distance and more remote. For example, as a social services director of a large English county I had, at its largest, overall responsibility for all social work and social care provision to children and to families and to disabled adults, including older people, within a population of 640,000 people spread across a geographical area where it took 2 hours to drive from the north to the south and 1 ½ hours from east to west. Services were provided by 3,200 employees within more than 150 service centres (locality offices, day centre services, residential homes etc).

Even with a commitment to spend half-a-day each week meeting with teams within their work locations and bases meant that I only got to meet with most teams every 12 to 15 months. It became more difficult and complex again with the development of integrated services and teams with other organisations, such as the local Health Services, as some colleagues might then be located in multi-professional teams with the work bases provided by other organisations, increasing the number and diversity of work locations to be visited.

The question which arose, and arises, is how to manage and lead at a distance? As managers and leaders how to get others to do what we want and need them to do, and how we want it to be done, even when we are not present, are unseen and may indeed have little direct contact? This is an issue for senior managers, but it is also of relevance to all managers including front-line managers.

It is also an issue of interest for all employed in the organisation. Managers may not be present, but an awareness of their position power and status is still pervasive. This may be a brooding and threatening unseen presence or an implicit impact giving confidence and reassurance that there is control and not chaos within the organisation and that at time of crisis managers will be supportively engaged rather than distanced and self-protecting.

As a consultant with the European Community funded Russian-European Trust for Welfare Reform it is an issue I explored with over 200 social services directors from across Russia and national policy makers in a 'master class' in August 2009 in Siberia. For some of these directors the communities and services for which they had a responsibility were hundreds of miles and days apart, accessible only by helicopter in the winter. It is also an issue I have explored with others in more recent workshops at Kingston, Leicester and Staffordshire universities with social care and social work managers.

Managers and accountability

In the United Kingdom, within a culture of inquiries (Butler & Drakeford, 2003; Stanley & Manthorpe, 2004) the consequences of a tragedy occurring after actions and omissions by front-line workers have previously almost exclusively fallen heavily on the front-line workers themselves. It was Diana Lees, the social worker for Maria Colwell in the early 1970s, who was pilloried by the majority report of the Colwell Inquiry (DHSS, 1974), the first of a genre of public inquiries following the killing of a child by carers. It was Lisa Arthurworrey, the social worker for Victoria Climbie in the early 1990s, who lost her job following the Laming Inquiry into Victoria Climbie's death (Laming et al, 2003).

In both instances, and for many of the inquiries in the years in between, the front-line workers carried the blame and the consequences for a child being killed. In each instance the top managers survived.

But it has changed. Following the death of 'Baby Peter' although the front-line social workers were dismissed, so were a whole tranche of managers, and it was the children's services director in Haringey, Sharon Shoesmith, who was most pilloried, harried and vilified in the press (see, for example, *The Sun*, 2008).

There is also an increasing pattern of children's services directors losing their jobs, from Surrey to Sandwell to Salford and elsewhere, when the services for which they are accountable receive a poor rating from the independent inspectorate or when a child is killed. In the judgement following the judicial 'review initiated by Sharon Shoesmith, the director of children's services in Haringey at the time of the death of 17 month old 'Baby Peter', the judge commented that

> the prospect of summary dismissal with no compensation and a good deal
> of public opprobrium is hardly likely to be an inducement for someone
> thinking of taking the job [as director of children's services] or, perhaps in
> some circumstances, continuing in it. (quoted by Butler, 2010)

In the two years to March 2010 almost half, 'more than 70' (Higgs, 2010), of the 152 local authorities in England had a change of children's services director.

So being at a distance from the front-line is no longer a defence or a safe position when a tragedy occurs or services are seen to be failing. Managing and leading well at a distance has become even more of a significant requirement if top managers are to survive in their roles. It is now an even greater self-interested concern of managers, although hopefully the ambition to successfully manage and lead is still largely driven by the wish and will to do the job well and to provide high quality services with a well-motivated and competent workforce.

'Management' and 'leadership'

But what is meant by 'management' and by 'leadership'? It is contested as to whether a distinction should be made between 'management' and 'leadership' as individuals, indeed all of us, are likely to be involved in both activities. But it may be helpful to conceptually discriminate between the two terms (Martin & Henderson, 2001; Jones, 2009; Skinner, 2010) to emphasise the different requirements which arise when managers are at a distance.

'Management', for example, might be seen to be primarily about the present, about what is done now and how it is done. It is about the delivery of current services and about current performance and quality and current economy, efficiency and effectiveness. It is 'transactional', concentrating on how current activities are undertaken with the manager monitoring and requiring activity which delivers on current standards and processes.

'Leadership', however, might be termed 'transformational' (for a discussion of 'transactional' and 'transformational' management and leadership see Burns, 1978, and also Adair, 2007). It is about having a vision of how a better performance and outcome might be achieved than within current horizons and understandings, and seeing how to progress from what is done now to how it could be done differently to achieve better results.

The *Every Child Matters* (HM Government, 2003) agenda within children's services, and the *Valuing People* (Department of Health, 2001) and *Putting People First* (HM Government, 2007) personalisation agendas within adult social care, are examples of creating a view of a different future, moving from children and adults seen as passive recipients of care to having competence and capability, and with more choice and control within their lives as active, contributing citizens.

This requires a step change from a paternalistic and sometimes patronising professionalism to a professionalism whose terminology and intentions are about assistance, being an ally alongside service users, and with expertise in enabling and facilitating. These new agendas – which have much in common across the United Kingdom (see: General Social Care

Council, 2006; Scottish Executive, 2006; Welsh Assembly Government, 2006) albeit with their roots firmly within the value-base and history of social work (see, for example, Biestek, 1961; GSSC, 2007) – are not about delivering and managing better current behaviours and services. They require leadership to change culture, understandings, actions and activities (Rose, Aldgate & Barnes, 2007).

The task is not *either* to ensure best performance in the here-and-now ('management') *or* to move forward on a journey with colleagues to create a potentially better future ('leadership'). Both are required (Harris, 2007; Lawler, 2007). To be a leader with no concern for current performance not only demonstrates an irresponsible lack of concern for the current use of resources and the impact for service users, but also provides a poor platform from which to move forward. To be a manager with no ambition or aspiration, or imagination, insight or intuition of what could be better and different, means being frozen in the present and

> the person at the top of the organisation may be in a leadership position, but may not be leading. They may be careful stewards of a legacy organisation. (Owen 2009)

Leadership and motivation

But how as a manager and leader to have an impact on how people behave, what happens and what services are like when you are not present? It is largely about how colleagues, in line management terms 'subordinates', are viewed and understandings of motivation and how to have influence. Whether acting as managers or leaders the results which will be achieved will be dependent on the actions and response of others. This is recognised by the workforce development councils in England for social care for adults (Skills for Care, 2006) and for children (CWDC, 2007).

McGregor (1960; and see Owen, 2009) described two theories of how people behave and how they should be managed. 'Theory X' was about people as inherently lazy, not trustworthy, needing to be told what to do and requiring close control and detailed direction. This may reflect the instrumental orientation to work for those with repetitive roles over which they had little say or opportunity to shape, especially in the 1950s and 1960s (Kynaston, 2007), where work provides the financial means for pursuing the all important goal of self-actualisation outside the factory or office, namely in leisure activities and family life. (Adair, 2006. p. 65)

In contrast, 'Theory Y' was about people as essentially proud, creative and wanting stimulation, and needing space and opportunity if they were to perform well. It is 'Theory Y' which reflects the models of Maslow (1954) and Herzberg (1968; see also Mayo 2001). In Maslow's hierarchy of human needs (discussed in Owen, 2006), which is not only about work but about life in general, it is argued that there are basic human needs for safety and for the physical necessities, such as food, warmth and shelter, but when these basic needs are met people will seek to satisfy higher level needs such as opportunities for achievement, approval and recognition, and for stimulation, self-esteem and 'self-actualisation', building and using one's competence and capacity.

If this is considered within the context of paid employment, it would mean that there are basic requirements which need to be met if someone is to be motivated and satisfied. These would include a reasonable and reliable salary and terms of conditions of employment, such a holiday entitlement, and acceptable working conditions, such as office or centre accommodation and addressing other factors which can cause stress and unhappiness, such as car parking and IT access and reliability. That these requirements may not be met for social care workers and social workers has been made explicit by Birmingham City Council (2009) and the Social Work Taskforce (2009).

When meeting with service teams when director of social services major concerns with which I would often be confronted were about unsatisfactory office accommodation, problems with car parking and not enough computers or unreliable information technology systems, including network unreliability and software programmes which hindered rather than assisted good working practice. The current largely pervasive concerns about the integrated children's system, which have been responded to constructively by the Social Work Taskforce (2009), would be a national example of a concern about the hindrance created by a not fit-for-purpose IT system.

But as a social services director I also came to understand that the model of a linear hierarchy of needs probably is not adequate. Although the motivational gain of a pay award might occur, the enhanced wage soon lost any motivational impact. A few months on and it would be forgotten or assumed as just the rate for the job. It did not create any lasting motivational benefit, although if pay rates were low in relation to those paid by neighbouring employers or to traditionally comparable occupational groups the continuing sense of grievance did have a lasting impact until the perceived injustice was rectified. What is probably important, therefore, is that meeting more basic needs may not be a motivator, but failing to meet them was a demotivator. However, at all times, receiving positive recognition and feeling proud of and valuing the work undertaken, was a motivator, and this was so for employees throughout the range of wage bands.

Yet what has been increasingly created over recent years, now often described as a culture of 'managerialism' (see Jordan & Jordan, 2000; Harris, 2003), are organisations which are more bureaucratic, procedural, and prescriptive of how employees should act, and with more recording and reporting required to monitor that procedures have been followed. The procedures undermine professionalism by giving priority to managerial power and priorities rather than to professional judgements (Exworthy & Halford, 1999; Pollitt, 1999; Hafford-Letchfield, 2006)). There is also preference for competition rather than cooperation (Payne, 2006).This is certainly so in social care and social work services with professional discretion, autonomy and judgement constrained and with the promotion of market-competition, where a concern with price can trump a concern for people and where a focus on cost can undermine a commitment to community.

The cult of managerialism reflected in burgeoning bureaucracy and prescription also has a danger of undermining the value-base, with its focus on respecting individuals and their differences and recognising their worth and potential capacity, and the perspectives of individual context combined with social context, which underlie social care and social work. All of this challenges and potentially undermines the social policy intentions described above about 'personalising' assistance and seeing people as having competence and with the status and esteem of making a contribution as active participating citizens within their communities. This all requires responsiveness, flexibility and creativity rather than regimentation and standardisation.

It also plays down the reality that, as well as being a practical occupation, social work must recognise and continue to develop its theoretical understandings of individuals in the context of social structures, something which is discarded if it is assumed that all is necessary is common-sense regulated by rules (see McLaughlin, 2008). Even when the rules are evidenced-informed they often deny complexity and leave little space for reflexion, despite the post-modernist world view of increasing complexity, fragmentation and uncertainty (see the discussion in Lawler & Harlow, 2005; Rogowski, 2010).

Organisational requirements for economy and efficiency may also overwhelm a concern for people in distress and difficulty. For example, the advent of call-centres as the contact point for services, and the increasing demarcation of different workers and teams for initial assessments, short-term work and then for longer-term contact reflects a focus on managing workflows but with disruption and a lack of continuity for service users – a major issue for a personal professional relationship-based service.

The growth of proceduralism and the bureaucratisation of practice is partly the consequence of the cult of inquiries (Butler & Drakeford, 2003; Jones, 2003; Stanley & Manthorpe, 2004) where inquiries following serious incidents almost invariably recommend more procedures to regulate practice. This is partly an attempt to generalise what is considered to be best practice, and this is also reflected in the burgeoning procedural requirements which follow new legislation. For example, the Children and Young Persons Act 1969 was followed by the government issuing a 63 page booklet of practice guidance. Contrast this with the 10 volumes which were issued to shape required practice following, twenty years later, the Children Act 1989 (Jones, 2010).

But the increase in rules and procedures is also about employers, and also now national inspectorates such as OFSTED, insuring themselves against complaint and litigation by regulating and routinising practice to try to cover any adverse risk. This then requires more measurement and monitoring by managers, and more reporting and reviewing by external inspectorates, to seek to ensure that procedures are followed and performance achieved in line with pre-determined standards.

The experience for employees within organisations where the overwhelming focus of the culture is on compliance is that they recognise that they are seen as more like McGregor's 'Theory X' workers, needing to be told what to do with detailed direction and close control, rather than proud, creative and stimulated 'Theory Y' workers. It may be that the organisations who base their culture and behaviours on Theory X reflect the limitations and lack of confidence and assurance of the organisation's top managers who because of their own anxiety and fears seek to create 'tight' and restrictive 'mechanistic' organisations rather than 'looser' more relaxed 'organic' organisations.

Self-actualising organisations

But what about those organisation which although mindful of performance targets, nationally determined regulations and procedures, and standards set by external inspectorates, still emphasise and work on the basis of a workforce which seeks and thrives on self-actualisation and is motivated by opportunity and recognition? What characterises these organisations?

Firstly, they are likely to be learning organisations rather than procedure-bound organisations. Senge (cited in Mayo, 2001) described a learning organisation as one which:

+ fostered a sense of personal mastery for those within the organisation
+ partly by building individual capability
+ but with people and teams learning together
+ leading to the creation of shared mental models (a common view) of how employees throughout the organisation should operate together
+ and with a shared vision (a common aspiration) embraced by all in the organisation.

Secondly, they are likely to be organisations where there is a focus on building and maintaining motivation. Adair (2006) described eight principles of motivation:

+ be motivated (as leaders) yourself
+ select people who are highly motivated
+ treat each person as an individual
+ set realistic but challenging targets
+ remember that progress motivates
+ create a motivating environment
+ provide fair rewards
+ give recognition.

Some of the above would seem to be circular (for example, build motivation by creating a motivating environment), but there is an affinity here with a changing emphasis in social policy and the promotion of changes in social work practice. For children and young people the *Every Child Matters* (HM Government, 2003) agenda emphasises that children and young people should be able to make a positive contribution. For disabled adults there is a promotion through policy of emphasising disabled people's value and potential (Department of Health, 2001; HM Government, 2007; HM Government 2010).

The common ground is about seeing people as having choice and control within their lives, and as being active and contributing citizens. It is a move away from the 'deficit model', heavily focussing on people's difficulties and problems, to a rebalancing where people are also seen as having competence, capability and capacity. At the time when social workers and others are asked professionally to re-set their mindset, their own work experience may be within organisations which emphasise what might be seen as deficits in their own practice, with this to be contained by restricting the choice and control they have within their work with a reduction in professional autonomy and space to practice.

Thirdly, organisations which promote a motivated workforce are likely to be organisations where managers and others understand and demonstrate emotional intelligence. Goleman, Boyatiz and McKee (2002) in considering leadership within organisations relate it to emotional intelligence (Goleman, 1996) which they describe as including:

+ self-awareness
+ self-management
+ social awareness
+ relationship management.

One might expect that social work, with its emphasis on empathy with and an understanding of others, and on building, maintaining and using relationships in the context of valuing others and recognising and accepting individual differences (see, for example, Barclay, 1982; Gilroy, 2004) might provide a strong emotionally intelligent foundation for those social workers who move into management and leadership roles (Jones, 2009; and see the discussion in Lawler, 2007).

Fourthly, they are likely to be organisations with some management and leadership stability, creating and continuing a culture which is inclusive for all in the organisation, with a consistency over time in values and vision and within an organisational atmosphere of trust rather than tension (Rogers and Reynolds, 2003). This is a somewhat different description from the very active, energised, excited management portrayed in much of 'In Search of Excellence' (Peters and Waterman, 1982), the 'new management' guru textbook of the 1980s. It is rather more the 'From Great to Good' (Collins, 2001) analysis of successful commercial companies, which Collins (2006) then applied to not-for-profit organisations, with the emphasis on leadership staying stable and continuing and consistent over time to build culture and a shared commitment.

The lessons from the above for management and leadership within social service organisations, including and especially those organisations where the responsibilities and work may often be related to crisis and risk, are noted below. The actions and behaviours below are of particular importance for senior managers managing and leading at a distance, but many of the messages are relevant for all managers. All can be encapsulated as being about a Theory Y emphasis on 'facilitating, enabling and involving' rather than Theory X's overwhelming emphasis on 'controlling and directing'.

The lessons also reflect the reality that within a widely dispersed service, with much activity unseen by managers, and especially senior managers, there is a requirement for 'distributed leadership'(see, for example, Rogers and Reynolds, 2003), with front-line workers required and empowered to use their judgement, take decisions and to act without continued and immediate reference to managers who are not immediately present and make be geographically distant (albeit new technologies may mitigate geographical distance). The experience, expertise and wisdom built and based on the realities of practice should also contribute to the shaping of organisational processes and priorities (Harris, 2003; Hafford-Letchfield, Leonard, Begum and Chick, 2008; Hafford-Letchfield, 2010).

The reality is also despite increased proceduralism, bureaucracy and performance monitoring, front-line workers and teams still create much of their own experience and meaning at work (Bilson and Ross, 1999). Recognising this as a manager at a distance, and working with it as a reality, is about seeking to participate in influencing and shaping this experience and meaning, being aware of and working with its presence and inevitability, and tolerating the uncertainty and diversity which results.

In essence, despite the critique that managerialism requires 'a managed workforce with no illusions about performance autonomy or ideals that service to clients is paramount' (Jones, 1999, p.47), and despite the squeezing of professional space, workers and their teams still significantly generate their own experience, to a greater or lesser extent in line with or in opposition to the management-described organisational goals and vision.

Leading and managing at a distance

- commit to staff training and development to enhance competence and confidence
- deliver the training whenever possible to teams and workers throughout the organisation together to create a shared commitment and impact and use training as an opportunity to build and transmit culture

---

- do not neglect planning and review, but within team and service business plans give space for individuals and work groups to define and shape at least some of their own priorities and the means to achieve pre-determined priorities
- and in the reporting and review process actively seek and follow through on the opportunities to give recognition and praise and to celebrate

---

- as leaders, be visible and accessible, especially to the front-line
- recognise others as 'colleagues' rather than 'my workers'
- be open to challenge and debate
- but all within a clear vision of direction

- insist on 'doing the basics well'
- consistently and fairly challenge poor performance

- focus on the quality of the front-line managers who have most influence on practice and create the day-to-day work experience for their team members
- know and acknowledge front-line realities

Joint reviews of social services

But does any of this really make any difference? In the late 1990s and early 2000s there was a significant investment in reviewing the performance of local authority social services in England and Wales. Each of the then 172 'councils with social services responsibilities' (CSSRs) were 'joint reviewed' by a team of inspectors from the Audit Commission and the government's Social Services Inspectorate. In addition to data analysis of performance information from the councils and large questionnaire customer satisfaction surveys of current service users, teams of usually three inspectors would spend six to eight weeks within each council meeting with service users and staff, reading case files, visiting services and seeing workers in action, and speaking with other agencies, with managers and with councillors. A detailed public report was prepared about each CSSR, and overview reports were prepared each year (see, for example, Social Services Inspectorate/

Audit Commission, 1999; 2001) as the review programme was rolled out. Alongside the overview reports themed reports were prepared, including a themed report (Social Services Inspectorate/ Audit Commission, undated) on leadership, human resource management and organisational cultures and how these were related to the perceived performance of each organisation.

The Joint Review Team reported that the councils who were doing well in providing social services:

- supported and developed their staff through good communication, training and supervision.
- were committed to learning from users and front-line staff about what works in practice.
- demonstrated leadership in delivering quality services.
- had a demonstrable commitment to change and improvement.

The importance of management and leadership styles, and the resulting organisational cultures, were seen to be directly correlated with the satisfaction of service users, the morale of staff and the scoring on key performance indicators.

The authority where I was the social services director for fourteen years scored as one of the equal top eight of the 172 councils, but with a comment that there was a tendency towards 'a culture of non-conformity' (Social Services Inspectorate/ Audit Commission, 2000) amongst front-line teams and workers. Rather than panicking about what might be seen as a negative comment, this was understood to reflect the 'loose' process of decentralisation, delegation and devolution with the front-line being active in contributing to constructively shaping their own work and processes, albeit within a 'tight' department-wide vision and direction of movement and a requirement and focus on 'doing the basics well'.

Concluding comments

What is dissonant is that when it is known from the major detailed inspection and review programme which was spawned by the then new 'New Labour' government in the late 1990s that a Theory Y understanding of behaviour and motivation was positively correlated with performance, much of the government's actions reflect more of a Theory X response.

There has been a burgeoning of detailed directives and the promulgation of more procedures. There has also been a move from the independent but developmental and learning style of the Commission for Social Care Inspection to the 'hit and run' tick box style of inspections of the Care Quality Commission and, in particular, OFSTED. Performance indicators have become the determinants of performance, rather than a tool for discussion, debate and development.

Rather as with managers, energised, manic but inexperienced and unconfident politicians may cause a lot of activity but with the consequence of the creation of chaos, uncertainty and clogged up, constipated organisations, focussed ultimately on procedures rather the performance (see Seldon, 2005; Toynbee & Walker, 2005; Jenkins, 2007; Mullin, 2009 for comments about the controlling culture of recent governments). Managing and leading at a distance, whether it is political or organisational management and leadership, ought to be based on respect and recognition for, and with an emphasis on the capacity, commitment and competence of, others rather than about an overwhelming emphasis on control and containment.

It is though a question of balance with the weighting to Theory Y but not totally disregarding as managers some Theory X requirements, especially about the non-negotiable requirements to 'do the basics well'. Indeed, managing and leading at a distance does require the availability of performance information to spot and explore variations in practice (see, for example, Jones 1996, for an account of using performance information to explore variations in child protection decision-making), and the same performance information is also of use to front-line teams to benchmark their own practice. Maybe there is a need for a 'Theory Z' emphasising the Theory Y characteristics of self-actualising, motivated colleagues but not totally ignoring Theory X requirements that there are some actions and behaviours which are required and are non-negotiable.

References

Adair, J. (2006) *Leadership and Motivation.* London: Kogan Page

Adair, J. (2007) *Leadership and Innovation.* London: Kogan Page

Barclay Report (1982) *Social Workers: Their roles and tasks.* London: Bedford Square Press

Bilson, A. and Ross, S. (1999) *Social Work Management and Practice: Systems principles.* London: Jessica Kingsley

Birmingham City Council (2009) *Who Cares? Protecting children and improving children's social care: A report for the Overview and Scrutiny Committee*, Birmingham: Birmingham City Council

Burns, J. (1978) *Leadership*. New York: Harper and Row

Burns, T. and Stalker, G.M. (1961) *The Management of Innovation*. London: Tavistock Publications

Butler, I. and Drakeford, M. (2003) *Scandal, Social Policy and Social Welfare*. Bristol: Policy Press

Butler, P. (2010) A Crisis in Child Protection, *The Guardian* (24 April, p.4)

Collins, J. (2001) *From Good to Great: Why some companies make the leap and others don't*. Bristol: Random House

Collins, J. (2006) *Good to Great and the Social Sectors*. London: Random House, :

Coulshed, V., Mullender, A., Jones, D., and Thompson, N. (2006) *Management in Social Work*. Basingstoke: Palgrave Macmillan

CWDC (2007) *Championing Children: A shared set of skills, knowledge, and behaviours for those leading and managing integrated children's services*. Leeds: Children's Workforce Development Council

Department of Health (2001) *Valuing People: A new strategy for learning disability for the 21st century*. London: TSO

DHSS (1974) *Report of the Inquiry into the Care and Supervision Provided in Relation to Maria Colwell*. London: HMSO

Exworthy, M. and Halford, S. (1999) *Professionalism in the New Managerialism in the Public Sector*. Buckinham: Open University Press

Gilroy, P. (2004) *A Personal Perspective on the Future of Social Work and Social Care in the UK*. Brighton: Pavilion

General Social Care Council (2006) *Options for Excellence: Building a social care workforce for the future*. London: General Social Care Council

General Social Care Council (2007) *Roles and Tasks of Social Work in England: A consultation paper*. London: General Social Care Council

Goldthorpe, J, and Lockwood, D. (1968) *The Affluent Worker*. Cambridge: Cambridge University Press

Goleman, D. (1996) *Emotional Intelligence*. London: Bloomsbury

Goleman, D., Boyatiz, R. and McKee, A. (2002) *The New Leaders: Transforming the art of leadership into the science of results*. London: Little Brown

Hafford-Letchfield, T. (2006) *Management and Organisations in Social Work*. Exeter: Learning Matters

Hafford-Letchfield, S. (2010) *Social Care Management, Strategy and Business Planning*. London. Jessica Kingsley

Hafford-Letchfield, T., Leonard, K., Begum, N., and Chick, N. (2008) *Leadership and Management in Social Care*. London: Sage

Harris, J. (2003) *The Social Work Business.* London: Routledge

Harris, J. (2008) Looking backward, looking forward: Current trends in human services management. in J. Aldgate, L. Healy, M. Barris, B. Pine, W. Rose, and J. Seden (Eds) *Social Work Management: Theory and best practice from the UK and USA.* London: Jessica Kingsley

Herzberg, F. (1968) *Work and the Nature of Man.* London: Stapels Press

Higgs, L. (2010) DCS turnover rate raises concern. *Children and Young People Now,* 4 May, www.cypnow.co.uk/bulletins/Daily-Bulletin/news/1000691:

HM Government (2003) *Every Child Matters.* London: TSO

HM Government (2007) *Putting People First: A shared vision and commitment to the transformation of adult social care..* London: TSO

HM Government (2010) *Building the National Care Service.* Cmnd 7854. London: TSO

Jenkins, S. (2007) *Thatcher and Sons: A revolution in three parts.* Harmondsworth: Penguin

Jones, C. (1999) Social work: regulation and management. in M. Exworthy and S. Halford (Eds) *Professionals and the New Managerialism in Public Sector.* Buckingham: Open University Press

Jones, R. (1996) Decision-making in child protection. *British Journal of Social Work,* 26, 509-522:

Jones, R. (2003) Delayering decisions, *ADSS Inform,* 24-26

Jones, R. (2009) Social work and management, in A,Barnard, N. Horner, and J. Wild (Ed.) *The Value Base of Social Work and Social Care.* Maidenhead: Open University Press

Jones, R. (2010) Children Acts 1948-2008: The drivers for legislative change in England over 60 Years. *Journal of Children's Services,* 4, 4, 39-52:

Jordan, B. and Jordan, C. (2000) *Social Work and the Third Way: Tough love and social policy.* London: Sage

Kearney, P. (2004) First line managers: The mediators of standards and the quality of practice. in D. Statham (Ed.) *Managing Front-Line Practice in Social Care.* London: Jessica Kingsley

Kynaston, D. (2007) *Austerity Britain 1948-51: Smoke in the valley.* London: Bloomsbury

Laming, H., Adjaye, N., Fox, J., Kinnair, D. and Richardson, N. (2003) *The Victoria Climbie Inquiry.* London: TSO

Lawler, J. (2007) Leadership in social work: A case of caveat emptor? *British Journal of Social Work,* 37, 123-141:

Lawler, J. and Harlow, E. (2005) Postmodernisation: A phase we're going through? Management in social care, *British Journal of Social Work,*

35, 1163-1174:

Lawler, J. and Bilson, A. (2010) *Social Work Management and Leadership: Managing complexity with creativity.* London: Routledge

Martin, V. and Henderson, E. (2001) *Managing in Health and Social Care.* London: Routledge

Maslow, A.H., (1954) *Motivation and Personality.* New York: Harper and Row

Mayo, A. (2001) *The Human Value of the Enterprise.* London: Nicholas Brealey

McGregor, D. (1960) *The Human Side of Enterprise.* Maidenhead: McGraw Hill

McLaughlin, K. (2008) *Social Work, Politics and Society: From radicalism to orthodoxy.* Bristol: Policy Press

Montgomery, V. (1961) *The Path to Leadership.* London: Collins

Mullin, C. (2009) *A View from the Foothills: The diaries of Chris Mullin.* London: Profile books

Owen, J. (2006) *The Leadership Skills Handbook.* London: Kogan Page

Owen, J. (2009) *How to Lead.* Harlow: Pearson Education

Payne, M. (2006) *What is Professional Social Work?* Bristol: Policy Press

Peters, T.J. and Waterman, R.K. (1982) *In Search of Excellence: Lessons from America's best run companies.* New York: Harper and Row

Pollitt, C. (1994) *Managerialism and the Public Services.* Oxford: Blackwell

Reynolds, J., Henderson, J., Seden, J., Charlesworth, J., and Bullman, A. (2003) *The Managing Care Reader.* London: Routledge

Rogowski, S. (2010) *Social Work: The rise and fall of a profession.* Bristol: Policy Press

Rogers, A. and Reynolds, J. (2003) Leadership and vision. in J. Seden and J. Reynolds (Eds.) *Managing Care In Practice.* London: Routledge

Rose, W., Aldgate, J., Barnes, J. (2007) From policy visions to practice realities: The pivotal role of service managers in implementation, in J. Aldgate, L. Healy, M. Barris, B. Pine, W. Rose, and J. Seden (Eds) *Enhancing Social Work Management.* London: Jessica Kingsley

Seldon, A. (2005) *Blair.* London: Free Press

Skills for Care (2006) *Leadership and Management: A strategy for the social care workforce.* Leeds: Skills for Care

Skinner, K. (2010) Supervision, management and leadership: think piece. in Z. Von Zwanenberg (Ed.) *Leadership in Social Care.* London: Jessica Kingsley

Social Services Inspectorate and the Audit commission (1999) *Getting the Best from Children's Services.* Abingdon: Audit Commission

Social Services Inspectorate and the Audit Commission (2000) *A Report of the Joint Review of Social Services in Wiltshire*. Abingdon: Audit Commission

Social Services Inspectorate and the Audit Commission (2001) *Delivering Results: Joint Review Team Fifth Annual Report*. Abingdon: Audit Commission

Social Work Task Force (2009) *Building a Safe, Confident Future: The Final Report of the Social Work Task Force*. London: Department of Children, Schools and Families

Stanley, N. and Manthorpe, J. (2004) *The Age of Inquiry: Learning and blaming in health and social care*. London: Routledge

The Sun (2008) It's Not Enough, 2 December, pp.1, 4-7:

Scottish Executive (2006) *Changing Lives: 21st Century Social Work Review*. www.21csocialwork.org.uk

Social Services Inspectorate and the Audit commission (undated) *People Need People: Realising the potential of people working in social services*. Abingdon: Audit Commission

Toynbee, P. and Walker, D. (2005) *Better or Worse?: Has Labour Delivered?* London: Bloomsbury

Welsh Assembly Government (2006) *A Strategy for Social Services in Wales Over the Next Decade: Fulfilled lives, supportive communities*. Cardiff: NHS Wales

The body of this chapter was first published in 2010 in *Social Work & Social Sciences Review* vol. 14(1) pp.59-75. Ray Jones was thenProfessor of Social Work, Kingston University and St. George's, University of London.

6

Managers:
Are they really to blame for what's happening to social work?

Sharon Lambley

Introduction

Social work has traditionally mediated between the state and citizens but changes to the welfare system over the last 30 years have directly impacted upon the social work role, and how social workers engage with service users. Lymbery (2001) asserts that

> The recasting of welfare by the New Right affected the way in which the state has chosen to interpret its mediating role in respect of social work and a more coercive and restricted role has been constructed. (p.377)

As a result 'social work practice has been subject to increased managerial control and social worker levels of autonomy have been reduced. This has created a sense of crisis which has been experienced particularly within Social Services Departments (Lymbery, 2001). Jones (2001) supports this view arguing that social work has been transformed and downgraded. He blames managers for this situation arguing that they have responded compliantly to the neo-liberal agenda, are bullies, have lost touch with the welfare ideals of social work and they can no longer be relied upon to support state social work.

There is evidence to support the assertion that the social work role has been eroded or transformed by management practice. Research by Dustin (2007) for example suggests that care management had transformed the social work role through administrative processes that emphasise targeting, financial assessments and the co-ordination of care packages. In children and family's social work, Munro (2010a) argues that over-standardised administrative systems and performance management priorities have distorted social work practice, leaving social workers unable to exercise their professional judgement. She identifies a culture of blame that has led to defensive social work practices and suggests that social work management is one contributory factor to why this is happening. She takes the view that practice appears to be dominated by management performance requirements rather than professional concerns. Research by Broadhurst et al (2010) however suggests that

> whilst social work practitioners are obliged to comply with risk reduction technologies .... Informal processes continue to play a critical role in shaping decisions and actions in this relationship-based profession. (p.1046)

What is interesting about this research is that the authors were not suggesting that social workers were unaffected by the excessive performance monitoring and audit demands but that they continued to use discretion and make decisions based upon their experiences with service users, regardless of these constraints. Harris (2003) also suggests that some social workers are working creatively and moving beyond the constraints of performance management, rather than being subordinated by it. Dustin (2007) found some evidence of social workers using discretion, although this varied from team to team, and was dependant upon whether 'the manager respected them and the social worker was able to make a case for their plan' (p.66). Developing this idea further, Evans (2010) asserts that some social workers and managers in Older People and Mental Health teams are working collaboratively despite the constraints imposed by managerialism and his work challenges the assertion that managers have all the power and social workers have none. He suggests that the manager-worker relationship needs to be examined more closely as managers are a fractured group who do not act simply as 'policy lieutenants' and social work organisations are not 'well oiled policy implementation machines'. This paper seeks to explore these contradictory positions and examines the view that managers are to blame for the significant changes in social work organisation and practice.

The role of social work

Social work is located between competing political ideologies that shape and define social problems and solutions. It is a contested term (Dickens, 2010). This is because social work is constructed from ideas that individuals hold about the world (Payne, 2005). For example, structural theorists such as Mullaly (1997) argue that social work is a project, with its own mission, ideology, and progressive theory. From this perspective, social work seeks to overcome structural barriers, and thereby transform society. The changes that have been imposed upon social work in recent years however, have led many supporters of this view to argue that social work is in crisis (Jones, 2001), and that its role within society needs to be reclaimed (Ferguson and Woodward, 2009). These views suggest that social work managers implementing neo-liberal policies, are to be blamed for what is happening to social work (Jones, 2001).

Another viewpoint put forward by Harris (2008) argues that welfare regimes are important as they shape how social work is constituted and enacted. From his perspective, social work is a contingent activity that can be positioned at different moments in time in response to a combination of events and ideas. The dominant discourse at these moments shapes social work. For example, the introduction of recent austerity measures in Britain has seen a re-emergence of a discourse from the last economic recession where the poor were portrayed as over dependant upon the state, as 'work shy' and in some cases not deserving of state help and support. This compares with state social work in the past, where the poor were portrayed as victims of inequalities and injustice and state help was made available to redress these imbalances. Current narratives support the rationing of services, and the withdrawal of welfare benefits. Social workers are required to assess individuals and families to decide if they meet the eligibility criteria for state support and refuse those who are not eligible. Given the expansive roles that social workers held in the past, it appears that the social work role today has been more narrowly re-positioned within society. Wilson et al (2008, p.3) argues however that social work, which is characterised by complexity, uncertainty and risk can resist any narrowing of practice and continue to build relationships with service users 'even when the wider socio-political context in which they are located is not conducive'. Social work maybe dependent upon the context from which it emerges and in which it engages (McDonald et al, 2003) but it can respond proactively rather than be subordinated by change.

The social work role in Britain can be compared to social work elsewhere. The International Federation of Social Workers (2000) defined social work as promoting 'social change, problem solving in human relationships and the empowerment and liberation of people to enhance well-being. Utilising theories of human behaviour and social systems, social work intervenes at the points where people interact with their environments. Principles of human rights and social justice are fundamental to social work'(www.

ifsw.org). This definition is wide to encompass a world view of social work that reflects the interface between people, their environment, social work principles, theories and activities. This view of social work is compared with a view within the Social Work Task Force (SWTF, 2009) report which asserts that

> When people are made vulnerable – by poverty, bereavement, addiction, isolation, mental distress, disability, neglect, abuse or other circumstances – what happens next matters hugely. If outcomes are poor, if dependency becomes ingrained or harm goes unchecked, individuals, families, communities and the economy can pay a heavy price. Good social workers can and do make a huge difference in these difficult circumstances. (p.16)

Here, social work appears highly functionalist as social workers are concerned with what happens to vulnerable people, regardless of how or why people become vulnerable in the first place. Service users are framed as problems reflecting current political concerns about how vulnerable people generate costs to society, and good social work is said to reduce these costs through interventions. When comparing these two views of social work the Task Force view appears to confirm Shardlow's (2007) assertion that the scope of social work in many other countries is more expansive than in Britain, and reinforces views that social work has been eroded.

Service users views of social workers are that they provide support, control and personal change and

> The first is valued by service users; the others are contentious and particularly in work with children and families seem to be occupying an increasingly central role in social work. (Beresford, 2007, p.7)

This is not unexpected given that service users have criticised social workers for being oppressive, (Ferguson and Woodward, 2009), wary of the power social workers hold and how this is used. Beresford (2007, p.3) suggests that 'service users draw a distinction between social work and social workers.' What makes social work more acceptable to them is the extent to which good practitioners mediate underlying problems in its ideology and organization (Branfield et al, 2005). This places a big responsibility and creates large challenges for such practitioners. Beresford goes on to suggest that service users value social workers that use a social approach (sees the person in a broader context), a relationship based approach (builds trust and supports empowerment) and can utilise personal qualities to good effect (listens, non-judgemental, warmth, etc). He makes the point that service users are unhappy about the reduction in social work contact with service users and the quality of this contact. This is mirrored in the criticisms by social workers of performance management systems which standardise practice, and generate narrow ways of practicing which are then enforced by managers (Dustin, 2007). Both service user and social worker expectations and behaviours are now understood within performance management discourse, frameworks and a wider neo-liberal context that has to be navigated, despite criticism of this context.

Whilst performance management attracts much criticism in all areas of social work practice, societal and organisational blame has created additional problems for social work (Munro, 2010b). The high level of media interest and societal concerns relating to the management of risk in children and family services in particular has created a hostile environment, as according to Brownbill (2010) social workers attract more blame than other professional groups when things go wrong. Cohen (2002) suggests that the media play an important role in apportioning blame. Mass-Lowit and Hothersall (2010) argue that

> *The Sun's* coverage of the Baby Peter case demonstrates very clearly what the potential dangers are for any government or its agents (in this case, Haringey Council) of apparently failing to manage significant risk .... If the risks are known or predictable, then the issue becomes one of apportioning blame if bad things happen, even if their occurrence was in fact unavoidable. (p.41)

Munro (2010b) suggests that this situation has generated a blame culture and managers are contributing to social work problems as they exert more control over social workers which has led to defensive practices and increased risks to children.

The role of social work within society therefore has been framed by a neo-liberalist paradigm which has re-positioned social work, and concerns are being expressed that performance management may be dominating professional concerns through the narrowing of expectations in relation to the social work role and the increased standardisation and management control over social work practice. In a role where social workers are required to implement government policies that reduce state social work support. To understand how social workers are responding to these challenges we need to look further at what is happening in practice.

What is happening within social work?

Academics have developed models of practice that can provide insight into what is occurring in social work. Payne (2005) has developed a three dimensional model which is similar to a two dimensional model developed by Mullaly (1997). The first dimension identified by Mullaly (1997) is a *conventional approach* which focuses upon helping vulnerable people to cope or adjust to their situation. Payne (2005) refers to this as individual-reflexive. Social workers who adopt this approach strive to maintain people during difficult periods in their lives, so that when they recover, they can continue with their lives. A second dimension identified by Mullaly (1997) is a *progressive approach*, which Payne (2005) refers to as socialist-collectivist. Social workers who adopt this approach see themselves as empowering people to get what they need and engage in challenging inequalities and social injustices as they seek to transform society. A third dimension identified by Payne (2005) is the *reflexive-therapeutic* approach, where social workers focus upon supporting and enabling service users to overcome personal difficulties in their lives. Payne suggests each of these three perspectives represents social work activities, which are critical as well as complementary in relation to each other (p.11).

Payne's (2005) three dimensional model allows us to examine the perspectives and activities of social work. For example a social worker who incorporates all three dimensions in their practice but who is working in a role where the social work task is perceived to be one dimensional, may react by resisting pressure from his/her manager to work in a one dimensional way. Alternatively a social worker may decide to comply, or be required to comply. Where collaboration is possible social workers may be able to negotiate and agree with their manager to work in ways that enable them to draw upon all the three approaches using their professional discretion. These strategies mirror similar strategies found in education where head teachers and teachers were faced with unintended policy outcomes and practice dilemmas (Hoyle and Wallace, 2005).

Social work literature is full of examples of these strategies being used by social workers. White et al. (2009, p.12) for example, summarise how social workers in referral and assessment teams who were trying to safeguard children and meet performance targets, found that it was only possible to offer a service to those children and families that met strict eligibility criteria, and use rationing strategies for the remaining cases. The impact of performance targets they suggested was profound in these situations where relationship based practice struggled to remain relevant within a time-operated system. Social workers had to adopt strategies that ensured that individual-reflexive or conventional approaches did not come to dominate their practice particularly as performance management is already restricting what they can offer. However it may be difficult to respond in any other way than with compliance, given the scrutiny that some managers exert over social work practice. Jones (2001) argues that social work managers should challenge these situations, as they create low morale and high levels of stress for workers, and this situation is not good for service users. He blames managers for accepting this situation.

A second response by social workers is covert resistance. There is a range of ways in which social workers might undertake resistance. White (2009 found that

'... workers often mystify or conceal their knowledge of service users in order to acquire resources ('dressing up assessments...') (p.139). Collinson (1994, p25) refers to this as strategic manipulation of knowledge and information. Second ....is to deliberately delay paperwork or assessment plans so that managers are manipulated into taking a course of action...Third, apparent cooperation with a social work task may often conceal resistance. Such forms of resistance centre of 'destabilising truth and challenging subjectivities and normalising discourses' (Thomas and Davies, 2005, p.727).

A similar response but one that is more open, is overt resistance. Broadhurst et al (2001) highlighted the tension that existed between social workers and managers in the following quote (p.11)

Social worker: My manager said to me 'why haven't you finished that yet?'... and I said 'well the health visitor hasn't called me back...and they said, 'well, no, if you've decided that its family support, then the outcome won't change, whatever they say. I said 'I disagree' and of course that information informs my assessment. I'm not putting my name to that', (p.11)

The social worker in this scenario refused to accept the managers attempt to take away professional discretion and to assert management power over social work practice. In both overt and covert resistance social workers were not compliant. The relationship between the social worker and manager is adversarial (either overtly or covertly) as managers and social workers battle for control over practice. In this scenario it is possible for social workers to appear to use a dimension of the practice model managers wish them to use, but to actually extend the range of activities through resistance strategies.

A third potential response is collaboration. Evans' (2010) suggestion that local managers often chose to co-operate with practitioners because giving practitioners control over decision-making and practice ensures that the work is completed. Local managers and professionals worked together to promote professionalism, and this was achievable as senior managers were occupied with organisation performance rather than the details of professional practice. Local managers encouraged social workers to exercise professional judgement and were able to offer professional support and guidance rather than act simply as agents of hierarchical control, which was valued by social workers (Evans, 2010). Social workers are encouraged to use discretion and to exercise professional freedom and judgement and be mindful of performance requirements which require them to adapt their practice. In this scenario it would be possible for social workers to openly use any combination of the three dimensions outlined in Payne's (2005) model.

The social workers who adopt resistance and collaboration strategies challenge the prevailing view of 'management domination and control of practices' (Evans, 2010, p.2) but it must be tempered by evidence that front line practice has become more regulated and restrictive, (Kirkpatrick, 2006). Compliance maybe the only option as Jones (2001) points to evidence of management bullying and stressful work environments as managers assert their authority over social workers. The role that managers play therefore needs further examination.

Management in social work

The transformation of social work is based upon

> a new spectrum of values – of freedom rather than equality, individualism rather than community, efficiency rather than justice, and competition rather than cooperation. (Ranson and Stewart, 1994, p.48)

These values are problematical for social work as they are ideologically at odds with the values espoused by social workers and are embedded within social work and employer codes of practice (GSCC, 2002). Adherence to these codes currently remains a requirement of professional registration and complements existing social care policy and legislation. This complex mix of values and expectations of social work provides the context within which social work management is located and practised.

Lawler and Bilson (2010) suggest that administration, which preceded social work management, was based upon negotiation, mediation and consensus. This approach could accommodate social work values. These authors have developed a model that explains the difference between administration and social work management. They start by identifying a rational-objective category which lies at one end of a continuum with a set of characteristics that include a rational, linear and bureaucratic orientation, a utilitarian ethical position, as well as views of change that are predictable, planned and managerially determined. Management 'know how' is generalist rather than managers having a specific understanding of social work and they assume that the external environment is stable and that a knowable reality exists. Within social work organisation, at a senior level in particular, managers can be found at this end of the continuum. As managers of the new social work business (Harris, 2003) they are focused upon managing systems that control finance, information and resources to deliver strategically planned outputs that achieve performance targets (Evans, 2010). They rely on tools that standardise practice, rational approaches to developing the business and collate data even though these tools simplify and standardise complex work, and exclude practice dilemmas. The rational-objective category contrasts with the reflective-pluralist position where social reality is constructed, where management practice is specific to social work, and change is considered unpredictable, conflictual and emergent. Management work includes social, emotional and reflective orientations, and the ethical position is constructivist and compassionate.

In Dustin's (2007) work the characteristics of the rational-objective category was evident at the front line, where care managers were subject to management practices that controlled worker activity to achieve planned targets. Dustin (2007) details the effects of what she described as the McDonaldization of social work upon social work practice. Social workers struggled to work in ways that conformed to their codes of practice and in ways that made important aspects of their work visible. Social work practice deals with real people's lives, which are messy and often complex and social workers have to engage with that complexity and be able to respond flexibly using knowledge that sometimes go beyond the 'rational' into spheres of knowing that can be difficult to articulate, let alone identify and measure. In trying to simplify this work, social work managers can create tensions for social workers which can result in their complying with management pressures, and adopting narrow practice approaches. Some may adopt resistance strategies. Where managers take a reflexive-pluralist position, and understand the complexity of the task and its demands upon social workers, it is possible for them to adopt strategies which enable them to collaborate and work with social workers (Evans, 2010). However, these managers must also know how to manage upwards as senior managers may seek to overlay professional issues with performance and organisational concerns.

Politicians require managers to balance resource allocations, legal, policy and risk considerations, service user expectations and social work values within complex and often hostile environments that are over stretched. Managers know that the decisions they make will have life changing consequences for citizens. The development of social work management as a subject area has been informed by audit and inspection reports and public scrutiny when things have gone wrong as well as policy literature that is critical of managerialism. However, there has been little or no critical research into what works in social work management and this has left a group of workers in need of evidence to enable managers to reflect and develop appropriate management responses and practices.

How management is practised therefore can affect the strategies that social workers adopt. For example, if a manager is not interested in professional concerns and does not enable social workers to challenge decision making, managers are likely to find that social workers may adopt covert resistance strategies. This can be problematic, particularly if managers are focused upon organisational concerns and they use coercive strategies of control to achieve organisational objectives (Evans, 2009). Such managers perceive social workers to be self-interested and in need of monitoring. This approach is similar to McGregor's (1987) theory X approach used in Dustin's (2007) research. She found that managers who adopted a theory X approach took away discretion from social workers, who were required to focus upon activities whether or not that activity was purposeful. This domination approach is not appropriate in social work which is an ethical and relationship based activity. Evans (2009) also identifies a discursive approach, where managers are sceptical of the management rhetoric, and are critical of coercive approaches. These managers choose not to act compliantly, but rather collaborate with social workers. As Evans (2009, p.150) puts it:

> The discursive approach, then, locates actors within fields of tension – sites within which organisational and management practices can reflect professional strategies and concerns alongside increasingly influential managerialist ideas and concerns, to 'produce new focal points of resistance, compromise and accommodation' (Clarke & Newman, 1997, p.76).

It is within this view of management practice that critical management approaches can be found. The research suggests that management responses are as varied as social workers responses to the changes that have been imposed on them. It is possible therefore to understand how Munro (2010b) could argue that social work practice is dominated by management rather than professional concerns and why Jones (2001) has criticised managers for responding compliantly to neo-liberal reforms, or why social workers have been able to resist and adapt their practice (Broadhurst et al, 2010).

Lawler and Bilson (2010) assert that some social work managers are adopting management approaches that do not fit comfortably with social work values and that the impact upon social workers can be demoralising. One worker in Dustin's (2007) research for example said:

'I personally would love a supervision where one can also have reflection and also be able to be honest about the issues you are facing, the way you're considering or resolving them, but it's very much down to targets and actions.' (p.64)

The impact upon services users of inappropriate social work management can be damaging. White (2009) drawing on research by Gupta and Blewett, (2007) says

What is measured is paper output not work with children. All managers care about is getting the assessment finished on time ... We are scrambling around to find more children to be adopted or else we lose our three star status and hundreds of pounds, yet adoption may not be right for these children. (White, 2009, p.34)

However not all social work managers were adopting management approaches that are unsuitable. Dustin (2007) found examples where social workers were well supported and service user requirements were not sacrificed to performance targets. Similarly Ferguson and Woodward, (2009. p.74) highlight a case where there was collaboration at the front line, between social workers and managers, and between senior and front line managers. This is contradicted by Evans (2010) who found managers in social services to be a fractured group. It appears that where social work management worked well, social workers were able to use their professional autonomy, decision making and discretionary approaches to best effect.

What these examples demonstrate is that managers would appear be responding in different ways to the demands being placed upon them. The responses from social workers to these management approaches are illustrated in these quotes below

Cynicism: '*I think they (senior managers) see social workers as there to, yes, assess the needs, because that's what we're obliged to do; but then as much as possible to limit, to ration what we can do to meet the need as cheaply as possible, as quickly as possible and as long as we get the paper work done then they're happy.*' (White, 2009, p.155)

Blame: '*There's something missing at senior level in recognising that we really need to work hand in hand and sometimes it feels like we're actually fighting against each other.*' (Ferguson and Woodward, 2009, p.74) and;

'*There is a huge gap between managers ... who are trying to implement what we've been talking about and their understanding of what actually good practice is*' (pg 72).

Understanding: of the difficulties facing managers; '*I wouldn't want to be a manager. I have found my little niche. I do what I can. I don't feel I can compromise myself, to the extent that I would have to, to go up the career ladder*', (White, 2009, p.61)

These examples illustrate the variety of responses that managers are making and how these are perceived by social workers and go some way to explain why managers may be blamed for what is happening to social work

Conclusion

In care management it is generally agreed that the transformation of social work is complete (Lymbery and Postle, 2010). However Dustin (2007) highlights some areas where social workers and social work managers adopted collaboration strategies but this was not representative of her overall findings. It has been suggested that the personalisation agenda (HMG, 2007) is bringing new challenges, particularly in relation to the protection of vulnerable adults and the management of risk, which will require social workers to re-engage with more complex ways of working, but this will be challenging for social workers and managers. Dustin (2007) found management practice largely reflects Theory X approaches, as managers used the performance management frameworks to assert control over social work practice. McGregor's (1987) work is interesting in that he argued that there was a link between the style of management a person adopts and their attitudes to human nature and behaviour. In the case of theory X, McGregor (1987) argues that managers believe that workers are basically uninterested in working hard, in thinking for themselves and prefer to be told what to do. In highlighting that social work practice is being delivered supported by theory X management, Dustin (2007) exposes some serious problems relating to the value base being adopted by managers in care management and raises questions as to how these approaches are affecting service users, although some indications have already been presented in this paper. She highlights some variations in practice, and in particular describes one manager who adopted a theory Y approach which is the antithesis of theory X; this manager worked collaboratively with social workers. It appears that the values informing her social work practice were also informing her management practice. In children and family social work the picture is more complex. The impact of blame on social work practice is an additional problem, which when added to performance management, is creating a situation where managers appear to be increasing their control over the means and ends of practice, (Derber, 1993). The colonisation of social work by inappropriate management approaches at the front line of social work appears to be undermining social work practice and according to Munro (2010b) reducing the scope for professional judgement and flexibility, which is making it difficult for social workers to learn from practice and is increasing the risks to children. Whilst social workers may wish to respond to inappropriate management practice through resistance strategies so that they can create space for decision making and discretion, this may not always be possible. Evans and Harris (2004) suggest that it is necessary to look at each situation on a case by case basis because what is happening is contingent upon 'beliefs about a manager's desire for, and ability to secure control and workers ability to resist control and seek discretion' (p.871). Where social work managers fail to appropriately support social workers, the social workers may feel justified in blaming managers and respond by adopting what they see as appropriate strategies to alleviate the worst effects of inappropriate management approaches. However, not all managers are responding inappropriately and collaboration strategies are being adopted when both managers and social workers on the front line shared professional concerns and are able to adapt management performance requirements (Evans, 2010) This situation was also found in education (Hoyle and Wallace, 2005). It would be useful to understand more about the conditions for collaboration, along with some analysis of how the demands of the different roles are worked through in the lived experiences of social workers and managers. Whilst the prevailing view is that managers are largely responding compliantly to the changes in social work, it is clear that in practice the picture is far more complex.

References

Beresford P, (2007), *The Changing Role and Tasks of Social Workers from Service Users Perspectives: A literature Informed Discussion Paper*, London: Shaping our Lives National User Network.

Branfield, F., Beresford, P., Danagher, N., and Webb, R. (2005) *Independence, Wellbeing and Choice A response to the Green Paper on Adult Social Care: Report of a consultation with service users*, London: National Centre for Independent Living and Shaping our Lives

Broadhurst, K., Wastell, D., White, S., Hall, C., Peckover, S., Thompson, K., Pithouse, A., and Davey, D. (2009) Performing 'initial assessment': Identifying the latent conditions for error at the front-door of local authority children's services. *British Journal of Social Work*, Advanced Access. available January 18th 2009. doi: 10.1093/bjsw/bcn162

Broadhurst, K., Hall, C., Wastell, D., White, S., and Pithouse, A. (2010) Risk, instrumentalism and the humane project in social work: Identifying the informal logics of risk management in children's statutory services. *British Journal of Social Work*, 40, 1046-1064

Brownbill, T. (2010) Kyhra tragedy: Don't blame the social worker, blame the killers, *Community Care*, 31st March, available from http://www.communitycare.co.uk/Articles/2010/03/31/114192/khyra-ishaq-dont-blame-the-social-worker-blame-the-killers.htm [accessed September 2010]

Clarke, J. (ed) (1993) *A Crisis in Care: Challenges to social work*, London: Sage / Open University

Clarke, J., and Newman, J. (1997) *The Managerial State*, London: Sage

Cohen, S. (2002) *Folk Devils and Moral Panics*. London: Routledge

Collinson, D. (1994) Strategies of resistance power, knowledge and subjectivity in the workplace. in M. Jermier, D. Knights, and W. Nord (Eds) *Resistance and Power in Organisations*. London: Routledge

Derber, C. (1993) *Managing Professionals: Ideological proletarianism and post-industrial labour. Theory and Society*, 12, 3, 309-41

Dickens, J. (2010) Social work in England at a watershed – as always: From the Seebohm Report to the Social Work Task Force. *British Journal of Social Work*, Advanced Access.available October 7th 2010. doi:10.1093/bjsw/bcq112

Dustin, D (2007) *The McDonaldization of Social Work*. Basingstoke: Ashgate

Evans, T. and Harris, J. 2004) Street-level; bureaucracy, social work and the (exaggerated) death of discretion, *British Journal of Social Work*, 34, 871-895

Evans, T. (2009) Managing to be professional? Team managers and practitioners in modernising social work. in J. Harris and V. White (Eds.) *Modernising Social Work, Critical Considerations*, Bristol: Policy Press

Evans, T. (2010) Professionals, managers and discretion: Critiquing street-level bureaucracy. *British Journal of Social Work* Advanced Access. available June 10th 2010. doi: 10.1093/bjsw/bcq074

Ferguson, I., and Woodward, R. (2009) *Radical Social Work in Practice Making a difference.* Bristol: Policy Press

General Social Care Council (2002) *Codes of Conduct for Social Care.* London: GSCC

Gupta, A., and Blewett, J. (2007) Change for Children? The challenges and opportunities for children's social work workforce. *Children and Family Social Work*, 12, 2, 172-181

Harris, J (2003), *The Social Work Business.* Abingdon: Routledge

Harris, J. (2008) State social work: constructing the present from moments in the past'. *British Journal of Social Work*, 38, 662-679

Harris, J. and White, V. (Eds.) (2009) *Modernising Social Work, Critical considerations.* Bristol: Policy Press

HM Government (2007) *Putting People First: A shared vision and commitment to the transformation of adult social care.* London: HMG

Hoyle, E., and Wallace, M. (2005) *Educational Leadership, Ambiguity, Professionals and Managerialism,* London: Sage

Jones, C. (2001) Voices from the Front Line: State Social Workers and New Labour, *British Journal of Social Work*, 31, 547-562

Jones, C. and Novak, T. (1993) Social Work Today, *British Journal of Social Work*, 23, 195-212

Kirkpatrick (2006) Taking stock of new managerialism in English social services. *Social Work & Society*, 4, 1

Lawler, J., and Bilson, A. (2010) *Social Work Management and Leadership: Managing complexity and creativity.* Abingdon: Routledge

Lymbery, M. (2001), Social Work at the Cross Roads, *British Journal of Social Work* 31, 369-384

Lymbery, M., and Postle, K. (2010) Social work in the context of adult social care in England and the resultant implications for social work education. *British Journal of Social Work.* Advanced Access. available April 9, 2010. doi:10.1093/bjsw/bcq045.

Maas-Lowit., M., and Hothersall, S. (2010) Protection. in S. Hothersall, and M. Maas-Lowit (Eds.) *Need, Risk and Protection in Social Work Practice.* Exeter: Learning Matters

McDonald, C., Harris, J., and Wintersteen, R. (2003) Contingent on context? Social work and the state in Australia, Britain and the USA, *British Journal of Social Work*, 33, 191-209

McGregor, D. (1987), *The Human Side of Enterprise.* Harmondsworth: Penguin

Mullaly, B. (1997) *Structural Social Work Ideology: Theory and practice.* Oxford:

Oxford University press.

Munro, E. (2010a) The Munro Review of Child Protection Part One: A systems Analysis, London: Department for Education

Munro, E. (2010b) Learning to reduce risks in child protection. *British Journal of Social Work*, 40, 1135-1151

Payne, M. (2005), *Modern Social Work Theory*. (3rd ed.). Basingstoke: Palgrave

Ranson, S., and Stuart, J. (1994) *Management for the Public Domain Enabling the learning society*, London: St Martins Press

Rogowski, S. (2008) Social work with children and families: Towards a radical/ critical Practice. *Practice*, 20, 1, 17-28

Shardlow, S.M. (2007) Social work in an international context. in M. Lymbery, and K. Postle (Eds.) *Social Work: A companion to learning*. London: Sage

Social Work Task Force (2009), *Building a Safe, Confident Future: The final report of the Social Work Task Force, November 2009*. London: Department of Children, Schools and Families. http://publications.education.gov.uk/default.aspx?PageFunction=productdetails&PageMode=publications&ProductId=DCSF-01114-2009 (accessed December 2010)

The International Federation of Social Work (2000) http://www.ifsw.org/f38000138.html (accessed September 2010)

Thomas, R and Davies, A (2005), What have feminists done for us? Feminists theory and organisational resistance. *Organisation*, 12, 5, 711-740

White, S., Wastell, D., Peckover, S., Hall, C., and Broadhurst, K. (2009), *Managing Risk in a High Blame Environment: Tales from the 'front door' in contemporary children's social care*, London: London School of Economics and Political Science / University of Oxford.

White, V. (2009), Quite Challenges? Professional practice in modernised social work. in J. Harris and V. White (Eds.) *Modernising Social Work, Critical considerations*. Bristol: Policy Press

Wilson, K., Ruch, G., Lymbery, M., and Cooper, A. (2008) *Social Work An Introduction to contemporary practice*. London: Pearson Longman

This chapter is an amended version of an article first published in 2011 in *Social Work & Social Sciences Review* vol. 14(2) pp.6-19. Sharon Lambley was then a Lecturer in the Dept of Social Work and Social Care, School of Education and Social Work, University of Sussex.

7

Developing communities of practice:
A strategy for effective leadership, management and supervision in social work

Ivan Gray, Jonathan Parker,
Lynne Rutter, and Sarah Williams

The situation in 2013

The major developments in social work since we wrote this paper in 2010 mean that developing communities of practice has become an essential issue that needs to be addressed urgently if intended reforms are to be successful. Without such attention we would argue that changes may well undermine services and practice rather than enhance them. The social work profession is facing one of the most significant periods of reform in its history. Following an arguably media-induced decline in public and Government confidence after publication of the inquiry into the death of Peter Connelly, a Social Work Reform Board (SWRB) was established to develop strategies for educators, social workers and the agencies that employed them to implement the recommendations of the Social Work Task Force (2009) and make their services 'fit for purpose' in the 21st Century.

The SWRB has established a Professional Capabilities Framework (PCF), Employer Standards and a framework for qualifying education and continuing professional development (SWRB 2010 and 2011). A new College of Social Work is now fully responsible for the PCF, introduced in 2012 as the single way in which social workers should think about and plan their careers and professional development. The College say the PCF should provide a backdrop to both initial social work education, an Assessed and Supported Year in Employment (ASYE), and continuing professional development after qualification (TCSW 2012).

At the heart of the reform agenda, ostensibly, is the recognition that social workers practise in uncertain and complex situations in which risk can never be completely eliminated. Both the Social Work Reform Board and the more recently published Munro Report (2011) stress the importance of moving away from top down, target driven management towards a more creative and flexible approach to service provision that enables social workers to learn from their experiences and have more freedom to exercise their professional judgement. Whilst the experiences of social workers that we have spoken to may not reflect this in reality it does represent an aim and has gained mainstream support (Williams, Rutter and Gray, 2012).

'The media is the message', of course, and we should all ask to what extent the changes themselves and the way they are being implemented will empower professionals? We would argue there are good grounds for suggesting this fundamental issue has been ignored or that the expressed aim of increased professional freedom is merely rhetoric. Current approaches to professional change do not empower. They are top down and not owned. They are bureaucratic and technocratic. ASYE is onerous for newly qualified social workers. The PCF despite its pretensions is just another set of occupational standards that offer nothing that the previous occupational standards could not have provided and, like any approach based on standards, is in danger of offering only more control.

Munro's (2011) over-influence could be construed as an unwelcome lurch towards the cult of the charismatic leader and the notorious bickering between the College of Social Work and BASW has been unseemly and divisive. We have more professional quangos than we started with and a fragmentation of responsibilities that can only confuse and impede change. The demise of the GSCC represents the downgrading of the profession to just another 'health' profession, without recognition of its distinctive features and needs and its focus, not on health, but on the social side of human life. The demise of the post-qualifying framework gives freedom in theory to employers, but offers little to professionals and could be seen as little more than benign neglect. In sum the agenda fails to regulate where regulation might help, offers regulation where it isn't necessary and despite its avowed intent fails to liberate professionals in any respect.

Improvements in individual and organisational learning set against a backdrop of improved cultures for learning are not just a desirable part of the reform of social work but an essential foundation on which to build these recommended changes. If social workers are to be given more freedom to exercise professional judgement they must be encouraged and supported to think for themselves and make situation-responsive, evidence-informed judgements. Learning is therefore not just something that happens at the beginning of a career or in an occasional training course, which quickly becomes a low priority or even stops. Learning should be something that happens every time a social worker speaks to a service user, works alongside another professional, engages in supervision or encounters any new situation. A social worker's knowledge and skills must evolve over time to ensure that they keep pace with new developments and are flexible enough to respond to unexpected and complex situations. It follows that if real change is to happen within the profession, all social workers must be encouraged to take personal responsibility for keeping up to date and for critically reflecting on their experiences to gain a deeper understanding of how they can provide a more effective service (Williams, Rutter and Gray, 2012).

However, improving the way that individual social workers learn is only half the story because services are provided within an organisational context. Individual learning must therefore be shared and developed in order to inform the knowledge and skill base of organisations as a whole. Taking a communities of practice approach to learning places service users and carers needs at the centre of reform because it ensures that the people at the frontline with direct experience of providing services are able to learn from each other and provide managers and policy makers with valuable insights into what works and doesn't work in practice. Improving the way that organisations learn will, in many cases, require major shifts in attitude and approach from people working at all levels, but most particularly from those with leadership and management responsibilities who are in a position to drive forward the necessary changes and create a culture in which all forms of learning can thrive.

For instance Munro's emphasis on case review as a means to organisational learning is a very positive but, unfortunately, probably represents an unrealistic proposal. She is right to see value in communal problem-solving and process improvement based on systems thinking and involving the multi-disciplinary team. However, this is not to be achieved by methodology alone. Empowering and mobilising teams as organisational problem solvers demands major cultural change.

We suggest, in this chapter, that a community of practice approach allows social work to develop a 'superordinate' learning culture this combines professional and managed learning cultures, which are perhaps getting all the current attention, with humanitarian and democratic learning cultures. The desired features of a humanitarian and democratic learning culture can be summarised as:

- Group trust
- A democratic and inclusive team
- Group problem solving

- Team support and challenge
- Expression of emotion
- Shared resources and expertise
- An outward looking team

The Reform Board's emphasis on improving supervision through introducing standards is also in danger of over-individualising learning and development. Munro is right to seek in case reviews a mechanism that could balance a tendency for supervision to locate practice problems and improvement with individuals (SCIE 2012) but, we could argue, what is required is a cultural change that recognises the importance of the wider community of practice. What is encapsulated within the idea of case review is a more fundamental development that also changes the nature of supervision, i.e. supervision recognises the social context of practice. Both the perspective of supervisor and supervisee and their actions need to recognise the crucial significance of and the need to influence and develop the wider community of practice and their understanding and efforts should be directed to this end.

References

Munro, E. (2011) *The Munro Review of Child Protection: The Final report-a child centred system. London: Dept for Education*

SCIE (2012) *At a glance 01: learning together to safeguard children: a systems model for case reviews Available from: www.scie.org.uk/publications/ataglance/ataglance01. asp*

Social Work Task Force (2009) *Building a Safe and Confident Future-The Final Report of the Social Work Taskforce. London: Department for Children Schools and Families(DCSF)*

SWRB (2010) *Building a safe and confident future: one year on. London: Social Work Reform Board. Available from: www.education.gov.uk/swrb*

SWRB (2011) *Standards for employers and supervision framework statement [Online] Available from : http://www.education.gov.uk/swrb/social/a0074240/ professional-standards-for-social-workers-in-england*

TCSW 2012 *The Professional Capabilities Framework (PCF). London: The College of Social Work Available from http://www.collegeofsocialwork.org/pcf.aspx*

Williams, S., Rutter,L., and Gray, I. (2012) *Promoting Individual and Organisational Learning in Health and Social Care. London: Sage*

Developing communities of practice:
A strategy for effective leadership, management and supervision in social work

Introduction

Social work in the UK has developed in a paradoxical way during its short history. Social work aims to enhance people's autonomy, self-direction and independence yet this has been juxtaposed with the social monitoring and regulatory mechanisms of a state regulated and approved profession (Payne, 2005; Gray et al., 2008).

Recently, the radical reform of the public sector has had a significant impact on social work (Jordan and Jordan, 2006; Parker, 2007). Changes in policy and practice have led to the rationalisation of services and reprioritisation that has resulted in the fragmentation of some services and the integration of others (Blewitt, 2008). Accompanying these changes has been a rise in managerialism and bureaucracy underpinned by a belief that services improve through inspection and regulation (Hafford-Letchfield, 2006). The focus, therefore, tends to be on performance management and measurement rather than professional judgement and practice (Martin et al., 2004; Penhale and Parker, 2008).

Negotiating a pathway through and managing such ambiguities and complexities requires models that maintain the values of social work and promote practice consonant with the agreed definition of social work, yet can also facilitate the development of services, social work practice and their management.

This paper argues that developing communities of practice may provide a bridge between managerialism and authentic practices. It argues that effective, participative leadership can develop and support a community of practice even in an unsympathetic organisational culture. Whilst in other organisations leaders will probably not be equipped or orientated to lead a community of practice, a confluence of social work values, groupwork and community building skills, political awareness and a congruent learning culture/history, might make it a real possibility in social work and provide an attractive leadership model for team leaders. It posits that there is pressing need for research into communities of practice as they might have considerable potential as a leadership model for social work..

Learning organisations and learning cultures in social work

The concept of learning organisations has been given some attention in social work (Gould, 2000; Gray et al., 2008; Hafford- Letchfield et al., 2008) whilst it is receiving increasing attention from policy makers as an ideal to be strived for (DfES/DH, 2006). Attempts are being made actively to develop organisations as learning organisations (SCIE, 2004) and to 'enable work based learning' as a communal provision that can have a significant impact on professional competence (GSCC, 2006); this despite considerable pessimism as to their likely success of learning organisations in social work (Gould et al., 2004).

Senge's (1990) hugely influential work identified the features of a learning organisation. Mobilising teams and individuals seeking to maximise their effectiveness as learners are crucial components of his model, but it is in essence a top down, managed approach. An alternative approach is developing communities of practice, which focuses on the micro-level activity on which organisational learning processes depend. It can either be seen as a valuable companion theory to learning organisations, in that it might be used as the basis for mobilising teams, or it could be seen as an alternative 'bottom up' approach. However, communities of practice as an approach is relatively underdeveloped (Fuller et al., 2004).

Wenger (2006) defines communities of practice as groups of people sharing common interests, concerns and responsibilities and engaging together and improving their practice as a result. He also acknowledges the development of shared resources within these communities. This definition allows for communities of practice to encompass networks of people from a number of different organisations, for instance social workers with a particular specialism might link up to develop their practice. However, in his earlier work Wenger identified communities of practice as natural working groups within an organisation that apart from facilitating learning provide *'ways of ameliorating institutionally generated conflicts'* (Wenger, 1998, p. 46). They also help socialise the workplace and whilst they may extend beyond work teams they can encompass them. This earlier focus on working groups allows the possibility of a leadership strategy that is based on developing social work teams as communities of practice.

A key question is how might a community of practice be developed and led? Hawkins and Shohet (2000) argue for the importance of a learning and development culture to support effective supervision, so developing a learning and development culture may offer a good starting point. As a first step this will require determining the parameters of a learning and development culture.

Learning cultures and communities of practice

Several different learning cultures can be identified in social work (Gray et al., 2008). By learning culture we mean a culture in which learning and development are valued, encouraged and seen as fundamental to the organisation's successful operation. For instance, by introducing registration for social workers with re-registration dependent on the demonstration of continuing professional development; the General Social Council (GSCC) can be seen to be striving for a *professional learning culture*(GSCC, 2002, 2007). 'Investors in People' is best described as creating a *managed learning culture* where training and learning activity is directed towards service strategy and business plans (Hoque et al., 2005). A therapeutic community can be seen as aspiring to a *humanistic leaning culture*(Barber, 1988); and Total Quality Management, that seeks to address the negative impact of organisational hierarchy and power on workers' involvement in organisational problem solving, can be seen as aiming to create a *democratic leaning culture* (Marinez- Costa and Jiminez- Jiminez, 2009). Each culture has a range of principles (see table 1).

Each identified culture has its particular theory of learning, specific objectives, unique learning processes and defined outcomes. For example, it can be argued that currently in social work a professional and managerial learning culture dominates whereas in the past a humanistic and democratic learning culture may have been more influential (Tsui, 2005).

To foster communities of practice, Wenger (2006) suggests there is a need to minimise prescription, set the context in which communities can prosper, value the work of community building and development and make sure participants have access to the resources they need to learn. In stressing the social and communal nature of learning and the dangers of prescription, Wenger locates communities of practice in humanistic and democratic cultures.

However, in social work a 'super-ordinate' learning culture that encompasses all four organisational cultures, (table 1) may be both desirable and necessary. Professional and managerial cultures have to be accommodated but a communal humanistic culture is essential if the emotional nature of the work and the impact of society and community on the self and learning, is to be recognised. A democratic learning culture is also essential if, in a similar way, social work is to maintain awareness of and engage with the power differentials that can disempower users and carers. If a super-ordinate learning culture might be a goal, a key issue concerns how a community of practice might be led.

Leading communities of practice

After making a case for the importance of group processes and group leadership for communities of practice, Plaskoff (2006) identifies that leaders have an administrative role in setting up and facilitating meetings, and distributing information, but that otherwise their role is one of 'mentoring'. It is almost, for Plaskoff (2006), that leaders need to take a backseat when it comes to developing communities of practice.

So both Wenger and Plaskoff seem to advocate the emergence of leadership within teams, but a manager with a team of inexperienced staff might be waiting for a long time for something to 'emerge' and will need to be far more proactive. It is as if Wenger and Plaskoff have got stuck in seeing leadership as synonymous with control and the antithesis of a community of practice. In social work, this back seat role is not congruent with a manager's or leader's responsibilities to develop and supervise social work practice. Accepting that the use of power is a crucial issue, this does not necessarily negate pro-active leadership by a team manager, but demands a particular value-based approach.

For instance, Hersey and Blanchard's (1993) theory of situational leadership offers an approach to leadership which is congruent with social work values. It is centred on managers' roles in developing staff and is supported by concepts from group work theory. It is 'situational' in that leaders' behaviours need to vary according to the characteristics of the team, group or individual staff member. They see teams and groups of staff as being at different developmental levels that demand different leadership styles. So if a team or staff member is very new they may not understand the purpose of the work or be motivated to do it. They may not have the skills and knowledge to carry out the tasks and may need instruction and close supervision if they are to be able to function appropriately. An experienced team or staff member, on the other hand, may be more self motivated and well equipped to do the work, have a stronger value base, knowledge of essential procedures and objectives and the skills to practise effectively. So a

Table 1

Contending learning and development cultures and types of learning organisation

Professional learning culture (General Social Care Council)	Managed learning culture (Investors in People)
Professional college sets practice standards and practitioners have a long term relationship with their college	Standards are quality standards determined by managers
Professionals manage their own learning and development	Learning and development is the responsibility of line managers
Competence determined by experienced professionals using personal judgement	Competence determined by appraisal or assessment against published standards
Learning and development driven by personal career and practice agendas. Strong emphasis on professional value base.	Learning and development driven by business need and business case. Strong emphasis on cost effectiveness
Learning and development evaluated in terms of professional growth and development	Learning and development evaluated according to business outcomes and impact on the service
Supervision is focused on personal development	Supervision is focused on case and service management
Sanctions are removal of professional accreditation and judgement is made by peers	Sanctions are managerial i.e. progression, reward or use of capability procedures
Dialogue with a fellow professional, critical reflection and professional education are crucial vehicles for personal development	A range of training and development methods are used according to learning need and cost efficiency considerations
Professional are expected to contribute to professional development as a duty	Professional trainers and consultants are employed, relationships are commercial
Humanistic learning culture (therapeutic communities)	Democratic learning culture (total quality management)
Individuals are liberated by reflecting on their actions and the consequences of their actions for others and making choices. The community both challenges behaviour and supports individuals	Organisational and social expertise and creativity can be increased if the power relations that exclude some from problem solving and decision making are addressed.
Learning and development are natural human activities. Group influence and experiences can be mobilised to bring personal change.	Learning and development are natural human activities but power relationships in society seek to use them to control.
Competence is competence in life and is about self actualisation.	If groups are liberated they can make a contribution to social competence, that is to the capability of society or an organisation to learn and develop.
Learning and development is driven by social and personal needs that are inseparable.	Learning and development should be directed towards the social good.

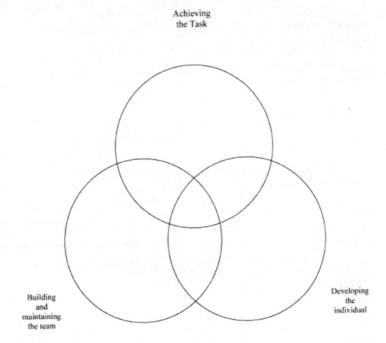

Fig 1. What a leader has to do from Adair, 1983, p.44

leader can allow them greater opportunity to participate in the management and development of practice and can delegate to them. Developed teams will require minimal facilitation.

The situational leadership model is compatible with the needs of a community of practice and would make leadership central to its effective development. Adair's action centred leadership model may also be of value here (Adair, 1983). Adair's action-centred leadership model identifies three interrelated areas of activity that are necessary for a team to function effectively. This provides a useful basis for analysing a team's performance and planning for improvement.

Adair's model can help synthesise the different learning cultures into a super-ordinate culture and so it could be particularly well suited to developing a community of practice in social work. The domains all overlap, so that whilst developing the team might include such things as building trusting relationships and positive regard between team members or creating a climate where problems can be raised and practice challenged, it overlaps with achieving core tasks. This means business planning and developing services are not only supported by team development but also provide a medium through which the team can develop. Supervision as part of personal development is also dependent on the effectiveness of the team and is a crucial forum for case management.

The model also emphasises task management, so that a community of practice will give attention to a range of 'soft' and 'hard' issues. Table 2 identifies some questions such a community of practice and their leader need to address, to define concepts and evaluate practice.

Leading communities of practice: Helping a community learn and develop its practice

A crucial challenge for the leader of a community of practice is how they help it to learn and develop its practice. Thompson (2006) stresses the importance of creating a culture which places learning at the centre of organisations, suggesting that effective leadership is needed to help remove barriers to learning and create an environment in which learning is valued and change is embraced. Although leadership can be provided by people at all levels within organisations, managers may take a principal role in providing leadership which achieves these objectives.

If managers are to promote and support the development of a community of practice approach within their team they need to have a specific skill set which must include a good understanding of how individuals and groups learn and develop their professional expertise and an ability to facilitate those processes. Furthermore, they will need a commitment to learning as a fundamental part of the delivery of high quality services and understand that it is not possible to deliver responsive services unless those delivering them are constantly updating and applying new knowledge and understanding to their practice. They will need the capability to build a shared vision, implement strategies for supporting and enabling individual and team growth and the capacity to encourage individuals to increase their confidence and skills to be involved in decision making and to take leadership responsibilities in their areas of expertise (Hafford-Letchfield *et al.* 2008).

Communities of practice are formed by people who strive together to learn and enhance their practice (Wenger, 2006). However, they are not necessarily groups deliberately convened for learning, and Wenger acknowledges that the existence of a community per se does not ensure that it provides an effective environment for learning and development. Having said that, our informal learning and our behaviour can be

Table 2

Achieving the task
How effective are our business planning processes?
Are we clear about our objectives as a team and our priorities for service development?
How effective are our quality management processes?
How is the team performing against performance measures, quality standards and business objectives?
How effective is our case management in supervision?
How effective is our multi-disciplinary working?
Is the team engaged in service development?
Are people who use services engaged in service development planning?

Building and maintaining the team
How effective are our recruitment processes?
What will be our needs in the short medium and long term in terms of skills and staffing levels?
What stage of development is the team at?
To what extent does the team have:
Trusting relationships between its members and positive regard?
A climate where problems can be raised and practice challenged?
Responsive and flexible leadership?
A good range of personalities and roles?
Procedures and ways of working that allow it to work effectively including resolving conflicts?
Good relationships and established working relationships with co-providers?
Good relationships and established working relationships with people who use services and carers?
Good relationships and established working relationships with the rest of the organisation?
Continuous team development and improvement?

Developing the individual
How effective is induction and probation
How effective is supervision in developing practice?
How effective is our management of training?
How effective is our CPD?
How effective is our appraisal?
How effective is qualifying and post qualifying training?
Is there shared training with co-providers?
Are individuals committed and motivated?

influenced at a fundamental level by the interactions we have with others and by the inherent beliefs and understandings of the communities in which we live and work. Social learning theories explain that within any social context people can learn from one another, from observation, imitation, and modelling (Bandura, 1997). Accordingly, team managers can use their understanding of group processes and social learning theories to put in place strategies to enhance the learning potential of such groups and communities of practice.

Plaskoff (2006) suggests that community building activities are critical if the potential to support learning within organisations is to be realised. He identifies a number of factors fundamental to the successful operation of a community of practice including trust, sense of belonging, equality and thriving relationships. He points out that in traditional hierarchical organisations trust can be undermined by the way that power is distributed and community building undermined by a lack of commitment to joint working. Managers striving to encourage a community of practice approach need to fully consider the way that they use and share their power, perhaps considering the early involvement of team members in community building processes such as agreeing priorities, philosophical underpinnings and common understandings.

Leaders may endeavour to work to adult learning principles and model the learning and development behaviour required by others. Leaders, acting as enablers of learning, need to allow for the individual and group variations in learning, and acknowledge the function and importance of the learning environment (physical and psychological). By working to the facilitative and supportive values embedded within adult learning principles, leaders become aware and take more account of the real issues, complexities and contradictions that practitioners face. By working co-operatively and meaningfully together in a community of practice, acknowledging the uncertainty of practice, as well as their own learning and development concerns, a meaningful learning culture is more likely to emerge.

It appears that a careful balance needs to be reached in terms of concentrating on the social, emotional and participatory dimensions of workplace learning and the focus on instrumental tasks (Lefevre, 2005).

Communities of practice and effective supervision

Effective supervision is both a means to achieving a community of practice and an outcome. One could see Adair's (1993) action-centred leadership as very hard to achieve without the dialogue between manager and team that social work's model of supervision generates. The Children's Workforce Development Council and Skills for Care have jointly introduced a supervision unit designed to provide a model of good practice and to assist in auditing and improving supervision by identifying relevant standards (SfC/CWDC, 2007). This is an important development aimed at improving the quality of supervision in a current climate that gives it considerable priority (Laming, 2009).

We would contend, however, that there are two futures for supervision that the unit might usher in. One where supervision becomes subject to scrutiny and audit, but the quality of practice really changes little- that is the unit becomes a monitoring tool - and one where there is an in-depth improvement in the quality of supervision – that is the unit becomes a developmental/educative tool. The latter is perhaps dependent on the standards being mobilised by a community of practice to bring change and is situated rather than universal.

This point has been well made by Hawkins and Shohet (2000) in arguing for the importance of a learning and development culture to effective supervision:

> ... a great deal of social work and indeed counselling and therapy is about creating the environment and relationships in which clients learn about themselves and their environment in a way that leaves them with more options than they arrived with... social workers, counsellors and therapists, etc. are best able to facilitate others to learn if they are supported in constantly learning and developing themselves. Hawkins and Shohet (2000 p. 137)

A community of practice is an effective vehicle for introducing complex changes arising from the Effective Supervision Unit (SfC 2007) because it:

- Engenders ownership and motivates the team
- Supports the personal development necessary to respond to the change
- Builds flexible teams that can adjust to the change
- Mobilises the team to problem-solve, drawing on both the leader's and the team's resources and facilitating creativity and innovation

Also, the culture a community generates supports the quality of relationships necessary for effective supervisory practice.

Interagency working and involving people who use services in case management and service design

One measure of team effectiveness is its ability to look outwards responding to the needs of those outside of the team and even welcoming them into the team. A team at an earlier stage of development may be inward looking, concerned with building trust and relationships and determining norms within the team. This can make it unresponsive to those outside of the team or even hostile (Mullins, 2007). Some teams can get stuck in a culture where they blame the wider organisation or co-providers for problems, giving themselves a sense of identity and togetherness in the process, but at considerable cost to their effectiveness.

The tendency for teams to become inward looking is seen by Total Quality Management (TQM) as generating many quality problems (Oakland, 2003). A TQM response is to establish 'quality circles' at the interface of teams or departments and encourage teams to either view 'the next process as the customer' or else focus on breaking down barriers between staff areas (Deming, 1994).In social work it is expressed as a drive towards multi-professional working (Barr et al., 2008; Quinney, 2006; Whittington et al., 2003).

Accepting that a higher performing and developed community of practice will be more outward looking, a constant challenge for the community is managing external relationships. The external relationship that offers the greatest challenge for social work is arguably with the people who use services.

Carr (2004) identifies a daunting number of problems that undermine the involvement of people who use services in developing service provision.

To be successful in building partnership and participation in service design and delivery, practice must be seen as a joint project (Beresford and Croft, 2002; Doel and Best, 2008). This shift is also the essence of personalisation and is one that demands major changes in practice and therefore in leadership and supervision to be successful (O'Leary and Lownsbrough, 2007). Personalisation could be construed as welcoming people who use services into the community of practice and that there is direct parallel here with the principles of therapeutic communities (Hinshelwood and Manning, 1979).

Communities of practice, like groups and teams have different levels of development (Tuckman, 1965). There are also different degrees of personalisation (Carr, 2008), suggesting that advanced communities of practice will be characterised by their inclusion of people who use services. In this way, the community will facilitate more advanced levels of personalisation and fuller participation of people who use services in service planning and design.

Learning organisations and communities of practice

Communities of practice offer an alternative perspective and approach to developing a learning organisation; a 'bottom up' approach in contrast to a 'top down' approach. It places team and group activity at the heart of service and practice development and it relies on team or group leadership to be effective.

Whilst it needs further exploration, the strength of a communities of practice approach is that a team or group leader may still be able to adopt it to good effect even in an unsupportive organisation. Even in an organisation dominated by managerialism it may be possible to create a 'micro- culture' of good communal practice. A leader may, however, need to give full attention to managing the interface with the wider organisation to ensure that its demands and imperatives do not undermine the community of practice and to ensure that the organisation does not come to see the community of practice as a threat. For instance, therapeutic communities as communities of practice can be seen to have been particularly prone to this conflict with the host organisation and therefore prone to closure (Hinshelwood and Manning, 1979). The high failure rate of early Total Quality Management initiatives could also be seen as resulting from the conflicts created by empowering work teams in a hierarchical organisation (Klein 1981; Thompson, 1982). However, a super-ordinate approach to developing a learning culture, that acknowledges organisational purpose and imperatives, may allow a community of practice to survive or even influence the development of the wider organisation.

Leading communities of practice: Understandings and skills

Table 1 clarifies the different cultures that must be accommodated to support a community of practice, generating community understandings

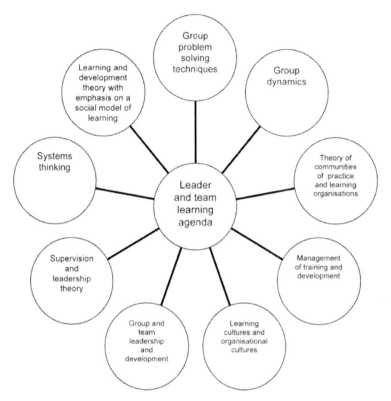

Fig 2. Leading a community of practice: The theoretical domain

and setting the agendas for community leadership.

In the super-ordinate model, all the cultures in order to be integrated must be shaped by a mixture of groupwork and leadership skills and learning and development skills driven by a humanistic value base. This overlays the cultures and is the ingredient that stops mechanistic approaches (Gray et al., 2008). Reflective leadership practice as well as reflective professional practice could also be seen as essential (Lawler & Bilson 2010)

This creates a demanding but social work congruent set of skills and knowledge for leaders or managers to acquire. Figure 2 shows some of the theoretical domains leading and contributing to a community of practice requires, accepting that an understanding of more general management theory is also a necessity.

The future of communities of practice in social work

Wenger suggests (1998) organisations are designs which construct their own discourses to justify themselves. Social work could be seen as locked into professional and managerial cultures, design initiatives and discourses. Learning organisations are on the contemporary managerial agenda. However, current policy initiatives do not reach for a super-ordinate model of learning culture, for communities of practice or for humanitarian and democratic learning cultures.

When exploring the SCIE organisational audit (SCIE, 2004) with team managers attending our leadership and management programmes many concluded that they thought that their team had the characteristics of a learning organisation, but the wider organisation did not. This may have been loyalty to their team or simply optimism but, alternatively, it could be that the model revealed to them their community of practice whilst identifying the weaknesses of the wider organisation. Beddoe (2009) also notes this phenomenon and suggests there is a failure of social services organisations to learn from individual teams.

Developing communities of practice is therefore perhaps a strategy for first line managers. It may allow a value driven approach that can create a rewarding work environment for a team and, even given the limitations of an unsympathetic host organisation, has the potential of leading to considerable improvements in service quality. Making the approach explicit for managers can only assist and being realistic about the limitations set by the wider organisation will not, in fact, undermine it as a model. Taking the Effective Supervision Unit (SfC/CWDC, 2007), team managers leading communities of practice may well take a set of standards that will otherwise just increase their auditing burden and, by making the standards theirs and their teams, create a major change in the climate of supervision.

To provide the maximum momentum to the development of communities of practice in social work there is a compelling argument for this demanding learning agenda to be provided to all the potential stakeholders of a community of practice. This would mean, for instance, explicit integration into social work degree programmes and the Post Qualifying leadership and management pathway (GSCC, 2005). It would need to begin to appear as part of in–house training and would have to be at the centre of the specialist level Post Qualifying unit 'Enabling Others' (GSCC, 2006). It links clearly with the Social Work Task Force (2009) emphasis on partnership Working

Social work practitioners are motivated by a strong value base that means they seek to empower others and should have a developed self awareness and awareness of others from their training in social work methods and their everyday practice together with groupwork understandings and skills. Social Workers bring the motivation, perspectives and skills that would support the development of communities of practice. Developing communities of practice could therefore be a crucial opportunity to reach for. An opportunity that may prove truly productive in enhancing service quality, improving performance and building a bridge between managerialism and professional values, practices and experiences.

References

Adair, J., 1983. *Effective Leadership.* London: Pan

Bandura, A. (1997) *Self-efficacy: The exercise of control.* New York: Freeman

Barber, P., 1988. Learning to grow: the necessity for education processing in therapeutic community practice. *Journal of Therapeutic Communities*, 9, 2, 101-108

Barr, H., Goosey, D. and Webb, M. (2008) Social work in collaboration with other professions. in M. Davies (Ed.) *The Blackwell Companion to Social Work.* (3rd ed.) Oxford: Blackwell (pp. 277-86)

Beddoe, L. (2009) Creating conversation: Social workers and learning organisations. *Social Work Education*, 28: 7, 722-736

Beresford, P. (2003) *It's Our Lives: A short theory of knowledge, distance and experience.* London: Citizen Press

Beresford, P. and Croft, S. (2002) Involving service users in management :Citizenship, access and support. in J. Reynolds ,et al. (Eds.) *The Managing Care Reader.* London: Routledge (pp.21-28)

Blewitt, J. (2008) Social work in new policy contexts: Threats and opportunities. in S. Fraser and S. Matthews (Eds.) *The Critical Practitioner in Social Work and Health Care.* London: Sage

Brown, K., Immins, T., Bates, N., Gray, I., Rutter, L., Keen, S., Parker, J., and members of the Project's Steering Group (2007) *Tracking The Learning and Development Needs of Newly Qualified Social Workers Project.* Leeds: Skills for Care.

Care Standards Act (2000). *Care Standards Act 2000.* London: HMSO

Carr, S. (2004) *Has Service User Participation Made a Difference to Social Care Provision.* Scie position Paper 3. Bristol: Policy Press

Carr, S., 2008 *Personalisation: A rough guide.* London: Scie. http://www.scie.org.uk/ publications/reports/report20.pdf [Accessed 19th August 2009]

Dale, P., Davies, M., Morrison, T., and Waters, J. (1986) *Dangerous Families.* London:

Tavistock

Deming, W.E. (1994) *Out of the Crisis*. Cambridge: Cambridge University Press

DfES/DH (Department of Health) (2006) *Options for Excellence. Building the social workforce of the future*. London: DfES/DH

Fuller, A., Hodkinson, H. Hodkinson, P., and Unwin, L. (2005) Learning as a peripheral participation in communities of practice: A reassessment of key concepts in workplace learning. *British Educational Research Journal*, 31, 1, 49-68

Gray, I., Parker, J., and Immins, T. (2008) Leading communities of practice in social work . Groupwork or management? *Groupwork* 18, 2, 26-41

Glendinning, C., Clarke, S., Hare, P., Inna Kotchetkova, I., Maddison, J., and Newbronner, L. (2006) *Outcomes-focused Services for Older People. Scie* Adults' services knowledge review 13. Bristol: Scie. http://www.scie.org.uk/publications/knowledgereviews/kr13.pdf [Accessed 19th August 2009]

Gould, N. (2000) Becoming a learning organisation: A social work example. *Social Work Education*, 19, 6, 585-596

Gould, N. and Baldwin, M.(2004) *Social Work, Critical Reflection and the Learning Organisation*. Aldershot: Ashgate

GSCC (2002) *Codes of Practice for Social Workers and Employers*. London: General Social Council

GSCC (2005). *Specialist Standards and Requirements for Post Qualifying Social Work Education and Training. Leadership and management*. London: General Social Council

GSCC (2006) *Specialist Standards and Requirements for Post Qualifying Social Work Education and Training. Practice education*. London: General Social Council

Hafford-Letchfield, T. (2006) *Management and Organisations in Social Work*. Exeter: Learning Matters

Hafford-Letchfield, T., Leonard, K., Begum, N., and Chick, N.F. (2008) *Leadership and Management in Social Care*. London :Sage

Hawkins,P. and Shohet, R. (2000) *Supervision in the Helping Professions*. Buckingham: Open University

Hersey, P. and Blanchard, K.H. (1993) *Management of Organisational Behaviour : Utilising human resources*. (6th ed.) London: Prentice Hall

Hinshelwood, R.D. and Manning, N. (1979) *Therapeutic Communities: Reflections and progress*. Abingdon: Routledge

Hoque,K., Taylor,S., and Bell, E. (2005) Investors in people: market led voluntarism in vocational education and training. *British Journal of Industrial Relations*, 43, 1, 135-153

Jordan, B. and Jordan, C. (2006) *Social Work and the Third Way: Tough love as social policy*. (3rd ed.) London: Sage

Klein, G. (1981) Implementing quality circles; A hard look at some of the realities. *Personnel Review*, November/December

Lawler, J. & Bilson, A., (2010) *Social Work Management and Leadership; Managing complexity with creativity.* London: Routledge

Lord Laming (2009) *The Protection of Children in England: A progress report.* London: TSO http://publications.everychildmatters.gov.uk/eOrderingDownload/HC-330.pdf [Accessed 1st)October 2009]

Martinez-Costa, M. and Jiminez-Jiminez, D. (2009) The effectiveness of TQM: the key role of organisational learning in small businesses, *International Small Business Journal,* 27, 1, 98-125

Martin, G.P., Phelps, K. and Katbamna, S. (2004) Human motivation and professional practice: Knights, knaves and social workers, *Social Policy and Administration,* 38, 5, 470-87

Mayhew, N., (2006) *Board Level Development- Beyond Change Management.* http://www.executive.modern.nhs.uk/inview/inviewarticle.aspx?id=58 [Accessed 15.02.09]

Morgan G. (2006) *Images of Organisation.* London: Sage

Mullins, l., (2007) *Management and Organisational Behaviour.* (8th ed.) Harlow: Prentice Hall

Oakland, J.S. (2003) *Total quality management- text with cases.* Third edition. London:Heinemann

O'Leary, D. and Lownsbrough H. (2007) *The Leadership Imperative.* http://www.demos.co.uk/publications/leadershipimperative [Accessed 22nd August 2009]

Parker, J. (2007) Developing effective practice learning for tomorrow's social workers, *Social Work Education,* 26, 8, 763-79

Payne, M. (2005) *Modern social Work Theory.* Basingstoke: Palgrave MacMillan

Penhale, B. and Parker, J. (2008) *Working with Vulnerable Adults.* London: Routledge

Plaskoff, J. (2006) Intersubjectivity and community building: Learning to learn organisationally. in M.A. Easterby-Smith and M.A. Lyles (Eds) *Handbook of Organizational Learning and Knowledge Management.* Oxford: Blackwell

Quinney, A. (2006) *Collaborative Social Work Practice.* Exeter: Learning Matters

Reynolds, J., Henderson, J., Seden, J. Charlesworth, J and Bullman, A. (Eds.) (2002) *The Managing reader.* UK: Routledge

SCIE (2004) *Learning Organisations: A self assessment resource pack.* London: Social Care Institute for Excellence

Senge, P.M. (1990). *The Fifth Discipline: The art and practice of the learning organisation.* London: Random House

SfC/CWDC (Skills for England) 2007. *Providing Effective Supervision.* Leeds: SfC http://www.skillsfor.org.uk/files/Effective%20Supervision%20unit.pdf [Accessed 14th April 2008]

Sinclair, I. (2008) Inspection: A quality-control perspective. in M. Davies (Ed.) *The Blackwell Companion to Social Work,* (3rd ed.) Oxford: Blackwell. (pp. 449-57)

Thompson, N., (2006) *Promoting Workplace Learning.* Bristol: BASW / Policy Press

Thompson, W. (1982) Is the organisation ready for quality circles. *Training and Development Journal*, December

Tsui, M., S. (2005) *Social Work Supervision: Contexts and concepts.* London: Sage

Tuckman, B.W. (1965) Developmental sequence in small groups, *Psychological bulletin* 63, 384-99

Wenger, E. (1998) *Communities of Practice. Learning, meaning and Identity.* Cambridge: Cambridge University Press

Wenger, E. (2004) *Knowledge Management as a Doughnut: Shaping your knowledge through communities of practice.* Ivey Business Journal, 68, 3, 1-8

Wenger, E. (c2006) *Etienne Wenger Home Page http://www.ewenger.com* [Accessed 19th December 2009]

Wenger, E. (2006) *Communities of Practice: A brief introduction.* http://www.ewenger.com/theory/index.htm [Accesssed 15th January 2010]

The body of this chapter was first published in 2011 in *Social Work & Social Sciences Review* vol. 14(2) pp.20-36. Ivan Gray was Senior lecturer in Leadership and Management, Jonathan Parker was Professor of Social Work, Lynne Rutter was Lecturer, Student Support and Library Skills, and Sarah Williams was Senior Lecturer, Practice Development, Centre for Social Work and Social Policy, School of Health and Social Care.

8

Leadership from the bottom up:

Reinventing dementia care in residential and nursing home settings

Garuth Chalfont and Trish Hafford-Letchfield

Introduction

The quality of dementia care in the UK has attracted a great deal of attention following allegations of poor levels of service in both people's own homes and care homes (Care Quality Commission, 2010; Manthorpe, 2009). This adds further to the bleak realities of inappropriate use of antipsychotic medication (Guthrie et al, 2010); the scarcity of funding for residential care (Laing & Buisson, 2009) and the disappointment felt by many over the National Dementia Strategy (National Audit Office, 2010; Banerjee, 2010). Rising predictions on the future prevalence of dementia both in the UK and globally have implications for the future trajectory of dementia care (Wimo et al, 2010) and indicate that a radical overhaul of the current system is required if these challenges are to be addressed. There is also a corresponding need for increased research and debate on any solutions (O'Connor et al, 2007) particularly with attention to the organisational development factors influencing current models of dementia care and which tend not to be stressed in the dementia care literature.

In 2011, the government announced significant investment in funding for dementia research. Priority areas included the evaluation of prevention and public health interventions, the influence of genes and the environment in the development of the disease, alternatives to antipsychotic drugs, stem cell research, and a better understanding of how the brain is affected by dementia (DH, 2011).

Notwithstanding any immediatebreakthrough in scientific research, there is now a substantial body of evidence to demonstrate that the most effective interventions lie in the purposeful development of services to support a person with dementia and their carers by addressing the diverse and individual nature of their experience (Kitwood & Benson,

1995; Kitwood 1997; Killick and Allan, 2001; Nolan et al, 2002). The transformation of dementia care envisaged in the UK national dementia strategy has also highlighted the necessity for strong leadership as essential to its success, particularly at a local level (DoH, 2009; DoH, 2010). Alongside a range of strategic activities cited to promote the social care needs of older people with dementia, we thought it timely to review how leadership in dementia care might be encouraged to evolve at a local level to complement strategic imperatives. The term 'leadership' tends to be endorsed uncritically in the policy literature (Lawler, 2007) so through a small research study, we explored with managers themselves what meanings they associated with this term in the day-to-day realities of their own practice and some of the findings from this study are discussed briefly here. A more detailed report of this wider study is provided by Chalfont (2008). This paper seeks to explore any associations made by these managers with styles of leadership and the subsequent creation of a suitable culture or climate in care settings seen to be effective in supporting and enabling those involved in delivering more person-centred care.

Background

This paper discusses two key concerns emerging from the literature which the authors see as particularly challenging to leaders and managers within homes delivering dementia care. As mentioned earlier, the discussion is informed by the key themes which arose from data captured through in-depth individual interviews with four managers working in the field. These themes were originally drawn from a much larger research study which investigated the impact of nature and the importance of environmental design in dementia care (see Chalfont, 2008). During this study however, some interesting data was captured in relation to leadership and the organisational climate or the so called 'softer' aspects of the dementia care environment. The researcher then decided to explore some of these aspects in greater depth, by interviewing a further small sample of residential home managers. Using a broad topic guide, in-depth individual interviews of four managers sought to explore their perspectives of what constituted effective leadership within institutional residential care settings. Transcribed data from these interviews were subject to content analysis (Bryman, 2001) from which three key themes were identified. The first theme concerned the influence of different factors on organisational climate specific to a care home environment. The second theme concerned how managers identified the presence and potential of leadership roles at different levels in the organisation and their views about how this could be fostered and utlised including what also hindered leadership development. The third theme related to what managers said about the practical challenges they encountered in relation to staff learning and development. Drawing on these three main themes, some associations were observed about the importance of encouraging participation in developing better quality dementia care from the 'bottom up' as opposed to the more 'top-down' approach implied by national policy. Whilst our sample is small, we have utilised some of the managers' narrative from the interviews by interspersing quotes throughout this paper in order to promote a fuller discussion of the relevant issues. Working through challenges confidently at a local level, we suggest, might contribute to the evolvement of more creative and positive dementia care practice. This might facilitate the evolution of the service in a way that reflects aspirations of improved dementia care coming 'from above', that is in policy declarations.

Firstly, we provide an overview of current issues and challenges in dementia care in the context of recent policy developments. Secondly, we discuss the potential features of leadership within dementia care settings. The manager's narratives are used to illustrate further the discussion about the experiences, issues and theoretical challenges discussed and provide some points of reflection in relation to promoting a positive person-centred culture.

Contemporary issues in dementia care

The number of people with dementia in England is expected to double within 30 years with an associated estimated cost of care rising from £15.9 billion in 2009 to £34.8 billion by 2026 (McCrone et al, 2008). Dementia covers a range of progressive, organic brain conditions which affect an estimated 800,000 people in England and is expected to increase (Alzheimer's Disease Society, 2012). People living with dementia present a complexity of needs, requiring a holistic approach which engages with support across traditional organisational boundaries. There are also significant patterns of inequality amongst older people with high support needs including: discrimination in service delivery; the failure of services to take a holistic approach which addresses different social, cultural, religious, spiritual, emotional or sexual needs: and a lack of voice, choice and control for those with dementia, particularly for those who experience language barriers (Blood and Bamford, 2010). Effective outcomes of care depend on focused co-ordination and co-operation between health and social care and their contracted agencies (Sheard & Cox, 1998, NICE and SCIE, 2006) as well as creative approaches to person-centred care (Hayes & Povey, 2010). Dementia continues to be a much stigmatised condition within our society despite recent media campaigns aiming to make it more visible (Dementia Awareness News, 2010). The Department of Health's National Dementia Strategy, *Living Well with Dementia* (DH, 2009) and its implementation plan provide an ambitious and comprehensive vision for people with dementia and their carers to be enabled to live as well as possible. Cited as an 'evidenced-based strategy' (Ministers Foreword, DH, 2009) it focuses on achieving outcomes for people living with dementia: to improve the public and professionals' awareness; to provide earlier specialist diagnosis and intervention through the provision of memory clinics; and to provide higher quality health and social care. Chalfont (2008) for example, refers to the importance of providing information and support about what helps to improve the quality of life for people living and caring for someone with dementia, alongside awareness raising and early diagnosis. He advocates publicising examples of positive experiences as many carers may have low expectations and therefore may settle unquestioningly for an institutional regime.

Many people living with dementia will spend some time in a care home and/or end their life in one (Laing & Buisson, 2009). Therefore demand for specialist care and support is expected to grow. Care homes are a key partner in planning to meet challenges to develop capacity and quality personalised services. There are around 18,000 care home places for older people in the UK, mostly provided by the private sector where 30% of beds for people with dementia are supplied by the largest ten providers (Laing & Buisson, 2009). Even if early diagnosis delays entry to a care home, the quality of care itself in homes will need to rise correspondingly. The *National Dementia Strategy* (DH, 2009) specifically identifies the need for improved quality of care in care homes (see objective number eleven). Major trends for the design, delivery and evaluation of services will need to incorporate the development of partnerships between service providers and users and their carers, to facilitate the movement away from the dominance of professional viewpoints (Gilleard et al, 2005). The reference to such partnerships has been actively promoted by the more recent Dementia Action Alliance (Alzheimer's Disease Society, 2012). Through its National Dementia

Declaration, the Alliance has placed strong emphasis on the importance of outcomes which relate to how people with dementia live in and feel part of the community. Greater emphasis is been placed on the role played by public services, families and carers to make communities more dementia friendly. Similarly, an historical overview of movements in nursing homes which have successfully facilitated culture-change interventions (Rahman, 2008) demonstrates the importance of strengthening the empirical base for achieving these changes, particularly those which are based on the active engagement of service users and carers. The UK *Dignity in Care* campaign (DH, 2006) similarly aimed to stimulate a national debate and create a national care system with zero tolerance of disrespect for adults with dementia. Outcomes from these studies and initiatives reveal the significance of developing leadership and management skills within the sector to take change forward particularly within smaller providers. A study by O'Driscoll (2006) into the impact of management on care homes for example, identified specific difficulties for staff and service users in getting support from their managers when managers are seen to be too involved in administration matters and as a result, become distanced from daily activities and contact.

In their review of progress made on the impact of the *National Dementia Strategy* (DH, 2009), the National Audit Office (2009) found that many local care home managers lacked an actual awareness of the strategy and that there was little participation in developing local services whereas this is expected to be a significant feature within care home managers' relationships with local commissioners. Similarly, those care homes consulted in the review reported that they had minimal communication about the *National Dementia Strategy* and revealed a lack of leadership in their own sector. Care home managers also identified lack of support from local specialist services which posed a particular challenge in their ability to provide good dementia care. The *National Service Framework for Older People* (2001) stipulated that specialist mental health services for older people should provide advice and outreach services for residential and nursing care providers and acknowledges that being an active part of the community care homes requires vital support from primary care services as well as from other mainstream services. Yet a review of implementation of the National Service Framework found that only 51% of teams provided training and several respondents from Community Mental Health Teams reported a lack of capacity to undertake such work (Tucker et al, 2007).

The liaison services described in the Dementia Quality Standards (NICE, 2012) continue to emphasise specialist services in acute and general hospital settings and the appointment of a dementia specialist coordinator, but care homes are not specifically mentioned here. The *Dementia Action Alliance* plan and the Alzheimer Disease Society's five year strategy, Delivering on dementia 2012–2017 (Alzheimer's Disease Society, 2012 also includes a key ambition to work with people affected by dementia, partners from business, the public sector and civic organisations, to define and develop dementia friendly communities.

As well as contributing to improvements in nursing or residential care, there is also evidence that more effective liaison services can potentially save costs (Ballard et al, 2001) which is an important factor in the current trajectory for the business planning side of dementia care in the UK population. There are a number of limitations that confront nursing and residential home managers in developing effective local strategies. Current developments in social care tend to concentrate on making strategic arrangements with less reflection upon the politics of organisational and professional change and their ideological imperatives (Carnwell & Buchanan, 2005). This can result in inadequate co-ordination of joint working arrangements and a lack of resources to support these at the local level. Local leadership therefore needs to be able to capitalise on potential for partnerships across local boundaries. There have been some good examples such as the formation of dementia partnership groups or local dementia 'summits' (see South West Dementia Partnership, 2010) illustrating the need for managers to find ways of developing their networking and political skills. To provide a meaningful strategy, one needs to focus not only on the outcomes specified in government legislation and policy but also on those outcomes which meet the needs of the local community and are determined by their actual involvement in defining these. Substantial support for the legitimate involvement of people using services within a model of participatory democracy must therefore acknowledge the potential of both managers and staff working in organisations to work in appropriately supportive ways (Postle & Beresford 2007). This is not an easy task where many care homes are often seen to be isolated without essential networks to their local community.

Finally, a more recent report which documents findings from thirty unannounced inspections to residential and nursing homes in Scotland (Care Commission and Mental Welfare Commission, 2009) makes uneasy reading about some of the progress for change being made in dementia care to date. Some care homes had fallen seriously short of best practice and people with dementia were not always getting the best possible care to meet their needs. Whilst 70% of people living in the homes visited had dementia, more than half had never gone outside of the home environment since their admission to it, for example for a visit or to engage in community activities. Further only 24% had any of their previous personal history documented by staff since their admission to the home and an even smaller number of these latter residents were involved in day-to-day decisions about their care. Most significantly only a third of care home managers had undergone a recognised training course on caring for people with dementia. The majority of care staff were generally unaware of best practice guidance and some felt that their knowledge was insufficient or that they did not have enough time to be able to give the care they wanted to (Care Commission and Mental Welfare Commission, 2009). Serious concerns have thus been raised over whether the workforce has the right training, support and leadership to enable it to provide the level of support needed to achieve the objectives of the Dementia Care Strategy, for example the All Parliamentary Group (HMSO, 2010) stated that 'the need for workforce development is profound' (p.2). Further, leaders within both service commission and provision are crucial to establishing the right tone and to providing guidance and support to care staff through the acquisition of good generic management skills in addition to good dementia care skills. One CSCI report (2008) highlighted that vacant managers posts provided a further reason for training not being implemented, resulting in an overall poor performance and a poorly developed climate. All partners therefore play an important role in creating working practices that enable positive outcomes for people with dementia.

One can only conclude from these limited studies that despite policy imperatives, and notwithstanding pockets of innovative practice in some areas, the care home sector remains relatively underdeveloped to take advantage of what is known about quality dementia care. Despite a range of recent campaigns, the issue of dementia and its fundamental association with upholding human rights, one might conclude that there has been partial failure to ignite the passion, pace and drive or to align leadership with the necessary funding, incentives and information to help deliver the person centred care much cited in the research and policy literature. We now go on to discuss some of these issues in more detail and with reference to our own study findings.

What types of leadership contribute to person-centred care?

A limited number of studies and theoretical debates have revealed the potential contribution of leadership and leadership style to social care organisations (Seden, 2003; Lawler, 2007; Hafford-Letchfield et al, 2008; Lawler & Bilson, 2010, Boehm & Yoels, 2010) highlighting a preference for more inclusive, distributed and participatory styles. The Department of Health (2008) refers to local clinical leadership as fundamental to its devolved management model - a prerequisite for improved provision of dementia care. In a review of the progress of the Dementia Care Strategy by the National Audit Office (2009), few frontline staff could identify leaders who were championing dementia, and few could give examples where the profile and priority of dementia at local level had been raised.

Within our own very small sample, we were able to explore different types of leadership which the four managers identified in the interviews. Leadership theories are very much associated with change and organisational development and as an essential agreement in being able to achieve transformation. As stated earlier, one of the themes to emerge from the interviews related to the type of leadership styles perceived as important or even desirable within the dementia care environment. We were particularly looking for any indications of transformational leadership which Senge (1996) describes as being present in individuals who learn to lead through critical thinking and who are equipped to achieving action and results in a wider context as well as a personal one. For example, all four managers interviewed made some reference to the type of leadership that is commonly referred to as 'transactional' in the leadership literature (Storey & Mangham, 2004). Our managers referred to a form of leadership likely to dominate in residential care by being based on an exchange approach in which the aims of the service and rewards are presented but tend not to provide staff with any expectation beyond the existing demands of the service. Whilst useful for some aspects of institutional care, these types of relations were explained by our interviewees as being related to expectations of the overarching owner of the residential service or expectations from 'head office'. One of the managers described this as follows:

I struggle with it, in what I've read and what I continue to read, the leadership at the top lacks real inclination to change. The system is still very much geared around the mental health model of service .... Are we really open to thinking differently and innovatively about the way that we do things, or are we kind of straight-jacketed into a way of thinking that's traditional, that's based on a very controlled medical model? (Manager 4)

Leadership theory places great emphasis on the interaction between leaders and followers (Bass, 1990; Avolio et al, 1999) where an authentic approach to leading is cited as desirable and effective in achieving positive and enduring outcomes in organizations (George & Sims, ,2007). Authentic leaders are thought to be those who know and act upon their true values, beliefs, and strengths, while helping others to do the same. Paying attention to employees' well-being at different levels is thought to show positive impact on follower performance (Ryan & Deci, 2001). The role that leaders play in follower engagement at work suggests that engagement is best enhanced when employees feel they are supported, recognized, and developed by their managers (Harter et al., 2002). Again this was something articulated by our management interviewees in relation to participatory approaches to leadership as illustrated below:

I think managers have to be open to listen ... to their staff who might not always be seen to be doing the right thing, but they see so much about us as managers that they can learn a lot from. I'm driven by the people for whom I work. Most staff have much more potential than we give them credit. (Manager 3)

This manager was clearly open to a consensus style approach in which mistakes were allowed and from which staff could learn. Donoghue and Castle (2009) used the Slevin leadership inventory (Slevin, 1989) to assess leadership styles within nursing homes. This is a survey instrument with a 50-item questionnaire consisting of statements answered using five-point Likert scales. Responses are based on how characteristic each item is of the leadership behaviour of the individual for example from 'to a very great extent' to 'to little or no extent.' The instrument aims to measure different leadership dimensions such as transactional or transformational leadership (Slevin, 1989). For example our capacity to make transformations or develop ways of knowing have affective, interpersonal and moral dimensions and the instrument attempts to measure these. Donoghue and Castles research demonstrated that those deploying a consensus management style were more likely to enhance employee satisfaction and that a consensus management style was associated with lower turnover amongst caregivers than where there was a more autocratic style for instance. Only 30% of their sample however exercised a consensus style and/or were moving towards a more transformational style. A transformational style was considered to be present and effective where staff was engaged in local governance and where managers were also given purposeful leadership training. Donoghue and Castle (2009) also noted that consensus management preserved the authority of the manager considered crucial to the organisation's best interest. Further to their study, an empirical study of leadership in welfare organisations in Israel conducted by Boehm & Yoels (2008) found that the contribution of leadership style to the effectiveness of social workers in welfare organisations was relatively weak compared with the contribution made through the empowerment of staff and team cohesion. The most influential component of staff empowerment in their study was the enhancement of staff knowledge and competence. Their study adds something to what we know about the personal and team aspects of organisational effectiveness and the importance of promoting a participatory and distributed style of leadership to foster these developments and which might be more suited to dementia care settings.

Within our own small study, the terms that managers used to describe themselves at work included 'change agents' and 'motivators', all common aspects of transformational styles. These descriptions were however tempered by a critical, realistic view mostly in relation to resource constraints but also by restraints perceived to be imposed from within the hierarchical management structures they worked within. The managers interviewed felt that their own preferred personal styles were not however modelled at the strategic level. Surprisingly to us, one of the themes that emerged in the discussion about the differences between management and leadership was the association made between leadership style and the traditions or background of the professional working in residential dementia care. One manager for example stated:

> *On the health side ... there's a much more management-traineeship type of approach... less grounded in on-the-ground delivery of services than say the social care services, where there are more people who have come through the ranks having worked with people, and are steeped in the values of what those kind of people's services are. I think that's a tremendous strength of the social care side in terms of management.* (Manager 1)

As our sample was very small, generalizations from these comments are invidious but the illustrative comments quoted here do call for consideration as to whether the social model of disability might provide a helpful framework for transforming dementia care (Gilleard et al, 2005). Likewise, Gilleard et al (2005) have considered whether application of the social model can help to reconsider the value of hearing and responding to personal experiences of those living with dementia and as a means of considering abilities instead of losses seen associated with dementia and to better understand the impact of public policy.

Towards a person centred culture in dementia care

Some of the factors discussed so far illustrate the complexity of issues behind concerns raised about the inconsistencies and lack of person-centred focus in the provision of care to people with dementia (National Audit Office 2007; Alzheimer's Society 2008; Ballard et al 2001). The concept of empowerment is widely embraced in the social work and social care literature as a process in which the older person with dementia acquires personal, organisational and community resources to enable them to gain more control of their lives and environment (Kitwood, 2007). For care staff, empowerment is seen to be an essential ingredient to achieve appropriate support for service users including the potential for autonomy and self-awareness at work; being aware of and recognising the demands for person-centred approaches, and the staff members own contribution and influence on the care environment. Empowerment of care workers involves a process in which they are given the opportunities to gain knowledge, skills and competence which increases their own sense of authority and responsibility to achieve the goals of the dementia care strategy and its underpinning evidence as well as to cope with the day to day challenges in the workplace. Managers interviewed in our sample for example made frequent references to the significance of interactions between managers which might promote empowerment. As one manager put it:

> *It can't be down to the manager to drive it .... I do think they are really stretched to the limits sometimes and carers face a high risk of burnout, and I think a lot of it is about support, supervision, training and involvement – feeling that you have a part to play in the service.* (Manager 2)

James et al (2007) suggest the term 'organisational climate' to refer to the estimations that people have of their jobs, co-workers, leaders, pay, performance expectations, opportunities and equity which impact on the individuals wellbeing. They argue that climate and culture are two different constructs although within the last decade have been discussed simultaneously in the organisational literature (Schneider, 1990; Holt and Lawler, 2005). The way in which people describe environmental objects in relation to themselves are seen as important aspects of culture. These are not only physical objects but include variables with a subjective, judgemental component that can be operationally defined. For example, the managers interviewed in our study made frequent inferences about the relationships between the environment and the atmosphere of the homes they worked in and inferred that the layout of the dementia care environment itself can determine spaces for more dynamic interaction, for example:

> *I think what makes x unique is its layout and location of its building because it's situated on a main road, there's lots of windows, there's lots for people to see, and there's lots of small rooms where people can interact better.* (Manager 1)

Holt and Lawler (2005) develop the idea of organisational 'climate' in social care which they suggest provides a means of identifying and indicating specific organisational initiatives which might impact positively on service delivery over time (p.32) and which has the advantage of making service improvements amenable to management. They see the culture of an organisation as being rooted in its values system and thus provide an aggregate view of what goes on there. They suggest that focussing on the climate however increased amenability to change even where this does not explicitly engage or reflect the organisations value system. Visible features of organisational climate may be described as peer support, relationships with supervisors such as those referred to above by the manager in this study as well as rewards and incentives (Holt & Lawler, 2005). Likewise, a different manager in our study highlighted this supposed link between the atmosphere and person-centred care:

> *By being person-centred with the service users we got round to being like that with staff. And there aren't many organisations like that so we found it really challenging when staff have been in one organisation for many years and come to us.* (Manager 3)

Locke (1976) proposed four latent factors that underpin personal and work-related values. These included; the desire for clarity, harmony and justice; a desire for challenge, independence and responsibility; desires for work facilitation such as leadership, support and recognition and desires for warm and friendly social relations. These correspond with empirically derived factors of organisational climate and culture illustrated in a number of studies of person-centred approaches in dementia care (for example, Kitwood, 1997) and their direct impact on service users. Kitwood argued against the depersonalisation that he observed to occur through a dialectical interplay between neurological alterations in brain function within people with dementia and their exposure to a negative social environment. He noted that these contribute to an unintended spiral away from well-being. More recently however, a three year study reported by Kelly (2009) in which she observed interactions between staff and service users on continuing care wards noted that this 'old style' culture is still very much alive. She documented the abusive, regimented and punitive task centred nature of experiences between nursing staff and older people and concluded that delivering a person-centred approach is extremely difficult without extensive support, mentoring and explicit organisational commitment to change. Further there is some evidence that the values and ethos of an organisation can provide major barriers to workforce development. Those management staff without good leadership skills or specialist dementia care knowledge may themselves present a barrier to recognising and promoting staff development. Current commissioning practices may also create barriers because of the working practices they tend to develop. For example, what appears to be a systemic failure within care homes on the surface might actually be related to low fee levels and which are also related to inadequate resources of time and skills or poor quality supervision for staff in the homes. All of these combine to undermine the personal development of care staff and the development of effective strategies to raise the quality of care.

As organisation culture often reflects the normative beliefs (that is, systems and values which furnish the ideologies) and shared behavioural expectations (that is, system norms) in an organisation, it may be that promoting positive group dynamics or interactions amongst people in a care setting will contribute towards collectively making sense of the environment at a systems level. Interviews with the four managers in our study all demonstrated a strong belief in the role of leadership in fostering work attitudes, and perceptions of staff and users about each other. For example, managers acknowledged the importance of giving attention to staff behaviour as being crucial to promoting job satisfaction and commitment to person-centred care. It was also seen to enhance the perceptions in individuals and teams of service quality and had an impact ultimately on turnover of staff:

> *I do not think I have any 'special' skills that cannot be used in any area of care. I think my management style is based around passion, respect, empathy, knowledge and understanding. You need this in all areas of care but you also need to be able to use these aspects of your management as a 'team player' with your staff to ensure the staff team work to the same vision, the same culture, if you like.* (Manager 2)

Leading a climate for learning in dementia care

As indicated above, building workforce capacity and capability for example through recruitment, retention and support for care staff working on the ground was the third key theme in the interviews reported here and highlights the importance of empowered local leadership for delivering transformational change. The creation of an informed and effective workforce for people with dementia is a key objective of the National Dementia Care Strategy (DH, 2009) in a context where there is a paucity of coherent, relevant training, high staff turnover and vacancies (Donoghue and Castle, 2009). Likewise, the stigma attached to dementia is reflected in the low status society gives to this work, which reduces morale and motivation. Staff turnover rates (23.2% in nursing homes, 20.5% in residential homes and 22% in domiciliary care) are around twice the 2004-05 NHS rate of 11.8 per cent, and the 2006 private sector rate of 12 per cent (National Audit Office, 2010). Staff turnover in care homes is frequently attributed to local economic factors as well as individual and organisational factors. Little is said however, in relation to the specific role of the care home manager. The creation of a new qualifications and credit framework may provide opportunities to develop a career path within dementia care (SfC, 2010) attributing higher status. Such as the recent knowledge sets which include dementia (SfC, 2011) recommended for continuing professional development for those working directly with people with dementia. A number of national leadership programmes are also now beginning to flourish, such as those provided by Dementia UK, the National Social Care Academy and the Bradford Centre. All of these factors are important features of a positive organisational climate.

However, staff learning is not just about achieving competence at the instrumental level. Effective learning requires reflection and thought in relation to organisational development where people are to interact in a collective learning experience for the development of knowledge about what constitutes effective care (Hafford-Letchfield et al, 2008). Collective learning is also achieved at both the explicit and tacit levels (Wenger et al, 1998). Emphasis on individual experiences of learning must somehow be integrated into the interpersonal experiences of organisational learning with an organisation as it starts to build a learning community or as referred to earlier, in building an appropriate culture for learning. Reed (2009) asserts that any attempt to change the 'norm' of organisational relationships brings about some degree of chaos at physiological levels as well as those at the personal, interpersonal and the organisational. Community building occurs through addressing integration of these elements (2009, p36). Such a culture promotes awareness, trust and accountability leading to benefits such as increased efficiency, job satisfaction and decreased absenteeism and attracts more motivated employees.

The Alzheimer Society (2008) echo these sentiments, recommending that the training needs of care staff in residential care should not only commend knowledge and skills but also capture the 'hearts and minds' of staff thereby enabling them to work 'with the person first, dementia second' (no page given). This illustrates further some of these differences between climate and culture that one needs to be conscious of. It recommends training that not only develops specific care competencies but is also geared to drive forward the quality of life of the residents who live in the care homes where they work. However, work based training as one solution is not without its challenges. Where staff turnover is very high problems may arise for the development and sustainability of skills which might then detract from genuine culture change. This is not the only challenge to address when it comes to introducing and maintaining gains observed on a training course. Carmeli and Vinarski-Peretz (2009) highlight the role of reciprocity and self-efficacy to avoid burnout among care staff for older adults with dementia alongside the organisational barriers. When moving towards a person-centred culture of care, one needs to be aware of the resistance that can occur for people returning from a training course. Having a critical mass of staff who can act as agents of change can make a difference to the impact of training:

> *Real meaningful change is often down to a small group of individual or an individual really driving something different ... whether they've got vision, they really understand where they want to get to and how they might get there.* (Manager 4)

A number of studies have already demonstrated the challenges in sustaining change, indicating the need for ongoing and sometimes external support to maintain benefits from training and to prevent slippage as staff resume their daily routines (Ballard et al, 2001; Hughes et al, 2008). Incentives in the form of rewards for staff, who work better and financial support to release staff to attend training, are more likely to support any change effort (Hughes et al, 2008). Solutions to some of these challenges require a more creative approach to addressing staff learning and development needs, particularly those which involve users and carers. Added value can be supported by work based coaching and mentoring led by skilled experienced dementia care practitioners in order to support the emergence of staff leadership skills (Whitby, 2008). We already know from some studies, as noted above, that without a fresh approach, the effects of training may readily dissipate and all that remains are the fine rhetoric of policy. The task of leadership is often expressed as being able to motivate people to achieve outcomes that benefit the individual, the team and the organisation and a balance between all of these are needed (Hafford-Letchfield et al, 2008). It can also make a significant contribution towards collaboration and collectivist approaches by promoting the leadership roles taken by users and other professionals during the learning and development process.

Conclusion

This paper has given a short overview of issues important in transforming dementia care by paying attention to the implied notion of leadership within residential and nursing home provision. We have tried to reflect these through the illustrative narratives and themes from the interviews with care home managers. Whilst a very small and partial sample, these do provide case examples from which the issues can be illuminated further. Change skills have been identified as key skills for managers and leaders and an understanding of providing opportunities for both managers and staff to develop a range of skills through which change can be recognised, implemented and sustained. It is well documented that the general lack of training and poor level of qualifications within the residential and nursing home sector, coupled with a lack of real tangible commitment to coherently registering, regulating, training and supporting the dementia care workforce, all combine to affect the quality of care and safety of the people living with dementia (Parliamentary Group on Dementia, 2009). There is a relatively sound theoretical framework and guidelines for 'person-centred care' – a perspective that espouses the value of all people with dementia irrespective of age, level of impairment, or those who care for them (Kitwood, 1997). It is also an approach that values the perspective of the person with dementia as well as recognizing the importance of all the relationships and interactions with others that support the person with dementia. The key priorities of high standard dementia care are well espoused within the Dementia Care Strategy in which there are significant guidelines for managers and staff to use and develop, not least those that require the active involvement of users and carers themselves. From a macro perspective however, given the regular publicised scandals in care, and the broader economic and social challenges that face public and private organizations, more positive and active forms of leadership in institutions and organizations need to be consciously and explicitly developed to restore public confidence. Whilst the implementation of the recommendations of the Dilnot review are pending (Dilnot, 2011), it must also be recognised that even these will not go far enough to reform the social care system in a way that has the positive impact required on people with dementia. Extra funding is needed to ensure that people with dementia and carers can access better quality as well as more care such as their inclusion in the personal budgets agenda. We must consider as a society where this money can come from. Resources should be shifted from inappropriate acute and residential care for people with dementia into the community setting. This would help ensure that the right support is available for people with dementia and carers such as early intervention and prevention services, and respite care services from a proper integration of health and social services in this significant and developing field of practice. Developments should support the development of consistency of quality care rather than pockets of good practice as demonstrated in those managers we interviewed for this paper. Simply expecting leaders to be more value-driven and to demonstrate integrity will be ineffective if concrete tools for implementing and measuring important aspects of leadership are lacking. In lieu of what we know about the contribution of leadership and the importance of a positive learning culture, such developments are very difficult to argue against!

References

Abraham, C. and Vinarski-Peretz, H. (2009) Burnout among care staff for older adults with dementia: and organizational factors. *Dementia*, 8, 4, 515-541

All-Party Parliamentary Group on Dementia (2010) *Prepare to Care: Challenging the dementia skills gap.London:* TSO

Avolio, B.J., Bass, B.M., and Jung, D.I. (1999). Re-examining the components of transformational and transactional leadership using Multifactor Leadership Questionnaire. *Journal of Occupational and Organizational Psychology*, 72, 4, 441–462

Alzheimer's Society (2008). *Home from Home: A report highlighting opportunities for improving standards of dementia care in care homes*. London: Alzheimer's Society

Alzheimer's Disease Society (2012) *Dementia 2012 Report*. available online from:

http://www.alzheimers.org.uk/site/scripts/download_info.php?fileID=1390

Bass, B. (1990). From transactional to transformational leadership: Learning to share the vision. *Organizational Dynamics*, 18, 3, 19-31

Ballard, C, Fossey, J, Chithramohan, R, Howard, R, Burns, A, Thompson P, et al. (2001) Quality of care in private sector and NHS facilities for people with dementia: cross sectional survey. *British Medical Journal* 323, 426-427

Banerjee, S. (2010) Living well with dementia: Developments of the national strategy for England. *International Journal of Geriatric Psychiatry*, 25, 9, 917-922

Blood, I. and Bamford, S.M. (2010) *Equality and diversity and older people with high support needs*. York: Joseph Rowntree Foundation

Boehm, A. and Yoels, N. (2008) Effectiveness of welfare organisations: The contribution of leadership styles, staff cohesion, and worker empowerment. *British Journal of Social Work*, 39, 7, 1360-1380

Bryman, A. (2001) *Social Research Methods*. (2nd ed.) Oxford: Oxford University Press

Care Commission and the Mental Welfare Commission for Scotland (2009) *Remember I'm Still Me*. Available from http://www.mwcscot.org.uk/web/FILES/Publications/CC__MWC_joint_report.pdf (accessed 4/10/2010)

Carnwell, R., Buchanan, J, (Eds) (2005) *Effective Practice In Health and Social Care: A partnership approach*. Maidenhead: Open University Press

Chalfont, G (2008) *Design for Nature in Dementia Care* London: Jessica Kingsley

Commission for Social Care Inspection (2008). *See Me, Not Just the Dementia*. London: CSCI,

Department of Health (2001) *National Service Framework for Older People*. London: DoH

Department of Health (2006) *Dignity in Care*. available from http://www.dh.gov.uk/en/Publicationsandstatistics/Publications/PublicationsPolicyAndGuidance/DH_4139552 (accessed 3/10/2010)

Department of Health (2009) *Living Well with Dementia*. (National Dementia Strategy) London: DoH

Department of Health (2010) *Quality Outcomes for People with Dementia: Building on the work of the National Dementia Strategy*. London: DoH

Department of Health (2011) *More funding for dementia research*. available online from: http://www.dh.gov.uk/en/MediaCentre/Pressreleases/DH_127899

Dementia Awareness http://www.dementiaawareness.co.uk/news (accessed 2/12/2010)

Dilnot, A. (2011) *The Future of Social Care. Report of the Dilnot Commission July 2011*.available online from http://www.dilnotcommission.dh.gov.uk/our-report/

Donoghue, C. and Castle, N.G. (2009) Leadership styles of nursing home administrators and their association with staff turnover. *The Gerontologist*, 49, 2, 166–174

George, B. and Sims, P. (2007) *True North: Discover your authentic leadership*. San Francisco: John Wiley

Gillieard, J., Means, R., Beattie, A., and Daker-White, G. (2005) Dementia care in England and the social model of disability: Lessons and issues *Dementia* 4, 4, 571-586
http://www.dh.gov.uk/en/Publicationsandstatistics/Publications/PublicationsPolicyAndGuidance/DH_4139552

Hafford-Letchfield, T., Leonard, K., Begum, N., and Chick, N., (2008) *Leadership and Management in Social Care*. London: Sage

Harter, J.K., Schmidt, F.L., and Hayes, T.L. (2002). Business-unit-level relationship between employee satisfaction, employee engagement, and business outcomes: A meta-analysis. *Journal of Applied Psychology*, 87, 2, 268-279

Hayes, J. and Povery, S. (2010) *The Creative Arts in Dementia Care: Practical person-centred approaches and ideas*. London, Jessica Kingsley

Holt, J. and Lawler, J. (2005) Children in Need Teams: Service delivery and organisational climate. *Social Work & Social Sciences Review* 12, 2, 29-47

Hughes, J., Bagley, H., Reilly, S., Burns, A., and Challis, D. (2008) Care staff working with people with dementia: Training, knowledge and confidence *Dementia* 7, 2, 227-238

James, L, Choi, R., Carol C., Ko, Chia-Huei Emily, McNeil, P. K., Minton, MK., Wright, M.A., and Kwang-il, K. (2007) Organizational and psychological climate: A review of theory and research. *European Journal of Work and Organizational Psychology*, 17, 1, 5- 32

Kelly, F. (2009) Recognising and supporting self in dementia: a new way to facilitate a person-centred approach to dementia care. *Ageing & Society*, 30, 1, 103-124

Killick J. and Allan K. (2001) *Communication and the Care of People with Dementia*. Buckingham: Open University Press

Kitwood T (1997) *Dementia Reconsidered: The person comes first*, Maidenhead: Open University Press/McGraw Hill Education

Kitwood T and Benson S (1995) *The New Culture of Dementia Care*. London: Hawker

Laing and Buisson (2009) *Care of Elderly People UK Market Survey*. London: Laing & Buisson

Lawler, J. (2007) Leadership in social work: A case of caveat emptor? *British Journal of Social Work* 37, 1, 123-141

Locke, E. A. (1976). The nature and causes of job satisfaction. in M.D. Dunnette (Ed.) *Handbook of Industrial and Organizational Psychology*. Skokie, IL: Rand McNally (pp. 1297-1350)

Manthorpe, C. (2009) We owe Gerry Robinson for highlighting bad practice.

Society Guardian, 16th December

McCrone, P., Dhanasiri, S., Patel, A., Knapp,M., and Lawton-Smith, S (2008) *Paying the Price*. London: The Kings Fund

National Audit Office (2007) *Improving services and support for people with dementia*: London: NAO

National Audit Office (2010) *Improving Dementia Services in England: An Interim Report*. London: TSO

National Institute for Health and Clinical Excellence, and Social Care Institute for Excellence (2006) Dementia: Supporting people with dementia and their carers in health and social care, *NICE Clinical Guideline 42*. London: The National Collaborating Centre for Mental Health

Nolan, M., Ryan, T., Enderby, P., and Reid, D., (2002) Towards a more inclusive vision of dementia care practice and research. *Dementia*, 1, 2, 93-211

O'Connor, D., Phinney, A., Smith, A., Small, J., Purves, B., and Perry, J. (2007). Personhood in dementia care: Developing a research agenda for broadening the vision. *Dementia*, 6, 1, 121-142

O'Driscoll, D. (2006) The dangers of 'ivory tower' management. *Community Living*, 20, 2, 18-19

Postle, K. and Beresford, P (2007) Capacity building and the reconception of political participation. *British Journal of Social Work*, 37, 1, 143–158

Rahman, A.N. (2008) The nursing home culture-change movement: Recent past, present, and future directions for research. *Gerontologist*, 48, 2, 142-148

Ryan, M. R. and Deci, E. (2001). On happiness and human potentials: A review of research on hedonic and eudaimonic well- being. *Annual Review of Psychology*, 52, 1, 141–166

Schneider, B. (1990). The climate for service: An application of the climate construct. in B. Schneider (Ed.),*Organizational Climate and Culture*. San Francisco, Jossey-Bass (pp.383-412)

Seden, J. (2003) Managers and their organisations. in J. Henderson and D. Atkinson (Eds.) *Managing Care in Context*. London, Routledge

Senge, P. M. (1996) *The Fifth Discipline*. London: Random House

Sheard, D. and Cox, S.(1998) *Teams, Multidisciplinary and Interprofessional Working and Dementia*. Stirling: University of Stirling. Dementia Services Development Centre

Skills for Care (2011) *Developing Skills: Supporting people with dementia*. available online from http://www.skillsforcare.org.uk/developing_skills/dementia/ supporting_people_with_dementia.aspx

Slevin, D. (1989) *The whole manager*. New York, Amacom

South West Dementia Partnership (2010) *Working Together to Improve Dementia Care: South West leads the way* http://www.southwestdementiapartnership.org.uk/2010/07/working-together-to-improve-dementia-care-%e2%80%93-south-west-leads-the-way/ (accessed 2/12/2010)

Storey, J. and Mangham, I. (2004) Bringing the strands together. in J. Storey, (Ed.) *Leadership in Organisations.* London: Routledge

Tucker, S. et al. (2007) Old age mental health services in England: implementing the National Service Framework for Older People, *International Journal of Geriatric Psychiatry* 22, 211-217

Wenger, E. (1998) *Communities of Practice.* Cambridge: Cambridge University Press

Whitby, P. (2008) Why is good quality residential care so very difficult to achieve? *Journal of Dementia Care,* 16, 2, 30-33

Wimo, A., Jönsson, L., Gustavsson, A., McDaid, D., Ersek, K., and Georges, J. (2010) The economic impact of dementia in Europe in 2008: Cost estimates from the Eurocode project. *International Journal of Geriatric Psychiatry,* 26, 8, 825-32

This chapter is an amended version of an article first published in 2011 in *Social Work & Social Sciences Review* vol. 14(2) pp.37-54. Garuth Chalfont was then Researcher, School of Architecture, University of Sheffield, and Principal, Chalfont Design Consultancy. Trish Hafford-Letchfield was a Teaching Fellow at Middlesex University.

8

Learning to lead:

Evaluation of a leadership development programme in a local authority social work service

William McAllan and Rhoda MacRae

The situation in 2013

The organisation has experienced unremitting change since the conclusion of the leadership development programme reported in this article. Organisational change has been influenced significantly by financial constraints and various policy imperatives, not least personalisation informing the redesign of services throughout the services within the organisation. Change has also featured at an individual level with 50% of the participants in the leadership programme having experienced changes in their job roles since the programme concluded. The drive for organisational change and improvement in service delivery continues at a fast pace with the expectation of closer integration of Scottish social care and health services in the near future. These drivers mean there has probably never been a time when leadership skills were more essential for social work services in Scotland. It is timely to ask if the impact reported in our article continues to be sustained at the level of the individual and, in wider operational terms, within the service.

Although there would have been merit in undertaking further evaluation activities to determine impact, lack of funds and time meant this has not been possible. Instead this is a reflective piece which draws upon the observations of the authors. These have been informed by a review of the projects initiated by the leadership development programme and discussions with the organisation's senior managers. First we will look at the organisational impact of the programme and then impact at the level of the individual participants.

The leadership development programme required each participant to design and implement a project which would improve organisational performance. The projects were seen as the vehicles which would connect individual leadership development with the organisation's goals and purpose and sustain activity in the day to day leadership behaviours of the participants. By the conclusion of the programme 45 diverse projects had been initiated but none had concluded. Therefore some measure of leadership sustainability may be deduced from the subsequent actions (or not) of the participants. Most projects were unlikely to have been initiated without the support of the leadership programme. For example, Working With Dads and Personal Growth And Change developed from concepts delivered directly by the programme. Some projects are likely to have been initiated regardless of the programme. For example, the Emergency Social Work Service was required to meet a gap in provision of statutory services. Even in these cases, the participant leadership skills of envisioning, influencing and managing change would be important in gaining the support of senior managers and overcoming inertia and resistance to change. A positive outcome is, therefore, presumed to arise from the completion of a project and its subsequent integration into the organisation's operations.

The review of the 45 projects found that 29 (64%) were completed and integrated into operational practice. Six (13%) projects were ultimately rejected by the organisation because they conflicted with the organisation's vision of how the service in question should develop. Seven (16%) were not developed to operational viability for reasons of the leaders' resignation, absence through ill health or a significant change to the leader's organisational role. The outcomes of three (7%) projects can not yet be determined. Two of these projects focused on raising awareness of particular issues and the third, concerned with improving the operation of the Blue Badge Scheme, is operating to a longer term timescale.

At an individual level the impact is less straightforward to determine, not least due to 50% of participants either leaving the organisation or changing their role. This more than anything emphasises the extent of change since the programme concluded: 42% (n=25) of participants have changed their work role; 8% (n=5) of participants have left the organisation to other employers or retirement.

The lead author recently undertook a training needs analysis with key members of the organisation's management team. Eight one to one interviews (n=8) were conducted with senior managers in April 2012 to elicit their identification of barriers to organisational effectiveness and to assess the need for leadership training. Three of these managers had been participants on the leadership development programme. All of the managers interviewed had received the IDI training but only the three who had been participants on the leadership programme could explain IDI and demonstrate application during the interview. Leadership behaviours were strongly present in seven of the senior managers which suggests that other leadership development programmes have had an impact on the organisation. Some interviewees were recent recruits and had received leadership training provided by previous employers such as NHS or other local authorities. Further, since the leadership programme's conclusion, some senior managers have undertaken doctorate level programmes which include leadership knowledge and skills such as managing change (see McAllan & Blair, 2011).

In conclusion, the authors found that, at the organisational level, 64% of the projects were completed and or integrated into the operational practice of the organisation. The use of projects appears to have provided a legitimate vehicle to enact learning and drive forward operation change and for the participants to practice new skills and to try different approaches. Impact is more difficult to determine at the level of the individual participants and would require further evaluation.

References

McAllan, W.J. and Blair, S.E. (2011) The potential to enhance practice: the value of a professional doctorate for social work practice. *Work Based Learning e-Journal*, 2, 1. http://wblearning-ejournal.com/currentIssue/E3008%20 rtb.pdf

Learning to lead:
Evaluation of a leadership development programme in a local authority social work service

Introduction

There has been significant investment and interest in leadership development for public sector staff in Scotland in recent years – not least by the Scottish Government. Although there is no single robust definition of leadership is available within UK organisations there would appear level of coherence in the various definitions, markers and standards of effective leadership (Alimo-Metcalfe & Lawler, 2001). This coherence can be seen in some of the leadership development initiatives that have been evaluated and have produced recommendations on the crucial and successful elements of developing effective leadership. Strengthening leadership was a key feature of Changing Lives (Scottish Executive, 2006a). Changing Lives identified that in order to achieve transformational change it was crucial to construct a national framework strategically to develop leadership and management at all levels to empower the social service workforce to develop creative solutions to meet people's needs. The Changing Lives Implementation Plan (Scottish Executive, 2006b) proposed five change programmes: Performance Improvement, Service Development, Leadership and Management, Workforce Development and Practice Governance.

It was in this context that South Lanarkshire Council Social Work Resources invested in a range of workforce development activities. Many staff within the social work service had had the opportunity to participate in other leadership programmes such as the 'Leading to Deliver' and a variety of post graduate programmes. However, it was felt that there was a need to develop training that focused on building not only leader skills but also leadership behaviours that can help address the practical day to day challenges of working collaboratively, influencing and engaging with others and becoming more self aware (Iles & Preece, 2006). After some scoping work on the learning needs of staff in respect of leadership, a trainer[1] specialising in organisational and people development was commissioned to design and deliver leadership training to 60 staff in 6 cohorts, in a 14 day programme between December 2007 and March 2009. It was expected that the leadership development programme would also assist in creating a critical mass of leaders that could accelerate the process of enacting initiatives and changes required to address key issues (Hannum et al., 2007; Alimo-Metcalfe & Lawler, 2001) as well as contributing to succession planning and the retention of talented staff.

Evaluating leadership development activities

The creation of specific leadership initiatives has been a key feature of the reform agenda in both central and local government. The Scottish Government has invested in a raft of leadership initiatives, conferences and activities. One of these was the Scottish Leadership Foundation (dissolved in 2008) and the Leading to Deliver Programme, a leadership development programme designed for social service sector staff. Evaluations of the different leadership development programmes have suggested that the features that support successful leadership development include: models that support distributed leadership such as the utilisation of networks; the use of action learning sets or communities fostered and supported for a sustained period of time (Dinham et al., 2009; York Consulting, 2008; Granville & Russell, 2005; Bowerman, 2003; Watkins & Marsick, 1993). Clarity about what leadership looks like in an organisational context; senior managers making explicit links between their investments in leadership development activities and improvements or changes they want to make need to be clearly expressed and supported as a priority by senior managers (Ford & Gardner, 2005; Tourish et al., 2007).

However other evaluations have found that leadership development activities are not always seen as beneficial. Tourish et al., (2007) found a lack of support from senior management, partly due to an inability to prove a direct impact on organisational performance for leadership development activities and a perceived lack of time to participate. A number of reports that discuss leadership development in the Scottish Public Sector recommend that leadership development activities be evaluated in order 'to track the investment and evaluate effectiveness of that investment – simple models such as the Kirkpatrick framework should be routinely applied' (Ford & Gardner, 2005; Tourish et al., 2007; Grint et al., 2009). They also suggest that leadership development activities should take place within a clear policy framework that is aligned with organisational goals and objectives (Ford & Gardner, 2005; Tourish et al., 2007).

A seminar series organised by the Scottish Government and the ESRC in 2008 brought together a number social scientists to present their thinking on emerging theories of leadership and how these may inform the development of leadership in the public sector. This found leadership development activities were fragmented across the public sector resulting in duplication of effort and a lack of sharing of ideas of what has worked effectively and little evidence that investment in leadership development has paid off. It highlighted how many of the issues public services have to face are often deeply complex social problems that sit across and between governmental departments and institutions so attempts to treat them through a single institutional framework are likely to fail. Further, many of the challenges facing managers of social services are 'wicked' problems, in that they are complex and require leaders to facilitate innovative responses rather than rolling out known processes (Grint et al., 2009).

It was this backdrop that informed the development, delivery and content of the South Lanarkshire leadership development programme - the primary motivation behind the investment in the programme was the need to strengthen leadership and management at all levels in the organisation. It was felt many managers operated in procedural loops of custom and practice and were not exercising leadership roles despite being in key positions to enact change within the organisation. It was felt that transactional managerial tasks were being delivered effectively but that this key group were poor at dealing with what Kotter (1990) describes as key leadership behaviours such as coping with change and instability. These were seen as important gaps at a time when social work provision was reconfiguring to provide more personalised services and funding constraints were demanding ever more cost efficient service delivery. It was important to assess whether and in what ways the programme impacted on participants' individual leadership practice, in particular to look for evidence of increased self awareness, improved communication within teams and with other participant colleagues and whether participants were enacting change to make a positive difference to social work services in order to evaluate the effectiveness of the programme, not least to inform further development.

It was acknowledged that whilst leadership and management shared common characteristics, leadership was concerned primarily with transformation and innovation (Skills for Care, 2008). It was with this in mind that the service wanted to develop leaders who could establish direction, articulate vision, inspire, motivate, energise and engage others and use research evidence to inform approaches and change. The senior management team wanted to support an accountable environment in which creative solutions could be developed by staff. The programme's strategy was to focus learning at the level of the individual participant but have each participant undertake a project which would require them to apply their learning to a real service challenge. As Alimo-Metcalfe and Alban-Metcalfe observe to ensure the leadership development activity is sustained into practice, it must be embedded in the day-to-day behaviours of managers (2008, p.22). In this way the projects would connect individual development with the organisation's goals and purpose. In summary, the organisation needed to develop confident, adaptive leaders with excellent communication and influencing skills who would challenge existing practice using evidence-based collaborative methods. The programme was also an opportunity to improve succession planning by including practitioners with the potential to be leaders ('successors') and ensure leadership was developed across all levels of the organisation (Senge, 1992)[2]. For clarity, the following terms are used: 'participants' are the managers and successors who took part in the programme; 'managers' are the supervisors of the participants; 'senior managers' are the director and heads of the various social work departments.

In light of this, the aims of the Programme were broad and ambitious. It was designed to:

+ Strengthen leadership among managers so as to improve services for council citizens and enhance partnership working with all stakeholders
+ Build self awareness and emotional intelligence as foundations for effective and value based leadership (Burgess, 2005)
+ Integrate leadership practice into a culture in which behaviours can be mirrored between managers and staff so as to influence the quality of encounter between staff and service users
+ Establish consistent shared principles, based on robust theory and applied in day to day practice, so as to be as relevant to the quality of staff interactions as they are to the quality of communication with service users
+ Build sustainable resources and skills into the service by coaching internal facilitators
+ Strengthen capability for team working and optimise individual and team strengths towards clear shared purpose and objectives within an optimistic and resilient culture

Table 1

Timescale for the programme

Date	Activity
November 2007	Launch event led by the Executive Director held for prospective participants and supporters.
December 2007	Introductory Information Day. Learning contract set with participants.
January 2008	Emotional intelligence inputs using the Interpersonal Dynamics Inventory (IDI) tool that measures and describes the impact a person's behaviour has upon the people with whom they interact[3]. Participants completed IDI profiles to provide insight into leadership style and adaptability.
March to November 2008	Five taught input days to 3 cohorts of 20 on Management and Leadership Theory by way of presentation, discussion, exercises and simulations.
March to November 2008	Six Action Learning sets to 6 groups of 10: facilitated peer group learning focused on real-world operational and strategic challenges.
August 2008	Project identification and design related to organisational objectives and including an analysis of current service, issue or proposal for performance improvement.
March 2009	Celebration of Learning and Application Conference Day attended by 390 delegates. Round table discussion between senior managers and participants about projects.
August to December 2009	Participants present progress reports to the Executive Director and Senior Management Team on the outcomes of their project work, barriers to change encountered and any further supports needed to facilitate change.

Evaluation

Informed by the reports suggesting that leadership development activities should be evaluated, South Lanarkshire Social Work Resources collaborated with the Institute for Research and Innovation in Social Services (IRISS) to undertake an independent evaluation of the programme[4]. A range of options were considered.

The main thrust of the evaluation was to look for the impact it had on individual participants' leadership behaviours and the impact that the individual was having within teams or service area through those behaviours and through project work. Impact was expected to be seen within 6-12 months of the programme ending. The theory of change approach has been used to gather data in order to test out whether and to what extent and in what contexts individual change leads to broader outcomes (Gutierrez & Tasse, 2007). However this approach is perhaps best suited to community based initiatives that seek multiple level outcomes across several programme areas; this evaluation was not focusing on the process of change. The programme was not quasi-experiential or experimental, nor was it measuring the return on investment, these aims may have required a different evaluation methodology than the one used. Although the evaluation would inform future leadership development activities, we were not looking at training design or the evaluation as a learning experience in the way Preskill and Torres describe (1999). The literature on models of training evaluation is dominated by the Kirkpatrick model (1983, 1994). Kirkpatrick's four stage model (1983) of evaluating training focuses on responses to learning from the most immediate to the most distant. Kirkpatrick's model has been extended to evaluate societal impact but this extension was beyond the aims and scope of the evaluation so not utilised. Having explored other approaches to evaluating the programme we concurred with Tamkin et al., (2002) 'Kirkpatrick's model remains very useful for framing where evaluation might be made' (2002, p.xiii). Thus Kirkpatrick's four stage model (response, learning, behaviour and impact) (1994) of evaluating training became the methodological scaffold for this evaluation.

However, the evaluation was cognisant that relatively little correlation has been found between learner reactions and measures of learning and subsequent measures of changed behaviour (Warr et al., 1999; Alliger & Janak, 1989; Holton, 1996). It also took into account the literature that states although knowledge tests may indicate learning they do not indicate whether and to what extent the learning has been applied, future performance or the attainment of soft skills (Ghodsian et al, 1997). An 'open systems perspective' (Grove et al., 2007) was useful, we adopted elements of this approach to explore three different but interrelated forms of change: episodic, developmental and transformative in the individual domain. In addition we looked for observable performance outcomes as a way of determining the transfer of learning to practice (Hicks & Hennessy, 2001). This allowed us to account for not only external knowledge and skills acquisition but also the more personal learning experiences, insights, reflections, understandings and how these influenced participant's leadership practice in the workplace. This meant the evaluation was more qualitative than quantitative, exploring the softer, experiential affects and applications of learning.

Methods

Table 2
Linking methods to programme objectives

Method	Objective of programme
Knowledge tests (*n*=40) on taught input prior to and after delivery of training.	To assess knowledge gain in relation to the principles of leadership
Semi-structured questionnaires (*n*=40) prior to and after delivery of training.	To assess whether expectations of programme were shared and met
Two focus groups with participants (*n*=16) at end of taught programme	To explore sense of ownership, shared principles of leadership, learning insights, perceptions of impact of learning at an individual level.
One to one interviews (*n*=5) with key stakeholders including senior managers.	To explore whether expectations of programme were shared and perceptions about whether its aims were being met.
One to one interviews with participant mentors (*n*=6)	To explore perceptions of and examples of impact of learning at an individual level
One to one interviews (*n*=12) with participants	To explore with participants their perceptions on the impact the learning had had on their leadership practice including their self awareness, communication and interaction patterns, team working, emotional intelligence, adaptability and enacting change.
One to one interviews (*n*=10) with line managers of participants.	To explore their perceptions on whether and in what ways the programme had had an impact on participants' leadership practice including their self awareness, communication and interaction patterns, team working, emotional intelligence, adaptability and enacting change.
One to one interviews with peer colleagues (*n*=11) of participants	To explore whether they perceived any changes in interaction style and approach, whether they were aware of the project work and or changes in working practices during and after their manager had been on the programme.
Follow up telephone interviews (*n*=12) with participants 6 months after programme completion	To explore whether any perceived changes in style, approach or practice had been strengthened or sustained.
Analysis of the project materials (*n*=10)	To evidence whether and in what way the projects had found solutions to an operational issue, used evidence or enacted positive change.

Findings

Preparing to learn, preparing to change

The literature on learning transfer suggests that participants need to be prepared for change as well as being prepared to change. Transfer of learning will be enhanced through making links between the individuals' and the organisation's needs, linking the programme learning goals to individual learning goals and clarifying and sharing expectations of the programme (Cherniss et al., 1998; Burke & Hutchins, 2007). The data suggested that for most participants this had been achieved.

All senior managers were very clear about the relationship between the programme and the goals and objectives of the social work service and the learning needs of its workforce. They were clear and actively supportive of the programme's ambition to facilitate experiential growth, reflection and development, to give participants an opportunity to influence operations through undertaking a project related to their role, responsibility and to organisational objectives. However managers and participants were less clear about the ethos of the programme. Managers would have benefited from being given explicit criteria to help them nominate staff, support to discuss with staff if it was a performance issue that was informing their nomination and attending the information day held before the start of the programme. Senior managers could have communicated more clearly the potential informal and formal value and rewards of participation to managers and participants.

Expectations about what the training would deliver are important, not least because if participants and their managers do not expect anything to change as a result of input then it seems likely that the transfer of learning will be negatively affected. There were, however, high expectations of this programme across the service. The vast majority of participants expected the training to increase their knowledge about leadership and management, increase their leadership skills and most expected that they would make changes to their leadership and management practice as a result of the training. Specifically most participants expected to have greater awareness of leadership styles, how their style affects their work and colleagues, have an increased ability to use new knowledge on leadership styles and skills to develop themselves and others. A significant number also expected to be given opportunities to practice new skills, learn from others and learn strategies to build on their strengths and overcome their weaknesses. Participants seemed less confident around expecting the programme to make a significant difference to their practice although they did expect that an increased self awareness would make them more effective in practice.

Reported Learning

Importantly the expectations of the participants were largely met. The majority cited an increased knowledge of and insight into their own adaptability and effectiveness, an increased awareness of different leadership styles and how to put different approaches into practice. The action learning sets were felt to be particularly valuable in enabling peer learning, gaining insight into how they and other colleagues approached challenges as well as giving many a greater understanding of the function and roles within the service.

The response to the taught element of the programme was less positive although the knowledge tests showed the teaching inputs significantly contributed to knowledge gain amongst participants, particularly on the difference between leadership and management, effective adaptive leadership, emotional intelligence and approaches to enacting change, all key aims of the programme.

The projects provided many participants with a vehicle to apply their learning in an area meaningful to them. They provided an opportunity to use evidence in an explicit and informed way to shed light on an operational concern and possible strategies to overcome it.

Reported changes in behaviour

Questionnaire and interview data from participants, managers, colleagues and senior managers conducted after the programme suggested that the programme had impacted on many participants' leadership abilities and behaviours. Most perceived the programme to have had greatest impact in relation to increasing their self-awareness about their own management and leadership style. The majority of participants felt they had a greater awareness of their style of interaction and communication and had increased their adaptability. Increased self awareness was prompting them to think more often about how they related to their colleagues, how their style impacted on their colleagues and affected their ability to manage and lead. Many talked of various ways they were trying to increase their adaptability.

For some this translated into making determined efforts to change the way they interacted with colleagues, for example, to be less directing, be more facilitative and help staff learn for themselves and by encouraging the staff they managed to take more responsibility.

I try and help them come up with the answers rather than me giving them or feeling I should be giving them all the answers

This seemed to take place mostly in supervision or team meetings although some had adjusted their 'office door' policy – for some this meant lessening the frequency of providing immediate responses, for others it meant taking more time to engage with staff and being more open to spontaneous dialogue. Whatever the changes, most participants seemed to be more proactive in thinking through the best way to approach an issue, a member of staff or a situation as well as reflecting on how well those went and how to resolve them more satisfactorily and effectively next time.

Application of learning was not only perceived to have happened by participants. Managers were able to cite examples of where they felt the programme had made a difference to participants. They too felt many participants were demonstrating an increased adaptability in their style and approach to problem solving, using the learning to manage operational change, using the learning to develop an aspect of service and using their increased self-awareness to relate to colleagues in more constructive ways. Some felt participants were also showing an increased tendency to reflect, be more confident in their decision making abilities and had improved their writing skills.

Importantly, these changes were also reported by half of participants' colleagues. These quotes illustrate the changes they saw in their managers since being on the programme.

new style of managing, talking less and encouraging us to try and come up with solutions

listens more, like if you go to the office they will ask us to wait rather than try and deal with it straight away, this is not a bad thing because it means they listen more and you feel you are really getting their attention

you see it at team meetings or in supervision, they encourage staff to take more responsibility

encourages us to find things out for ourselves and solve problems this has made me more confident

The projects offered further evidence of behaviour change as these were often the vehicles for participants to develop and practice their new found knowledge and skills and to influence change. Most participants reported to have involved their staff team to some extent in their projects and almost all participants had invited colleagues to the 'exhibition of change projects' where they illustrated their work. Some of the colleagues were very enthused by the projects and stated they had learned a lot from being involved, seeing how it was making a positive difference to service delivery and or team working. Although these data indicates some learning transfer, it was important to gather evidence of sustained learning.

Sustained transfer of learning at individual level.

Ten of the twelve participants followed up 6 months after the programme perceived a continued and sustained impact of the programme on their practice and style of leadership. One felt the programme had provided a solid platform to undertake further academic leadership education. Another felt the programme had prompted greater reflection on their career pathway and they had successfully applied for a more strategic position in the organisation. Another reported having more 'balcony moments' (ability to stand back and reflect on the bigger picture). Almost all felt their increased self awareness about their own leadership style had been sustained, and they reported using the learning to foster and maintain better collegial relationships.

Two of the twelve participants followed up maintained the programme had had little impact on their leadership style or practice as a manager. However, both felt that their project work had informed their thinking about service provision and one felt the information gathering process done in the course of the project would inform local service development in the future.

Moving beyond the individual:
Evidence of transformative change

The project work offered a way to evidence whether, to what extent and in what ways participants were using their learning to enact change and make service improvements. In total the programme generated 45 projects covering the full spectrum of social work services.

Table 3
Summary of Participant Projects

Eleven projects targeted work with children and young people:
Promotional work on the health care needs of young carers; changes to the ways child care reviews are conducted; earlier multi-agency intervention with children at risk of offending; working with fathers estranged from their children; reducing violent incidents in children's homes; supporting young people in crisis; improved support to child victims of sexual abuse; assessment of child neglect; support to people who adopt children; a review of the supported carers payment scheme; and improvements to child protection training.

Five projects aimed to improve services to older people:
Promotion of healthier eating for older people; increasing the choice of meaningful activities for older people in residential care; increasing access to day care services; reducing medication errors in residential homes; and a fall prevention programme with people at risk of hip fractures.

Four projects focused on home care services:
Improvements to communication with the workforce; health promotion of the workforce; the setting up of an overnight emergency respite service; and a more effective system for performance measurement and reporting.

Four projects were concerned with criminal justice services:
Development of community justice services; changes to the assessment of risk of re-offending; using feedback from service users; and supporting people who use illegal drugs and are otherwise unknown to social services.

Nine projects related to organisational change:
Improvements to the computer information system; changes to how goods and services are procured; changes to systems for monitoring contract compliance; improvements to the use of complaints from service users and carers; more innovative approaches to learning and development; changes in how the organisation supports students; promoting change in recruitment practice; proposals to change how front-line services are funded; and the setting up of an emergency 'out of hours' social work service.

Twelve projects were selected to explore whether in wider operational terms they had had an impact in the workplace. The data suggested that the majority had made a positive impact operationally. We found, like Boaden (2006) that many participants were better placed to utilise evidence effectively which is a factor not often cited in the leadership literature. Participants were evidently using their learning to take an enquiry approach in order to solve problems and address complex issues. There was evidence to support a refinement and improvement to processes and systems. Many of the projects were collaborative in nature with participants using the learning from the programme to influence others and engage others in change. Many projects involved extensive communication and collaboration and it was felt that through the project the communication between staff had improved and some staff reported feeling more involved and better supported in carrying out their duties. There was evidence to support the projects bringing about service enhancement. An example of this was in a home for older people, where the participant engaged the residents and staff to design a new way of providing a meaningful choice of activities to residents. The feedback from residents on the changes was positive.

There was evidence to suggest participants were able to sustain their learning through implementing the projects with some managers explicitly encouraging participants to apply their learning through encouraging further developmental projects. The evaluation underlined the importance of enlisting the active support and involvement of managers, as found similarly by Peters and Baum (2007) participants appeared to learn to lead on the job. Leadership development behaviours were strengthened by having the support and opportunities to enact learning through action orientated projects. The impact of this programme seems to have been considerably enhanced by the inclusion of projects designed to explore and address an operational challenge. The projects and participants all needed to be supported and encouraged to maintain momentum, especially when they came across hurdles or time delays. There was evidence to suggest they had support from one another, from some managers, some colleagues and the senior management team. One participant encapsulated the benefits of integrating the change projects into the programme

the organisation has benefited from us doing practical projects where the outcomes need to be evidenced, the project was a responsibility and made me talk to people in and out of the organisation that I may not have had the confidence to otherwise, it has shown me that I can influence change. (participant)

Discussion

This programme was designed with maximising the transfer of learning in mind. There is significant evidence that the programme met its aims although, as this evaluation has shown, it did not work for all participants. There are lessons to be learned particularly about the need to pay more attention to the selection process and the prior preparation of the participants' managers to support participant learning. There are particular features of this programme that have the potential to inform the way leadership development activities can be used not only to develop adaptive innovative leaders but to improve the provision of social services to citizens. Many of the participants, their managers and colleagues specifically mentioned how participants, rather than providing answers or use processes to manage issues. Participants were now more likely to ask questions, ask their staff teams to think through an issue, discuss issues in team meetings, encourage staff to raise issues in team meetings and reflect on issues before responding. Leadership success is rooted in persuading followers that at any one time the problematic situation is one of a critical, tame or wicked nature and adjusting behaviour to the appropriate authority form – command, management or leadership (Grint et al., 2009). The evidence suggested that many of the participants had learnt this and were actively trying to apply this learning to practice.

Although all the elements of the programme contributed to the transfer of learning there were particular features that stood out as being significant in this regard. This evaluation supports previous findings that action learning is useful for critically reflecting on leadership styles and behaviour and helping participants build constructive supportive learning relationships with one another. Discussing operational challenges, sharing lessons learnt, approaches and potential solutions in a collective way was reported to help participants reflect on their style of leadership in ways which facilitated them to be more adaptable in the workplace. Some talked about having more 'tools in their kit', of being more aware of what approach to use for different situations and with different colleagues. Learning also would appear to have been enhanced indirectly through putting both operational and support staff together on the programme. This gave some staff, often those less experienced, a greater understanding of the organisation as a whole, its structure, and greater insight into the various functions and roles of other staff and services. These insights seem to have positively affected the ability to work within and across the various strands of the service; it informed the approaches of participants to implementing change, facilitated confidence around joint working and seeking to influence change. Leadership in this case would appear to have been developed in the way Iles and Preece (2006) suggest, where the emphasis is on building relationships, networks and commitments. Thus it facilitated not only leader development but the development of leadership in the context of the collective action.

The project element of the programme proved a significant vehicle for the transfer of learning. It gave participants a practical opportunity to focus on an issue meaningful to their practice and or service, to use their learning and evidence gathering to influence and enact operational change. The projects were an effective process for both individual and organisational learning and development. Many were collective in nature and required concerted thinking and action over a sustained period of time. The findings support that leadership develop has to take place on the job, people learn to lead by leading. Leadership development requires both opportunity and support in the work settings (Peters & Baum, 2007). The findings suggested that many participants were effectively 'modelling' how to adapt to and influence change to staff through their project work. This finding underlines the importance of giving participants legitimised and proactive support over a sustained period of time to enact change, try new approaches, different ways of doing things in a collective fashion. Key to this was the decision by senior managers not to direct participants in the selection of project but rather to give participants the autonomy to decide where change and improvement was required. As Peters and Baum (2007) indicate development activities can create the potential but the context provides the opportunity to perform and apply that learning. The direct supervisor is key to creating local context and if they do not legitimise activities and allow participants time and resources to facilitate the application of what has been learnt, not much can be expected.

As Cherniss et al., (1998) state, continuous improvement of both learning programmes and staff is essential in maximising the investment of participants and the organisation. One way continuously to improve learning programmes is to evaluate their impact and use the findings to inform further development. The findings from this evaluation have shaped South Lanarkshire Council's approach towards leadership of the organisational and practice changes required to develop personalised services.

'The irony of leadership (as opposed to management or command) is that it is the most difficult of approaches as it implies the leader does not have the answer, it requires the leader to make the collective face up to responsibility, the answer is going to take a long time to construct and that it will require constant effort to maintain' (Grint et al., 2009:7). This is a difficult, possibly unpopular route when engaging in management or command would be easier. However, in times when change is the norm, leaders and managers in social services are required to do more, often with less and often in a different way. Perhaps those who have a responsibility for leading the social service workforce have to embrace a 'wicked' approach to the 'wicked' challenges faced. As Grint et al. (2009:2) state 'new demands on leadership in the Scottish public sector are not likely to be well served by traditional leadership development'. They suggest that public services need to embrace leadership and further to consider the potential of leadership less as a property of individuals and more as a collaboration that embraces active learning, critical reflection and active intervention rooted in sound evidence. Changing Lives identified that in order to achieve transformational change it is crucial to empower the social service workforce to develop creative solutions to meet citizens' needs. Aspects of this programme demonstrated that through investing in and giving opportunities to staff to enact change through using evidence, practice wisdom and professional knowledge can not only develop leadership at an individual level but it can also expand the organisation's capacity to enact basic leadership tasks needed for collective work (Hannum et al., 2007) .

Notes

1. Robin Burgess, Organisation, Leadership and People Development (www.robinburgessolpd.co.uk)
2. For a fuller discussion see Stevenson, H. (2010) Practitioner Leadership: how do we realise the potential within? In Zwanenberg, Z. *Leadership in Social Care*. London: Jessica Kingsley
3. IDI is the Interpersonal Dynamics Inventory - a tool that measures and describes the impact a person's behaviour has upon the people with whom they interact. www.idi360.co.uk
4. The evaluation of the Leadership Development Programme was one project amongst a number of 'demonstration projects' aimed to embed research and evaluation into social services activity, to increase capacity and capability of social service organisations to undertake and use research in order to improve outcomes for service users. IRISS completed their involvement during June 2009 and the original researcher undertaking the evaluation as an IRISS employee was then commissioned independently by Social Work Resources to complete the final stage of fieldwork (evidencing impact through observable

performance outcomes) and write up the evaluation findings. The researcher sought consent from all participants to gain access to their projects, to carry out focus groups and individual interviews. Attention was paid to ensuring participants' willingness to take part, informing the participants about the scope of the project and how the data would be used. Attention was also paid to issues of confidentiality and identifiability. It was important that all research participants felt comfortable with participation. The Social Research Association Guidelines (2005) provided the basis for the ethical conduct http://www.the-sra.org.uk/ethical.htm

References

Alliger, G. M. and Janak, E.A. (1989) Kirkpatrick's levels of training criteria: thirty years later. *Personnel Psychology*, 42, 2, 331-342

Alimo-Metcalfe, B. and Alban-Metcalfe, J. (2008) *Engaging Leadership: Creating organisations that maximise the potential of their people.* London: CIP

Alimo-Metcalfe, B. And Lawler, J. (2001) Leadership development in UK companies at the beginning of the twenty-first century: Lessons for the NHS? *Journal of Management in Medicine*, 15, 5, 387-404

Boaden, R.J. (2006) Leadership development: does it make a difference? *Leadership and Organisation Development Journal*, 27, 1, 5-27

Bowerman, J.K. (2003) Leadership development through action learning: an executive monograph. *International Journal of Health Care Quality Assurance*, 16, 4, vi-xii

Burgess, R.C. (2005) A Model for enhancing individual and organisational learning of 'emotional intelligence': The drama and winner's triangles. *Social Work Education*, 24, 1, 97–111

Burke, A. L and Hutchins, H. M. (2007) Training transfer: An integrative literature review. *Human Resource Development Review*, 6, 3. 263-296

Cherniss, C., Goleman, D., Emmerling, R., Cowan, K., and Adler, M. (1998) *Bringing Emotional Intelligence to the Workplace*, New Brunswick, NJ: Rutgers University, Consortium for Research on Emotional Intelligence in Organizations

Dinham, S. Abubusson, P., and Brady, L. (2008) Distributed Leadership as a factor in and outcome of teacher action learning. *International Electronic Journal for Leadership in Learning*.12, 4

Economic and Social Research Council, (2009) *Leadership in the Public Sector in Scotland*, Swindon: Economic and Social Research Counci

Ford, M. and Gardner, C. (2005) *Leadership Development: How government works.* Report prepared for the Auditor General for Scotland. Edinburgh: Audit Scotland

Ghodsian, D., Bjork, R.A., and Benjamin, A.S. (1997) Evaluating Training during training: obstacles and opportunities. in M.A. Quinones and A. Ehrenstein (Eds.). *Training for a Rapidly Changing Workplace: Applications of psychological research.* Washington DC: American Psychological Association

Granville, S. and Russell, K. (2005) *Evaluation of the Leadership for Learning Initiative.* http://www.scotland.gov.uk/publications/200

Grint, K., Martin, G., Wensely, R., Doig, B., Gray, P., and Martlew, C. (2009) *Mapping the Public Policy Landscape: Leadership in public sector in Scotland.* Swindon: Economic and Social Research Counci

Grove, J.T., Kibel, B.M., and Haas, T. (2007) An open systems perspective on evaluating leadership development. in K.M. Hannum, J.W. Martineau, and C. Reinelt *The Handbook of Leadership Development Evaluation.* San Francisco: John Wiley (pp.71-110)

Gutierrez, M. and Tasses, T. (2007) Leading with theory: Using a theory of change approach for leadership development evaluation. in K.M. Hannum, J.W. Martineau, and C. Reinelt *The Handbook of Leadership Development Evaluation.* San Francisco: John Wiley (pp.48-70)

Hannum, K.M., Martineau, J.W., and Reinelt, C. (2007) *The Handbook of Leadership Development Evaluation.* San Francisco : John Wiley

Hicks, C. and Hennessy, D. (2001) An alternative technique for evaluating the effectiveness of continuing professional development courses for health care professionals: A pilot study with practice nurses. *Journal of Nursing Management* 9, 1, 39-49

Holton, E. F. (1996) The flawed four level evaluation model. *Human Resource Development Quarterly,* 7, 1, 5-21

Iles, P. and Preece, D. (2006) Developing leaders or developing leadership? The Academy of Executives Programmes in North East England. *Leadership* 2, 3, 317-340

Kirkpatrick, D.L. (1983) Four steps to measuring training effectiveness. *Personnel Administrator,* 28, 11, 19-25

Kirkpatrick, D.L. (1994) *Evaluating Training Programs: the four levels.* San Francisco: Berrett-Koehler

Kotter, J.P. (1990) *A Force for Change: How leadership differs from management.* New York: Free Press

Martineau, J.W., Hannum, K.M. and Reinelt, C. (2007) Introduction. in K.M. Hannum, J.W. Martineau, and C. Reinelt *The Handbook of Leadership Development Evaluation.* San Francisco: John Wiley (pp.1-12)

Peters, L. and Baum, J. (2007) The importance of local context in leadership develoment and evaluation. in K.M. Hannum, J.W. Martineau, and C. Reinelt *The Handbook of Leadership Development Evaluation.* San Francisco: John Wiley (pp.261-283)

Preskill, H. and Torres, R.T. (1999) *Evaluative Enquiry for Learning in Organisations.* Thousand Oaks, CA: Sage

Scottish Executive (2006a) *Changing Lives: 21st Century Review of Social Work.* Edinburgh: Scottish Executive.
http://www.scotland.gov.uk/Resource/Doc/91931/0021949.pd

Scottish Executive (2006b) *Changing Lives: 21st century review of social work: Implementation Plan.* Edinburgh: Scottish Executive.
http://www.scotland.gov.uk/Publications/2006/06/27144954/

Senge, P. M. (1992) *The Fifth Discipline: The art and practice of the learning organisation.* London: Century Books

Skills for Care (2008) *Leadership and Management Strategy Update 2008: Transforming adult social care,* Leeds: Skills for Care

Tamkin, P., Yarnall, J. and Kerrin, M. (2002) *Kirkpatrick and Beyond: A review of training evaluation.* The Institute for Employment Studies (IES Report 392)

Tourish, D., Pinnington, A., and Braithwaite-Anderson, S. (2007). *Evaluating Leadership Development in Scotland.* Aberdeen: The Robert Gordon University, Aberdeen Business School

Warr, P. B., Allan, C., and Birdi, K. (1999).. Predicting three levels of training outcome. *Journal of Occupational and Organisational Psychology,* 72, 351-375

Watkins, K. and Marsick, V. (1993) *Sculpting the Learning Organisations: Lessons in the art and science of systematic change.* San Francisco: Jossey-Bass

York Consulting. (2008) *Evaluation of Leading to Deliver.* http:/www.scotland.gov.uk/publications/200

The body of this chapter was first published in 2011 in *Social Work & Social Sciences Review* vol. 14(2) pp.55-72. William McAllan was Training Manager, South Lanarkshire Council Social Work Resources, and Rhoda MacRae an Independent Researcher

9

Social work management in Ireland:
Time for education and training

John Leinster

The situation in 2013

Since conducting my research in 2008 there have been significant changes in the economic and social landscape which has had a deleterious effect on social work education and management practice. Two significant developments have had an impact on social work management in Ireland.

Firstly, the economic recession has become the dominant feature of the Irish social and political landscape. Part of the political response has been to reduce the number of people working in the public sector. Since 2009, social workers, like all public servants, have been affected by budgetary decisions which have reduced their salaries with further reductions through the imposition of additional income taxes. Social work in Ireland is funded either directly or indirectly through the state and anecdotally there has been a decline in the number of social work posts and a public sector recruitment embargo in all areas except child protection. This has made it more difficult for new social workers to enter the profession and narrowed promotional prospects of those in employment. As no research has been conducted into the number of social work posts in Ireland since 2005 it is difficult to ascertain the impact which the economic downturn has had on the numbers of practicing social workers.

The new economic realities have also prevented social workers from participating in further training. It has been reported by several organizations that their training budget has been severely reduced and the Health Service Executive (HSE) which is the principle employer of social workers, has reduced the training opportunities for all staff. Training budgets have been one of the first casualties of the recession and opportunities for post qualifying training have declined significantly.

Secondly, Despite the economic recession there has been one significant development in the area of social work education. In 2011 the National University of Ireland Galway (NUIG)established a Diploma in Practice Teaching, Supervision and Management. This initiative is important as it is the first time in Irish education history that Social Work Management has been formally taught at post qualifying level.

This three year pilot programme has an annual cohort of 10 established social workers who are enhancing their supervisory and management skills. While the number of students is relatively small it is one of the few postgraduate programmes exclusively open to social workers.

Social work management in Ireland:
Time for education and training

John Leinster

Introduction

The numbers of practising social workers in the Republic of Ireland have grown in recent years and social work in Ireland has now become a much more recognised and recognisable profession with its own accreditation system which conforms to international educational standards. There had been a continued increase in the number of practitioners up until 2008 when the impact of the economic recession resulted in budgetary constraints within the health services. Regardless of the current economic depression the areas in which social workers now practice are more extensive than before. Despite this expansion, within the context of social work education, Ireland has, with only a few notable exceptions, failed to develop a range of postgraduate programmes for social work graduates. Regarding the education and training needs of social work managers, there has been little recognition in the literature that these managerial positions require a set of specific management skills which are unique to the role.

Increase in social work posts

The social work profession in Ireland has undergone a period of transformation in recent years with the most recent figures showing a significant expansion in the number of social workers from 1390 posts in 1999 to 2237 posts in 2005 (National Social Workers Qualifications Board, 2006). This represents a 61% increase in the number of posts within a 6 year period. Although there are no figures indicating the increase in the number of managerial posts, it is reasonable to assume that the number of management posts also increased during this time. Consequently there has never been a period in Irish social work history when there has been such a large group of managers in the profession.

In some ways the situation of social work education in Ireland in the first decade of the 21st century resembles the state of social work education in

North America in the 1970s where questions were being asked about the suitability of experienced social work practitioners in providing effective management practices. Arising from this it was evident that at that time in America little or no attention had been paid to their training needs (Patti, 1977; Ellis, 1978). Slavin noted that:

> In the long line of development of social work, the latter part of the 1970s will be seen as a period that witnessed the coming of age of the conceptual and theoretical underpinnings for the administration of social services. (Slavin,1977 p. 245)

The lack of appropriate training provided by respective social work education programmes was further emphasised in a survey conducted by Egan and Bendick (1977), in which they stated:

> There is an increasing awareness in the social welfare field that managerial and analytical expertise is a major gap in the professional staff resources of public welfare agencies...the situation is said to exist because many agency managers are social workers whose professional education did not emphasise managerial skills (p.359).

Supporting Patti (1983), Rosenberg and Clarke (1987) who interviewed 14 social workers who had progressed to become executive managers in Canadian hospitals, argued that

> social workers are ill prepared for the transitional processes that normally occur in social work, that of moving from clinician to supervisor to manager. What needs to be strengthened in social work masters programmes are areas of strategic planning, financial management, financial accountability and general management skills to provide a basic level of knowledge useful to all social workers, a base that could be supplemented by later education appropriately specific to job tasks. (p.154.)

With the gradual expansion in the social work role over the last thirty years this statement could arguably now be made in relation to Irish social work management.

While the history of social work in Ireland has been documented by Skehill (1999, 2004) and Kearney (2005) the role and development of social work managers has been largely ignored. Due to the lack of research in this area it is difficult to gain an understanding of the role which managers perform, their range of supervisory responsibilities and the gaps in their education and training.

This exploratory research

This research aimed to explore the gaps the training and education needs of social work managers in Ireland (Leinster, 2009). The research was both quantitative and qualitative. The quantitative study involved distributing a questionnaire by email to 176 social work managers, with a total of 56 returned completed questionnaires amounting to a response rate of 32%. The qualitative research was carried out by running three focus groups with 15 managers and three individual interviews with managers. The research had a number of objectives. Firstly, to identify the extent and nature of their postgraduate education. Secondly, to obtain their views about their education and training needs and the required content of a programme which will meet these needs. Thirdly, to gain an understanding of the values, ethics and principles which may have informed their decision making in the absence of specific social work management training.

Research method

An e-mailed questionnaire pilot study was distributed to ten social work managers. They were asked to comment on the suitability and relevance of the questions and for suggestions, additions or amendments to improve the clarity of the questionnaire. Nine completed and returned the questionnaire by e-mail. The one who failed to respond cited pressure of work as the reason for her not participating. A number of amendments were suggested and accepted.

The sample study used non-probability selection, as the researcher had no control over the representation of the sample, but rather was reliant on the willingness of the participants to partake in the questionnaire (Babbie, 2001; Cournoyer & Klein, 2000).

The selection of respondents proved somewhat difficult due to, firstly, differing definitions of the notion of 'social work manager' and secondly, the use of listings of posts to make contact with respondents. The National Social Workers Qualifications Board, in a survey on social work posts in Ireland in 2005 (NSWQB, 2006), found that there were 236 social workers in management grades located within the sectors of Health/General, Local Authority and the Probation Service. However the definition of a manager differed slightly from the definition for this research, as the NSWQB counted Assistant Directors of Probation, while Principal Probation

Officers, who are a grade lower and more numerous than Assistant Directors, have been included in this exercise.

The NSWQB has a national database of all social work posts in Ireland and the respective grades. However due to the Data Protection Act (1988) they were not in a position to release any addresses or email contacts. Consequently the email addresses of those defined as managers for this research were obtained by telephoning each of them in the HSE social work area, each hospital and NGO. This task was made easier within the Probation Service where access to the email address of each Principal Probation Officer was willingly provided by senior management in the Probation Service. Thus the 176 questionnaires represent a sample of social work managers in Ireland rather than a complete list.

Amongst the 56 (32%) completed questionnaires there was representation from the HSE, Hospital Sector, Probation Service and NGO's. The one area which elicited no response was that of managers in the Local Authorities which totaled 22 or 9% of the managers in the NSWQB (2006) study. The Probation Service has 48 Senior Probation Officers and all their email addresses were made available. Of this total, 14 or 28% responded. However as the researcher did not have access to the email addresses of all managers in the other areas it was not possible to identify the proportion of the total population in each sector which responded.

Table 1 below represents the total number of returned questionnaires according to each of the four sectors and the percentage return from the questionnaire sample.

The group with the greatest proportionate response was the Probation Service while the HSE was less well represented despite having the greatest number of social work managers.

Table 1
Returned Questionnaires by Number and Percentage.

Organisation type	Questionnaire Respondents (*n*)	Questionaires returned (%)
Health ServiceExecutive	22	39
Probation Service	14	25
Non governmental organisation	12	22
Hospital Social Work	8	14
Total	56	100

Limitations in methodology

The research was affected by over representation from the Probation Service and under representation from the HSE. This created the problem of emphasising the opinions of managers who work in a relatively small area of the profession in Ireland, while at the same time failing to ascertain the views of a wide range of managers who work in the most populated area namely the HSE. The response was also numerically relatively small with only 56 respondents. This small response fails to truly capture the varied range of areas where managers are working. The use of email as a method of distributing and receiving the questionnaire excluded those managers who did not have an email address. It is difficult to ascertain how many managers did not have an email address. While the distribution process was made easier by the use of email, only one third of the questionnaires were returned by email, while the other two thirds were printed and returned by post. Thus a lack of competence or comfort with the technology may have discouraged some participants. The response rate amounted to 56 or 32% returning completed questionnaires.

Basis for the questionnaires

It may be debatable as to whether social worker managers are best placed to accurately identify their own training and education needs. However, as there has been no research conducted in this area in Ireland, it seemed appropriate to open up the debate by allowing managers to express themselves in a participatory and empowering way in starting the process of identifying their own educational needs. The research was influenced by previous researchers such as Scourfield (1980) who had previously surveyed managers in the field and by Menefee and Thompson (1994) and Menefee (1998) who researched what social work managers actually spent their time doing. They identified a diverse range of competencies and began to recognise that the social work management role demands a set of complex and wide ranging skills. Research conducted by Martin, Pine and Healy (1999) amongst practising social work managers attempted to ascertain if the MSW programs prepared managers for the role. Their findings were largely encouraging and emphasised the importance of providing specialist MSW programmes in Administration. Research conducted in South Africa, by van Bijon (1999), focussed on what the participants – practising managers participating in an MA (SS) (MH) (Mental Health) degree – actually did in their roles as managers. It was concluded that social work undergraduate training needed to include management theory, financial management and accounting, strategic management and organisational theory. On the basis of the above, questions were constructed to address issues under broad categories such as; qualifications and training, areas of work, range of responsibilities, reporting relationships, identification of training needs, prioritisation of management roles and responsibilities, and, employers support for additional training and education. These questionnaires formed the basis for the complimentary data gathering through focus groups.

Focus groups

Focus groups, defined by Kreuger (1994) as 'A carefully planned discussion designed to obtain perceptions on a defined area of interest in a permissive non-threatening environment,' were conducted to elicit the views of managers in a way which would complement the quantitative research information. A particular objective was to utilise this method to trigger thinking amongst participants to encourage deeper and wider discourse. To help ensure accuracy the focus groups were recorded using a digital recorder. One group was composed of Principal Probation Officers while the other two were composed of representatives from NGOs. Focus groups were planned to include respondents from both the HSE and the Hospital sector. However, as the focus groups were being set up, in the autumn of 2008, the global recession impacted on the economic climate in Ireland. As a direct consequence of this the HSE demanded immediate cut backs in its travel budget and within the HSE where the majority of managers work, an embargo on travel was imposed which affected both the HSE and hospital social work managers. While the focus groups were very accessible anyway to participants as they were timed to coincide with already scheduled regional meetings, the financial cutbacks made this method most timeous. For those organizations that had not scheduled meetings or who had cancelled meetings due to the cutbacks, focus groups were not possible. To reduce the effect of the loss of holding these two cancelled focus groups, three individual interviews were conducted with two local HSE managers and one manager from a local hospital setting. The three managers who were interviewed were selected because of their accessibility as they all worked in close proximity to Galway where the researched was based.

The focus groups were held in Dublin, Limerick and Roscommon after the information from the questionnaires had been collated. The resulting information gathered from the focus groups informed the following questions amongst others:

1. Have you participated in management training or education? If so what form did it take. How beneficial was it?
2. What do you base your decision making on in the absence of social work management training?
3. What are the values which determine your management decision making?

Research findings

Post graduate qualifications of social work managers

Analysing the data from the completed questionnaires, the majority of respondents/participants, 82%, have acquired additional postgraduate training or education. While this may not be particularly significant for social workers at a senior level, what is of importance is the nature of the further education they have pursued. The most common type of postgraduate education which respondents have completed is counselling (23%), mediation (13%) and Family Therapy (11%).

There were similar findings from the focus groups where participants reported the importance of acquiring additional training in traditional social work areas. The range of additional qualifications the focus group participants acquired extended from mediation, to Montessori teaching, research skills, life coaching, and a variety of specific counselling qualifications. Formal higher level management qualifications were conspicuously absent from any post graduate education undertaken by managers in the focus group sample. Amongst questionnaire respondents, only three had completed a Masters in Health Services Management which is a programme offered to managers working generally in the health services, rather than specifically geared toward social work managers. None of the respondents had completed any other recognised management qualification. It is remarkable that the nature of the participants' post graduate education and training has led to the vast majority of them enhancing their social work skills rather than their management knowledge and skills.

Responsibilities of managers

Table 2
Mean numbers of staff in teams supervised by the social work manager

Organisation type	Number of staff
Health Service Executive	23.0
Hospital social work	10.2
Probation Service	7.5
Non-governmental organisation	5.2

The research showed that within the social work management role there is considerable variation in the responsibilities of managers within and between the four main types of service in which they work; The Health Service Executive (HSE), hospital social work, The Probation Service and Non Government Organisations (NGO,s) (see Table 2). The specific question which gave the results represented in table 1 was:' How many staff are there in the team you supervise?' Note that the term 'supervise' was understood by the respondents to mean total staff number accountable to the manager.

The social work managers employed by the HSE each supervised teams which had an average of 23 staff while in contrast the managers working with the NGO sector supervised on average only 5.2 staff. Within these contrasting ranges managers working in the area of hospital social work had responsibility for managing and average of 10.2 staff and within the Probation Service each Senior Probation Officer managed a team comprising of 7.2 people. The range of staff included social workers, child care workers, administrative workers and others.

While these statistics point to a wide variation in the numbers of staff supervised in each of the organisation or section types, within each of the four organisational areas there was also a very wide range of managerial responsibilities. For example, one manager working in the HSE supervised 95 staff and another three managed more than 50 people. In stark contrast, three managers in the HSE do not supervise any staff, although their title was Principal Social Worker which is a senior managerial position and they were paid at a management grade. Thus within the HSE itself there is a very significant imbalance between the extent of their management responsibilities, yet they all have the same job title. Social work managers in the NGO sector supervise on average 5.2 staff members, the lowest number of any of the service types, significantly less than HSE managers and almost half of the number of staff which the social work managers in hospital supervise. While the numbers of staff which a manager supervises is a significant indicator of their scope of managerial responsibility, there are other areas of responsibility which are also important as discussed in the next section.

Differing range of responsibilities

Although they may have responsibility for supervising fewer staff, managers in the NGO sector indicated from the focus groups that they have a more diverse range of responsibilities. Five of the managers working in the NGO sector stated that they are chairpersons of various committees such as human rights committees, or are the designated persons with responsibility for managing abusive incidents within the organisation. These managers reported seeing themselves as senior managers because they participated as members of the senior management team. One manager described the difference between being a Social Work Team Leader with the HSE with responsibility for a small team of 6 Child Protection and Family Support workers and the contrast with his promotion to Head of Social Work in a large NGO. The transition meant that now, as a member of the senior management team, he was jointly responsible for (but not directly supervising) 950 staff in an organisation with a budget of €50 million. He described how ill equipped he felt participating in management decisions.

Key decisions made within organisations often relate to the way the finances are prioritised. Only a small percentage of managers have budgetary responsibility; 32% within their own department and 16% within their wider organisation.

Respondent opinion regarding their needs for future training

Respondents were asked to identify their further training needs from the following selection.

Table 3
Respondents identified training needs

Training Need	Percentage who Identified further training needs in these areas.
Supervision	39
Strategic Planning	59
Policy Making	36
Programme Development	38
Organisational Management	41
Financial Management	41
Staff Development	32
Staff Training	23
Human Relations	25
Mediation	18
Representing organisation at policy formulation	25
Service Delivery Evaluation	50
Programme Evaluation	50
Cost Benefit Analysis	52

The questionnaire asked participants to prioritise their training and education needs in fourteen areas including planning, finances, supervision, human resources, evaluation and policy formulation. The greatest need expressed by the cohort was for further training in the area of strategic planning, which was prioritised by 59% of the study group. Similar training needs were previously identified by Scourfield (1980), Phayane (1995) and van Bijon (1995). Cost benefit evaluation was seen as a significant training need by 52% of respondents along with service delivery evaluation, 50%, and programme evaluation, 50%. The areas of organisational management, 41%, financial management, 41%, and supervision at 39% were also recognised as high needs.

The areas of lowest priority in relation to further training were in human relations, 25%, staff training, 23% and mediation at 18%.

Only a minority, 16% of respondents, stated that they participated in management decisions relating to financial management within their wider organisation, while 32% had financial responsibilities within their team.

Arising from the focus groups, the areas where further training and education was identified centred on the need for enhancing supervision skills, case management, conflict resolution and the management of issues of a personal nature which spill over into the workplace. There was general agreement that interpersonal conflict was an area which presented managers with difficulty. Some said that dealing with conflict between team members, often referred to as 'personality clashes' was regarded as being particularly difficult to resolve. One manager commented, 'I feel comfortable working with the service users and their families but it is more difficult working with colleagues or managers and it is different when the issues are of a more serious nature and it is outside the supervision session. It could be an HR / Industrial relations issue and I am quite worried about it, rather than a practice or a professional issue. When a social worker comes and says ' there is an issue I have to talk to you about', my heart sort of sinks as it might be an issue to do with confrontation'

The importance of having an accessible human resources department for advice was voiced on two occasions by managers working in NGO's. Amongst participants working in the NGO sector there was a consensus that their Human Resource departments were easily accessible and offered sound advice which they followed. Within the larger statutory organisations the Human Resource departments were perceived as being more distant and less accessible and managers were more likely to rely on the advice of peers or a more senior manager for advice about what they described as a personnel problem.

Values which underpin management practice

One of the questions posed to the focus group participants was, 'What are the values which determine your management decision making?' In response there was a common understanding of the values, principles and ethics which underpin the practice of social work management. One manager responded by stating,

> *When it is finances the value system is value for money, when you talk about ethical values we talk about meeting the needs of the customer, we only exist to meet the needs of the people we serve.*

Another replied:

Knowing what service users want, respect for them – looking at what is possible – trying to inform the organisation of the needs of the service users out there and finding out what the expectation of the organisation are of the social work department.

One manager working in the area of disability with an NGO was very conscious that his focus was on ensuring that the needs of service users took priority. He reflected that the organisation has a

strategic plan incorporating each section of the agency and how each department fits in with the identified goals of the customers, the agency and our funders. There is clarity in the strategic plan about who is responsible to achieve the identified goals and the time scale and the results. Social work has a role to lead some goals, and identify the outcomes to achieve the goals.

In contrast one of the senior probation officers described how the service is drifting away from a client centred approach, in his opinion towards a

... broad, business based management - outputs, inputs. You could literally be in any form of commercial organisation. There is a drift towards doing what we do in terms of generic management principles rather than any specific social work input. When you reach a certain level of management it is about process, procedures, performance indicators. It is about familiarising yourself with the whole world of business and business concepts and then seeing how you can apply these business concepts to the work you do. For most of us with a social work background it is a new experience and there is a certain difficulty which comes with trying to integrate a business orientation with the social work end of things. The consensus is that social work gets lost in the middle of it all.

These quotations taken from the focus groups provide an example of how one manager who works with an NGO perceives the way in which the traditional values within social work that emphasise advocacy, self determination and individually chosen outcomes, have been retained within the smaller NGO. This is in contrast to the manager who works within the probation service which has undergone major growth in recent years with an enhancement in staff numbers and an expansion of its statutory role in relation to the management of offenders. This expansion, according to some of the managers, has been clearly undertaken at the expense of some core social work values. Another manager stated:

> I came from a business background into probation. When I came in five years ago there was a social work emphasis, the emphasis on corporate management wasn't evident. I think we have grown so fast and we are trying to put a corporate structure on ourselves and we haven't levelled off yet. We have emphasised getting good procedures but the other side, the client focussed side hasn't really caught up yet.

Conflicting expectations of organisations and the social work role

Bearing in mind that opportunities to participate in social work management training are largely absent, it was seen as an important exploration to gain an understanding of the influences which come to bear on the value systems which inform the decision making of social work managers.

Managers face conflict between the demands of the organisational expectations versus the demands of the people who use the services, articulated through the voice of the social worker. Social work is the primary profession which has a direct responsibility to act as advocates with and for people who use the services. The Irish Association of Social Workers' Code of Ethics validates this by stating in the second and third principles

> Social workers will advocate with and behalf of those whom society excludes and in doing so should engage with service users and facilitate them in contributing their views to such developmentsm... Social workers will strive to use their power appropriately within such relationships and will place special emphasis on the consideration of and promotion of service users' views in all decisions that are related to the quality of their lives. (Irish Association of Social Workers, 1992 p..2.)

The focus group conducted with senior probation officers was particularly enlightening in this respect as the probation service had commissioned a global human resources consulting group, Penna with the remit

> To equip managers of the Probation and Welfare Service with the necessary personal, interpersonal and leadership skills to meet their current role objectives and prepare them for future leadership roles. (Jones & Duffy, 2006)

This is the only specific management training for social work managers which this research identified. (see Penna, 'Learning for Leadership Programme, Programme Outline' at. www.penna.com).This programme was divided into four modules delivered over a 12 month period.

According to all six of the probation officers participating in that focus group, the training had some limited value but was in many ways not what they needed. The following quotation summed up the general consensus of the group:

For Senior Probation Officers there is a real deficit around support for practical issues. There is a loss of framework of what social work is about (in the Penna training). It is drawn to the organisational goals; the training is absolutely removed from the ethics and values of the social work profession. There is nothing about social equality; it is not about that, that's the real deficit in the management training within what is apparently a social work setting.

This attitude was also further reinforced in the eyes of the senior probation officers as they referred to the fact that the accompanying course outline failed to refer to the social work management literature. This they perceived as a serious omission.

The impact which this training had on their relationship to the organisation was very interesting. One participant commented that

We have two separate organisations. The seniors deliver the service, once a manager goes above the senior probation officer level they don't have a particular involvement in the delivery of the service.

Later the same person noted that

I speak two languages, I speak social work language to my team and I speak business corporate speak to my line manager and director, so it is a sort of schizophrenic existence.

When asked which language she was more comfortable with she stated

I would be more comfortable with the social work language.

While the participants' perception was that the training had failed, it is possible that there might have been a number of influencing factors that warrant some consideration here about this perception. The training programme appeared to not use content material that directly related to the area of work in which managers operated. Their perception was that it did not meet their needs precisely because it did not overtly take into account the ethical framework which underpins social work practice.

In their promotional information Penna state that their

> experience spans the entire Public Service (British), Including central government departments, agencies, local authorities, local government, non-departmental public bodies (NDPB), emergency services, the NHS and further and higher education. (http://www.penna.com)

So it appears that Penna had appropriately addressed the type of organisation that they deal with in relation to their work with the probation service.

The senior probation officers who participated in the focus group had roles as supervisors and line managers of probation officers and did not perceive themselves as leaders within the organisation. It might be argued then, that a type of training which directly addressed their roles as the line managers to probation officers would have been more beneficial.

It is unfortunate that the Penna training has met with this level of discomfort from the participants, as it appears to have much to offer the field of social work and social work managers and leaders in particular. It might be useful to surmise that there might not have been appropriate consultation between Penna, the senior management of the probation service and the senior probation officers themselves, about their training needs.

Discussion

A number of key points arising from the research warrant further examination.

Regarding their post graduate education, Irish social work managers have continued to enhance their social work skills rather than develop their management skills. Arguably the most available appropriate qualification, the Masters in Health Service Management, has to a large extent, not been utilised by social work managers. There may be several factors at play here. It may indicate that additional qualifications which enhance traditional social work skills, rather than management training or education appear to be advantageous when applying for promotion. This may be linked with a perception by senior organisational management that they might not be aware that social workers need management skills and in particular, social work management skills. It may also indicate that the rapid expansion in the employment of social workers and social work managers has run ahead of the ability of training institutions to provide appropriate training.

It appears that the lack of any formal management education or training has not prevented social work managers' promotion into their current position. As is evidenced in this research, social work managers themselves are uncomfortable with their lack of specialised management education and training. The senior managers of organisations need to not only become more acutely aware of this lack, but need to conduct assessments around the possible deleterious effects that it has on managers, their teams, and most importantly, the service users. They need to look urgently at using those assessments to put appropriate management training into place for their social work managers.

Organisations need social work managers who are fully equipped to deliver their services and if they are not being trained effectively as managers or leaders, they are not in a position to take up this leadership challenge. Effective and progressive service delivery depends on this.

Key decisions made within organisations often relate to the way the finances are prioritised. As discussed earlier, only a small percentage of managers have budgetary responsibility; 32% within their own department and of those, 16% also had financial responsibilities within their wider organisation. While only 32% of questionnaire respondents stated that they had financial responsibilities, only 41% of the total number of respondents identified this area as a further training need. Two issues are of immediate importance. Firstly, the fact that such a small proportion of social work managers are responsible for financial management is rather concerning. If social work managers are not included in the formal financial decision making processes in organisations, then their areas of service may be inadequately represented, resulting in a deterioration of service to those in greatest need. Secondly, the reason why they are not included needs to be examined further. Is it because they have no training in financial management, or that they have sought no training because their financial responsibilities are limited?

The Probation Service should be lauded for having the foresight to not only recognise the training needs of their managers, but to respond to that need by engaging with the Penna training. It is unfortunate that participants were left not feeling more skilled and empowered. Perhaps the learning from this experience could be taken up by all parties. Firstly, that the initial negotiation between the Probation Service and Penna could have identified the correct level of management participants for the training. Secondly, these early negotiations could have seen some value in Penna including some explicit material around social work ethics into their training. Thirdly, Penna and the senior managers of the Probation Service might have included the senior probation officers in the initial preparation to be clear about their needs and expectations. And, fourthly, the confusion around whether the course was primarily concerned with promoting management skills, or promoting leadership skills, could have been clarified and negotiated more successfully by all parties.

Regarding the values which inform their decision making in the absence of management education or training, the research has opened a discussion regarding how managers are influenced by the expectations of their management responsibilities and how they marry their decisions with the code of ethics determined by the profession. From the focus group discussions it was evident that social work managers are influenced by a value system which is influenced by the social work code of ethics. However it is also important to acknowledge that this area warrants a more thorough investigation and that no definitive answers were provided at this exploratory level.

Conclusions

Social work managers in Ireland have to date had few opportunities to further their training or education in the specific area of social work management. Amongst the group of managers who participated in the research, few had acquired recognised management qualifications despite their onerous responsibilities. Their range of managerial responsibilities is so varied as to be highly inequitable, both within specific organisations and between organisations.

The participants' prioritisation of their training needs in the areas of strategic planning, cost benefit evaluation and financial management was particularly powerful and needs to guide organisations and the profession, toward building better managers. The Probation Service's training initiative might have been more useful given the confusions of the target level and possible early negotiation problems, but certainly needs to act as a good example to other organisations.

While the issue of the social work Code of Ethics and the role it plays in informing management decision making is not recognised in the literature in Ireland, this research suggests that social work managers believe that it plays a crucial role in developing their management capacity.

To the distress of social work manager participants in this research, there was a complete absence of any social work management training or education. Their explicit desire to engage in relevant training is evidenced in this research. The establishment of social work management programmes, which marry management skills with social work ethics and values, is long overdue. Thus, better training of social work managers will result in more effective service delivery.

References

Babbie, E. (2001) *The Practice of Social Research*, Belmont: Wadsworth

Cournoyer, D. and Klein, W. (2000) *Research Methods for Social Work*, (3rd ed.), Basingstoke: Palgrave Macmillan

Data Protection Act (1988) Dublin: Government Publications,

Egan, M. and Bendick, M. (1977) Management training for public welfare agencies. Why the need remains unmet. *Administration in Social Work*, 1, 4, 359-67

Ellis, J. (1978) Skill training for social welfare management: developing a laboratory model for field instruction. *Administration in Social Work*, 2, 211-222

Jones, M. and Duffy, C. (2006) Probation Service Learning for Leadership Programme. Unpublished training handout

Kearney, N. and Skehill, C. (Eds.) (2005) *Social Work in Ireland: Historical perspectives.*Dublin: Institute of Social Administration

Kreuger, R. and Casey, M. (1994) *Focus Groups:A practical guide for applied research.* (4th ed.) Thousand Oaks, CA: Sage

Irish Association of Social Workers (1992) *Code of Ethics.* Dublin: Irish Association of social Workers

Leinster, J. (2009) National University of Ireland Galway. Unpublished M.Litt

Menefee, D. and Thompson, J. (1994) Identifying and comparing competencies for social work management: A practice driven approach. *Administration in Social Work*, 18, 3, 1-25

Menefee, D. (1998) Identifying and comparing competencies for social work management II: A replication study. *Administration in Social Work*, 22, 4, 53-63

National Social Workers Qualifications Board, (2006) *Social Work Posts in Ireland Report No.3.* Dublin: National Social Work Qualifications Board

Penna Consultancy. Learning for Leadership Programme. Dublin. http://www.

penna.com

Patti, R. (1977) Patterns of management activity in social welfare organisations. *Administration in Social Work*, 1, 5-18

Patti, R. (1983) *Managing Social Programmes in a Developmental Context*. New Jersey: Prentice-Hall

Phayane, J.S.M. (1996) Training needs of managers. Pretoria: *Department of Welfare, Sport and Recreation. Developmental Social Services Chief Directorate*

Rosenberg, G. and Clarke, S. (1987) Social workers in health care management: The movement to leadership. *Social Work in Health Care*, 12, 3

Scourfield, R. (1980) Educational preparation for social work administrators: A survey. *Journal of Education for Social Work*, 1, 3, 245-257

Skehill, C. (1999) *The Nature of Social Work in Ireland: A historical perspective*, Ceredigian: Edwin Mellon

Skehill, C. (2004) *History of the Present of Child Protection and Welfare Social Work in Ireland*, Ceredigian: Edwin Mellon

Slavin, S. (1977) A framework for selecting consent for teaching about social administration.*Administration in Social Work*, 1, 3,245-257

Van Biljon, R. (1999) Towards education and training in social work management: Needs and Necessity. *Social Work*, 35, 4.

The body of this chapter was first published in 2011 in *Social Work & Social Sciences Review* vol. 14(2) pp.73-94. John Leinster was Head of Social Work, BOC Services, Renmore, Galway, Ireland.

Appendix: The questionnaire

Questionnaire

Identifying the Training Needs of Social Work Managers

1.	**First some facts about you**		
1.1	Gender:		Female
1.2	What Age Are You:		

1.3   What social work qualifications do you have: **Please ✓**
BA Social Science ☐
BA Arts ☐
Diploma in Social Work ☐
CQSW ☐
MSW ☐
Other – Please Specify Below:

1.4   What year did you qualify as a social worker

2.	**Qualifications and Training**

2.1   What additional postgraduate qualifications do you have:

Qualification	*Please ✓*	*Year Obtained /Expected*
PhD	☐	
MBA	☐	
Masters in Health Services Management	☐	
MSc in Health Services Management	☐	
Masters in Health Promotion	☐	
M. Litt	☐	
M. Phil	☐	
MA	☐	
Other – Please Specify Below:		

2.2   **Training Details**

Training	*Qualification*	*Year Obtained /Expected*
Family Therapy	Certificate	
Counselling	Certificate	
Medication Studies	Certificate	
Addiction Studies	Certificate	
Family Support	Certificate	
Community Development	Certificate	
Advanced Diploma in Child Protection and Welfare	Certificate	
Diploma in Practice Teaching	Certificate	
Other – Please specify:		

2.3 Which of the following skills and knowledge from your Postgraduate Education and Training facilitated your role as a Social Work Manager?

Advanced supervision skills ☐
Advanced skill development ☐
Advanced your knowledge ☐
Advanced your theories and ethics ☐
Advanced your competencies ☐
Increased self awareness ☐
Increased level of reflective practice ☐

3. Job Overview

3.1 **Job Title?**
Head Social Worker ☐
Principal Social Worker ☐
Other

3.2 **Do you Work?**
Part Time ☐
Full Time ☐

3.3 How many hours are in your official working week?

3.4 Name and address of the organisation you work with?
Organisation Name:

Address:

3.5 Type of Organisation :
Statutory ☐
Voluntary /Community ☐

3.6 Please tick the main area in which you work (*please tick one box only*)

Child and Family ☐
Foster care ☐
Adoption ☐
Child and Adolescent Psychiatry ☐
Adult Psychiatry ☐
Medical ☐
Older People ☐
Mental Health ☐
Addiction ☐
Refugee / Asylum Seekers ☐
Unaccompanied Children ☐
Travelling Community ☐
Intellectual Disability ☐
Sensory and physical disability ☐
Community Development ☐
Probation & Welfare Service ☐
County Council ☐
City Council ☐
Defence Force ☐

5.4   What opportunities does your organisation provide for additional Management Training?
Full Payment of Fees	☐
Part Payment of Fees	☐
Study Leave	☐

5.5   How are your training needs identified?
Yourself	☐
Training Manager	☐
Your Line Manager	☐

5.6   What are the expectations of your organisation?
Presentation on training received	☐
Implementation of training	☐
Other - Please Specify:	

5.7   In which of the following areas do you feel you need further training?
Supervision	☐
Strategic Planning	☐
Policy Making	☐
Programme Development	☐
Organisational Management	☐
Financial Management	☐
Staff Development	☐
Staff Training	☐
Human Relations	☐
Mediation	☐
Representing your organisation at policy formulation	☐
Service Delivery Evaluation	☐
Programme Evaluation	☐
Cost Benefit Analysis Evaluation	☐

5.8   Does your agency have a policy to promote the training needs of Social Work Managers?   Yes

5.9a   Rate in order of significance the components of a Social Work Management Course?
(Where 3 is highest rating and 1 is lowest rating)

Advancement of Skills	Rating of 1
Advancement of Knowledge	Rating of 1
Advancement of Value Base	Rating of 1

5.9b   Are you familiar with any Social Work Management Course delivered currently?   Yes
If *"yes"* please specify:

Once you have completed this questionnaire you must save it as "completed questionnaire document" and return to me at jlnuig@gmail.com.

Thank you very much for completing this questionnaire. If you would like to add any further comments please feel free to do so.

Comments:
